A12 to Heaven

Can anyone help in the darkest hour?

> "The two girls had grown so close to each other, it was almost as if they had been travelling on parallel roads that had now converged. One night they were travelling together on one road: it turned out to be a narrow one that led straight to Heaven."
>
> *Chapter 11*

Phil Stoddart

Lastword Publications
Lowestoft, Suffolk, UK
www.lastwordpublications.com

First published 2008, by Lastword Publications
Revised publication and second print September 2009
www.lastwordpublications.com
Lastword Publications works with authors and musicians, businesses and charities to provide professional results with maximum impact.

ISBN 978 0 9559439 0 4

Useful website links:
www.lowestoftcommunitychurch.co.uk
www.philstoddart.co.uk
www.lastwordpublications.com

Biblical quotations are taken from the New International Version
© 1973, 1978, 1984 by the International Bible Society.

Design and production by The Upper Room 020 8406 1010

Foreword

When the appalling news reached us of the loss of two teenage girls in the Newfrontiers church in Lowestoft in a road accident, I shuddered and prayed for the family, as I know hundreds of other people must have done. I could not begin to comprehend the horror, the pain, the mind boggling enormity of losing not one but two daughters at once. How ever can a family cope with such a crisis? Can they ever return to normality? Can they articulate what has happened to them?

The answers to these and other questions that begin to surge into one's mind are contained in this remarkable book. Phil's response, as the father of the two girls, was to write the story of his own childhood, his journey into the Christian faith as a young man, his marriage, and involvement in church life. This provides a context for the terrible events which happened on July 1st 2006. One is allowed to share the story of growing maturity in Christ, the development of a happy, secure family and the tearing loss through his eyes. Much of it is delivered in extracts from his own diaries and those of the two vibrant, healthy and normal young Christian girls.

This book will be a help not only to those who have experienced the death of loved ones in road accidents, but for any who are grappling with the questions that inevitably arise because of traumatic situations. It will not necessarily answer all the questions: eg why our child? Why now? Why didn't God prevent it? But it communicates God's loving presence in the midst of it, his supernatural peace, and the slow process of healing. Phil is honest; he is not super spiritual; he is not 'over it' yet, but he has retained faith and hope in a loving God. I recommend this moving and helpful book.

Wendy Virgo, Newfrontiers UK

A newspaper comment

'When a drunk driver crashed and killed Jennifer Stoddart, 15, and her sister Claire, 18, you would have expected their father to be mad with grief and anger. Instead, Phil Stoddart has written an online blog to show how his faith has helped him to survive.

Recalling the dreadful moment when Jennifer lay desperately injured on a life-support machine, Mr Stoddart wrote: 'This was the moment God met with us in that little room. I prayed because I knew God could bring her back if he wanted. I heard his calm, reassuring voice again "no, she's home with me"'.

As for the man who killed his daughters, Mr Stoddart wrote, simply: 'I think about you often and what you must be going through. We are all guilty to some extent. Your crime will be greater than some, it will certainly be less than others.'

We don't see it voiced much these days, but faith walking hand-in-hand with forgiveness is a truly inspirational thing.'

The Daily Mail. Saturday June 9th 2007

A cause for debate

'Of course, atheists and agnostics will not believe it was the voice of God that Mr Stoddart heard. How can we when we do not believe in a God that speaks individually to us? But so what? What does it matter whether we believe it or not? Or whether Richard Dawkins and every other militant atheist who ever fired a broadside at religion thinks his faith is a delusion? If it has given strength to a mother and father to bear an unimaginable loss, it can only be a good thing. Their faith also gave them the strength to forgive the man who had killed their daughters – something that would be beyond most of us, I suspect. But how much better than being eaten away by anger and bitterness for the rest of their lives.'

John Humphrys, Author and BBC Television Broadcaster
(Extract from 'In God We Doubt.' Hodder & Stoughton)

An e-mail from a friend

I am sure that people have written books before on things such as these; that have been grief poured out but without the sweet and profound message of the cross and of the love of God. Also of course the assurance of Heaven and its beauty that is Claire and Jenny's reality now and will be ours in time. On finishing your book, I found myself (through the tears) sitting looking out at the hills around us and thanking the Lord for you, for Heather and for your four children and overwhelming gratitude that he has set "eternity in our hearts" (Ecclesiastes 3). I was glad that it was real and that there was a meshing of your honesty in the grief with the goodness of God. It never read as trite or unreal.

Judith Forster

The local church

On the tragic day of the car crash, Phil and Heather invited us, their wider church family, to walk with them. So many unanswered questions… these seemed inappropriate and unnecessary to ask as we began supporting this remarkable couple and their family. We soon realised that they would never be the same again and neither would any of us.

We are all affected forever by this event. We are not the same. It is a significant part of our journey of life. We believe somehow we are richer in God, more able to be used by him for more things affecting more people. Seeing clearer the eternal significance of all we do as a church – we've become more compassionate, more real, more vulnerable and more broken by love.

Phil said only days after the incident, "Once you have been broken by the love of God, nothing else; despair, anger, pain or bitterness can break you as there is nothing left to break".

It was humbling to witness Phil and Heather putting their complete faith and trust in the Lord Jesus. It was clear that they were being upheld by his love and comfort and they described very powerful intimate encounters with him. The Lord Jesus continues to sustain them and us, and all who trust him.

As with all who mourn, the roller coaster of emotions called the grieving process continues to be very real. Heather and Phil are not in denial of the pain and anguish of such a great loss but both are demonstrating faith with forgiveness. This has amazed the local community, as has the sense of togetherness within the church family as demonstrated through acts of kindness and love. We continue to witness the mighty hand of God upon us through these uncharted waters.

Rob Clarke and Mike Betts
Leadership Team, Lowestoft Community Church

The Stoddart family... and God

'I think God is really with me, giving this amazing sense of peace and exams have not really been too bad, although the worst are still to come. I think keeping up reading my bible even when I've been busy (like tonight!) is really important.'

Claire's diary

'I fully trust God and know that whatever happens, he has a plan for me.'

Jenny's diary

'Thanks God for Claire and Jenny. Excellent lives. We're so proud of them. They brought fun and friendship to so many people.

We're thrilled to think of them walking with you. You brought them so much joy on earth, how much more is their joy now. What an awesome God you are'.

Dad, Mum, Amy and Tom (Funeral Order of Service)

Contents

Preface

This is both a sad and glorious story. Sad, because it involves death and grief at times too heavy to bear; glorious because alongside the suffering there is joy and a provision from God that I never thought possible. Throughout this account it will be revealed that those who trust in him receive both strength and joy in the darkest of places.

They say that the worst kind of bereavement is the one where a child is lost. I heard this a number of times from a variety of sources, including the psychiatrist who assessed the damage caused to us, the parents. I didn't really agree with any of them at the time. For me, the worst loss is to lose your spouse. After all, at least we had each other to share our loss with, but for people who lose their partners of many years it must be so lonely. I'm not sure if I agree with them even now.

What I do know is that to lose loved ones is a dreadful experience that some people are unable to cope with. On many occasions I have wanted to die and considered how I might do it. At times I have lost all zest for life, my thoughts and dreams have been haunted and my stomach has churned over and over. Yet my story is about how knowing Jesus personally is sufficient to meet the deepest needs. He is able to shine in the darkest of places and to replace tears of despair with those of utmost joy.

Wishful thinking? I can only say I believe it more now than ever before. I have met Jesus in a new way since that horrible day and am looking forward with joy to being re-united with my girls in Heaven. I have good reason to believe that he is faithful and true. This trust provides the foundation for my hope and is what enables a believing family to climb a mountain and walk in the face of a storm. No one removes the obstacles but there is one who strengthens and guides. He is the great comforter and it is my belief that our testimony will bring much comfort to others who also walk dark paths.

1 Crash

Could be me, could be you

Why do some people live and some just die before their
time but when is their time?
I have a life expectancy and I wish I hadn't.
All we hope for is based on how others have fared.

99% of the time you'll live
The cars crash into other people
Unknown names appear in the headlines
If I didn't know them, well does it matter that much?

Strangers die and my life goes on
Seemingly random pot-shots, indiscriminate targets and
I keep being avoided
It's always someone else, but my eyes are everywhere.

Is this it?
Is this the car that's going to do it or is it that one
If I go in a plane maybe that'll be it, perhaps that person
walking towards me will do it?
I have no control,
Anything could happen and it just might
One day my daughters, another?

Is there anything I can do?
Drink, stay in but then there's old age.
Can I prepare in any way?
Maybe I'll ask the evolutionists.

Excuse me Mr Ape-man I want to know a way to live
without having to look over my shoulder
I want a reason to know I can love someone without
having to fear losing them.

I'm scared of the unknown
I'm always an instant away from death
You know all about the species
So surely you have the answers.

Silence. Oh I get it. Live for today, live while you can
Better to have lived having lived
Than not to have lived at all.

Dust to dust, nothing matters
Well I've never known a dog to consider its mortality
If I am ultimately pointless
Why do I bother to live at all?

I have no answers for why people die when they do
I only know that outside of God and life beyond death
Life can have no meaning and I protest.
Dust may be only dust … but people?

Two daughters were lost to me in a car crash in the early hours of July 1st 2006. Altogether, five people died while three survived, including the driver of the other car who had been drinking and lost control. My girls Claire and Jenny, aged 18 and 15, were hit head on in a hundred mile an hour collision. Claire was driving a little blue Vauxhall Astra and her good friend Carla was in the front passenger seat. Both were to die as a Renault Laguna appeared at the top of a hill they were climbing on the A12 in Bythburgh, Suffolk. The Laguna was on the wrong side of the road and Claire had no time to react; it must have been a sudden blinding glare from the headlights, a moment of shock and then bang, that quick. In the back was Jenny, sat between Adam and Sarah who survived. Jenny was wearing a lap-belt and I am aware that she may have survived had she been wearing a full shoulder seatbelt as the other two were. Even so, her injuries would have crippled her for life.

Imagining the crash is a horrible thing but nevertheless I believe that the moment it happened, they met their creator in person for both had put their trust in Jesus, and in the moments that followed they left this earth to be with him. What a journey, the one that starts out as an innocent venture on earth and ends up in Heaven itself!

I had every reason to be proud of my children. They had found God for themselves and were happy in what they were doing.

I marvelled at Claire and Jenny's enthusiasm for school work and they mixed with nice people. Often they would have friends round and there was never a time when either my wife Heather or I would worry about leaving the house to them. Sure, we might come back to a bit of mess, but we never feared for real damage to the house, or any of the dodgy activities that many teenagers indulge in. It is only after reflecting on their lives and reading through their diaries that I realise what an amazing blessing they were. I took all this for granted and remember talking to someone shortly before the car crash about feeling stale and bored with life. The person was shocked to hear it and exclaimed; "Why? You have everything, a lovely family, a good church and God. What more could you want for?" I was jolted by that response and it has risen to attack me on a number of times since.

Friday 30 June 2006 *The night before*

I recall feeling quite fed up on the night of June 30th 2006 while sat alone in my dining room staring at two burning candles on the window sill. It was the evening before the England team were due to play Portugal at football in the quarter-finals of the World Cup and like any other England fan I was looking forward to the game apprehensively. Which England was going to turn up? The team that could defeat any other or the usual team, the one that played like strangers, seemingly sapped of energy and commitment?

I don't know why I lit those candles, but I must have spent over an hour just staring at them while lost in gloomy contemplation. As football anxieties faded from my mind, even more sombre thoughts set in. Twenty one years after meeting Jesus, my Christian life was full of ups and downs. I had experienced enough of God to be fully convinced that he was who the Bible said he was. I'd experienced his power, I personally knew people who had been healed of incurable illnesses. One case was a friend who had developed cancer of the lymph nodes in five places and who had lost all his hair from the chemotherapy which hadn't worked. By prayer alone he was now well. I also had been in meetings where dramatic things had happened. In short, I had no problem with believing God; it was how to walk in the light of such knowledge that bothered me so.

Living for God is both joyful and hard, an on-going struggle in which you become a battleground. The Spirit of God has made his home in you and yet it is up to you to make the daily choice to listen and respond accordingly to his promptings or not. It isn't about church or fellow Christians pushing you; there are no "control" measures in place or dodgy manipulations to blackmail you into doing the "right" thing.

Knowing God is personal. Just like anyone, I don't really need people to tell me I'm doing wrong, I instinctively know it. With God this is magnified. Without him you are spiritually 'dead' yet you still have a strong sense of right and wrong. With him, it's more, so much more. You are spiritually alive and offending him does not sit nicely with you. This is even though you have received unconditional forgiveness through Jesus for past, present and future wrongdoing. Even though you have the freedom to do wrong, your very conscience holds you captive. Offend the awesome God after what he's done for me? No, no, no, I hate sinning.

Being a Christian brings great joy into your life, but it also brings great challenges. And of late I had been struggling. No big deals, no murders, no robberies, no adulteries, just plain old selfish living, self-seeking at the expense of others. A lazy, 'let other people do it' attitude was getting me down. So late into the night I sat there, staring at two candles on the window sill and not feeling too happy about myself.

Saturday 1 July *The early hours*

The A12 between Lowestoft and Ipswich is notorious for accidents. Like so many roads in Suffolk it twists and turns and rises and falls, with street-lighting confined to small villages and some crossroads. Late at night the road is often empty and it is easy for drivers to lose concentration and veer slightly to the left or right.

On the night of the Red Hot Chilli Peppers concert at the home of Ipswich Town Football Club, the A12 was a bit more busy than usual. It had been an amazing concert and five happy youngsters were part of a steady stream of cars returning home to Lowestoft.

Claire had not been looking forward to driving. After all, there was the Ipswich traffic to navigate and the difficulty of finding a place to park. Driving back on the A12 was probably least on her mind but nevertheless she must have been quite pleased with herself by the time the car reached Blythburgh.

Whatever Claire was thinking, in the space of a few seconds it no longer mattered. The things of this world had suddenly come to an end for herself, Jenny, Carla and two other people in the car that had hit them. The driver of this car suffered a broken leg amongst other injuries but otherwise was ok. Sarah was terribly injured and came close to dying while Adam amazingly only broke his thumb.

As for us, some ten miles away, the telephone rang a short time later in the early hours of the morning. It was Ipswich hospital telling us that they had Claire and she had been in a car accident. They would give us no indication of her condition, only that we needed to get there. My wife Heather was immediately sick while my thoughts were of broken bones. She phoned my brother-in-law Bernard and he came round to look after our other children, Amy aged twelve and Tom only five, while we left Lowestoft and drove down the A12. We played worship songs as we went and tried to phone Jenny who we thought was coming back from the concert in another car. There was no reply.

Presently just after Blythburgh we saw a diversion set up and a fire engine nearby. We went through the diversion, realising that this must be where the crash had taken place. I got out the car to talk to the policemen who were approaching us and said who I was. They told me the driver of the Vauxhall Astra had been air-lifted to James Paget hospital in Gorleston. I knew this would be Claire and so the person at Ipswich must have been Jenny. The hospital obviously didn't know which of our girls they had.

I fell to the ground, so weak, so desperate while Heather looked on at the mashed up car that our girls had been in. The police wanted to drive us to the hospital but I realised that this would delay us from being able to get back to Amy and Tom. So I drove and we prayed and focussed as best we could, already sensing the presence of Jesus, strengthening us, assuring us.

Ipswich hospital

We found the hospital, parked and walked in. At reception we were met by a nurse and shown into a small room where we waited for the results of a brain scan from Addenbrooks. They had Jenny breathing but only artificially. They would let us know more shortly and left us with a cup of tea. We were offered company I think, but declined. We knew in our hearts that Claire was dead and I sensed that Jenny was gone too.

I found it hard to sit down; it was too oppressive and confined so I wandered out for a few moments in the fresh morning air. 'Lord I so need you'. I went back in quickly and sat with Heather who could barely move and we prayed. And then it happened, a few precious moments where God met with us in that little room and let me know for sure. Both girls had gone to be with him and I think Heather knew as well from the look in her eyes.

Yet unexpectedly, it was not fear and dread that began to bear down upon us but calm and peace. We were assured they were with Jesus and an unyielding conviction of this was present. Strength came into me and focus and purpose so that when a nurse returned with the verdict from Addenbrooks, I was ready for it. She told us that Jenny was brain dead and moments later took us to see her.

When we got to the bed there was a curtain around it. We asked to be alone because I wanted to pray over her with no interference. Finally we stood either side of the bed and looked on her face. There was a swollen look to her but peaceful as though sleeping. I prayed because I knew God could bring her back if he wanted. We prayed but I heard his calm, re-assuring voice again saying, "no, she is home with me".

We said goodbye and looked at the bed again. I realised she was no longer there, for the body is only a house and the occupant had departed. We left the bedside and asked the nurse not to keep the life support on for our sake. Our main thought now was getting back to Amy and Tom our other children as quickly as possible, but there was organ donation to discuss.

We took telephone calls and signed forms that enabled both hospitals to remove what they wanted from the girls. There was no point being sentimental about it and our minds were as clear as crystal. If the organs were to be used to help other people live better lives, they had to be removed pretty quickly. Uncannily both girls had only recently happily discussed their deaths during a car journey. They had decided on how they wanted their funerals to be and had both indicated that they would want their organs donated.

For Christians such decisions are not really that hard. If we truly believe that our bodies are just dwelling-places for our souls, then we will not be too peturbed about what happens to them once the soul has departed. This is within reason of course; it is right to respect the body and give it a decent burial, but it should not be seen as more important than the life of another person.

Homecoming

The strength we had known at the hospital and on the road back to Lowestoft disappeared by the time we reached the house of our good friends Mike and Sue Betts. All the leaders of the church were there and we just collapsed into their arms. I think they were crying too as the sorrow of what had happened finally overcame us. We cried and then we prayed and once again the amazing presence of Jesus brought strength to our minds and bodies.

We drove across town on what was now a fine summer's day and arrived home to find a large crowd of people there. It strikes me now as similar to the scene in the gospel of John when Lazarus had died and people were comforting his sisters. My first reaction was to hug people as words seemed useless. There was a mix of Heather's family, folk from church and Claire's sixth form school friends. I guess no one knew where else to be. At that point, I thought Sarah had passed on as well, as indications from the accident scene police were that only one person in the Astra had survived. At least that's how I thought I heard it.

I went and sat with the sixth formers in the garden for a while in an eerie silence, but it was hard to stay in one place. Where does one put oneself, how can you hide from knowledge? The doorbell rang, it was two of Claire's closer friends in tears; we hugged but that just set me off again. I remember staggering back to the garden and falling face down in a mass of tears, the loss once again overwhelming me. Again, people drew in to offer comfort as I lay there so glad not to be alone.

"Get up", insisted a desperate voice from within my head, for the mental turmoil was too dreadful to bear. The only remedy seemed to be to keep moving from one place to another.

I sat back against the garden fence and considered the small groups of people before me, heads bowed down with the weight of the world upon their shoulders. Nobody was prepared for this; death was a stranger to so many of us.

Worn out with sorrow I closed my eyes, only to be immediately confronted by a sense of brilliant light. As I gazed with my mind's eye I sensed the presence of Jesus, his clothes shining white and an aura of comfort and acceptance radiating from him. Instantly I understood my heavenly father was not going to abandon me. Contrary to my five senses, the mighty, radiating presence of Jesus was there before me and his strength would be enough for I had none. In fact I felt so weak that it seemed my whole body was in the process of closing down. Yet all I had to do was focus upon him, stood there like a mighty captain guarding a wounded soldier, gesturing defiance to the situation. I was utterly in his hands and he both knew and accepted it completely.

Later on in the day a policeman, or Family Liaison Officer to give a more descriptive title, arrived for the first of many visits to support us as much as was possible. Ian's first job was to drive us to the Gorleston hospital to identify Claire. Our other daughter Amy wanted to come too and we also brought along our good friend Debbie. I didn't really want to take Amy, for in my mind I wanted to protect her. After all, she was so young, just a few weeks short of her thirteenth birthday, but what protection was there? Even though we were united in our grief as a family, each one of us now had a loneliness within that no one else could touch. Besides, she said she needed to say goodbye and I would have been a fool to deny her.

When we arrived, we found Claire's body had been prepared in such a way as to make it look presentable and peaceful.

I stepped forward and prayed on behalf of all us, a prayer of thanks for her life and a resolute acknowledgement that death was merely a passing through from one place to another. Only a Christian can say this with real conviction; I was not voicing a desperate hope, I was uttering a complete truth. Amy stepped forward to say her goodbyes and I was so proud of her in that moment. She was standing up to the grim challenge before her. Something in my spirit knew she would not fall, that whatever her age or maturity of faith, it would be no barrier to God. He would be more than sufficient to see her through this.

Thus the day came to an end. I telephoned my parents and sister in Birmingham and was particularly disturbed by the anguish in their voices, the utter disbelief at what had happened. By evening our trusted friend Mike believed it important that we eat. I remember us trying to eat some Chinese food but barely being able to move our mouths. We must have cast pathetic figures to the people around us. I could barely swallow a morsel and the meal ended up being mostly wasted, but the important thing was to eat as an emphatic physical first step to recovery.

The Joy of Christ

In the next few days we had to formally identify Jenny which meant our policeman having to drive us past the crash site once again on the way to Ipswich. At least it gave Amy the opportunity to say goodbye to her and I think it was important for her to do that.

Flowers and cards poured into the house, the flowers just kept turning up on the doorstep and the cards were from many people we did not know. We discovered that many churches were praying for us and that brought us much comfort. People from our church turned up regularly in the days that followed. They cooked us meals and spent plenty of time with us. Some of them were also in mourning as they were good friends with Claire and Jenny. We allowed the closer friends to read the girls' diaries and discover some of their thoughts. Chris was gutted to discover that Jenny wanted him to baptise her but didn't think he would and Abi found out just how highly Claire thought of her.

With Heather and myself being teachers, there were a number of colleagues from our respective schools that regularly visited us, as did some of the girls' school friends. These people were most welcome as they had good hearts and tried to bring the best comfort they could offer, but there is nothing quite so refreshing as having the people of God around you in such dreadful times. People with no clear faith can be kind and stand with you in so many ways but they cannot help you with death. For them, what lies beyond is unknown and so they can only hold your hand. A Christian knows death for what it really is and so can help to ease the pain and even confront it. Particularly soothing are those who have a deep walk with God, those who are used to experiencing his presence and power. There is inside them a joy and a peace that darkness cannot overcome; they are beacons of brightest light to those who walk in the darkest of places.

Yet despite the sadness of loss, it was the joy of the Holy Spirit that was the prevailing feature of our house. We laughed and joked together and spoke with increasing awe of the wonders of Heaven that were now upon Claire and Jenny. The agony of death was unable to overpower us and to me it was blatantly obvious that the Lord of Life was moving freely amongst those who knew him. On one occasion I saw in a vision Jesus take hold of mine and Heather's hands and together we began to step forward. As we walked, I noticed a number of our Christian friends walking with us. There was a purpose about us and in some way it seemed that every step we took proclaimed the victory over death.

If only I could say that this joy was so dominant that grief ran away. The reality was that joy and grief occupied the same house. Even some time on, I would still describe myself as being on a roller-coaster between the two, but back in those early days, the awful and utter sense of loss would at times overwhelm me. My body seemed to give way to a physical nausea in my stomach and my mind would collapse into a pit of sheer misery, but always the hand of Jesus would pull me up and as I became more aware of him the joy would surge. One thing I can say without doubt is that the tears shed within the majesty of his presence outnumbered by far those that fell from despair.

Funeral

We began our preparations for the funeral with two issues mostly on our minds: whether to go for cremation or burial and what sort of service to have. Initially I was all for cremation as

I didn't like the ideas of the girls bodies lying under the ground and becoming a focal point for people to remember them by. As far as I was concerned, the girls had discarded their bodies and were now in Heaven. Therefore I didn't want a grave to visit, anymore than I would want to visit a derelict house where the occupants had long since left.

My point of contact with the girls was now caught up in my relationship with Christ. So often when I met him in prayer

I had a sense of meeting with them also; for my perspective had changed from being purely on Jesus to also taking in something of Heaven. On a number of occasions I became absorbed with visions of paradise, a beautiful land of intense colours and beauty. I was aware of people enjoying green pastures and waterfalls and I identified them as Christians who had died and I knew Claire and Jen to be amongst them.

So cremation seemed quite attractive as a way of minimising the focus on what had been left behind. It was therefore quite a surprise to me to find that objections were raised to this. Amy was a most vocal antagonist to the idea and Heather's parents also expressed disappointment. We discussed it with Rob Clarke, a good friend and one of our church leaders and as we prayed my opinion changed dramatically.

It was hard to put my finger on exactly why, but apart from respecting the preferences of other family members, cremation started to bother my conscience. Walter (Heather's dad) said that burial was biblical and backed it up with some verses, but I didn't see any clear instruction in them one way or the other. What I do know is that the moment I changed my mind, it seemed everyone was relieved. Rob, Heather and even the funeral director were pleased and I also felt something of an affirmation in my spirit that God himself didn't want cremation.

I am still not really sure why it mattered so much and I know that many Christian families have chosen cremation for their loved ones. Where choice is available the issue seems more to do with conscience than theology and surely no person in their right mind would suggest any harm can come from whatever choice is made.

However, I am aware that the grave has since become an important focal point for many people who knew Claire and Jon. It would have been mean of me to deny them that opportunity just because I was so firmly focused elsewhere. And I must admit, there have been times when I've been glad of a grave to visit; there seems something substantial about it, something more wholesome than an urn of ashes.

The second issue of the funeral service was also one that had to be considered in the context of other people. Death, like birth and getting married, is a communal affair and should not be the sole domain of those directly affected. When I see couples announcing they are going to get married in a far-away land like Bermuda, it saddens me somewhat. What about the people who cannot afford to travel that distance, those people who have shared in the couples' lives; do they not have a share in the happy day also?

For the funeral we had to consider our relatives and friends, those that were perhaps uncomfortable with our way of doing church and also those with little understanding of Christian beliefs. There were Claire and Jenny's school friends to think about and also people from the local community who wanted to be there, perhaps to be consoled as well as to show support for us.

In the end we opted for two services, a morning burial for family and close friends and an afternoon thanksgiving service that would be open for anyone to attend. The vicar of St Michaels, an Anglican Church, had kindly offered us a burial plot in the graveyard and in my mind it is the most beautiful location in Lowestoft. The building is medieval and is situated in land that overlooks the Broads. It is a delightful area to walk in and is a place where one can sit in peace and breathe in the fresh country air and smile at the beauty of creation.

On the morning of Monday 17th July, we left our house for St Michaels, accompanied by some of my family from Birmingham and also Heather's family. I remember being quite relaxed and light-hearted as we travelled the short distance in the hearse. I felt sorry for the funeral staff who were obviously used to conducting themselves as people who walked on eggs. They were unaware of how strong the hope of Jesus was in our hearts as they trudged along with heads bent low.

There were about a hundred people in the church as we sang a few songs, including 'How Great Thou Art'. The verses are truly amazing and only someone who enjoyed a dynamic relationship with Jesus could have written the words. The glory of creation, the sorrow of the cross, the victory over death and the second coming of Jesus flow from one to the other and steadily build a joy in my heart that wells up to overflow.

As I worshipped I saw Jesus and tears of gratitude fell from my eyes. The coffins were a difficult sight as they lay together raised up on some sort of pedestal at the front of the church. Yet Mike spoke so clearly on our hope in Christ that it was hard to be shaken. Even as we walked in procession to the burial spot, the tragedy of the situation seemed to have trouble breaking in. The bodies were lowered into the ground, one coffin on top of the other and we prayed a little before leaving.

Eventually we arrived at a reception prepared for the funeral guests at Mount Pleasant Gospel Hall. The Hall is the home church of Walter and Margaret, who are Heather's parents and so outstanding in their support. We chatted for a while and ate before leaving for the afternoon service at our home church. Between five and six hundred people were assembled there, which was far too many for the main building, so the service was relayed via video link into the other hall.

Looking around I saw many people from our church and from the girl's school. There were a number of mine and Heather's teaching colleagues present and staff from Hoseasons Ltd and Adventure Island where Claire and Jenny worked. Our policeman, Ian, stood out by virtue of his uniform and it was good to see him there. He proved so helpful to us, particularly in assisting with all the practicalities and legal chores of death. I certainly had not expected this level of help from the police and the only thing I could fault him on was his annoyingly loyal support of Chelsea Football Club!

Also present were a small number of local and regional press. Ian had warned me from the outset that the events of the car crash would not pass by quietly. Sure enough, even on the first day they visited our house and knocked on nearby doors in the hunt for extra information. Some were certainly insensitive to what had happened, but most of them, and in particular the local reporters, gave us the space we needed.

So I was not too concerned about their presence at the funeral and in fact quite welcomed it. For in my heart I knew that Jesus was going to bring something special from the tragedy. Neither the accident nor the goodness of God was going to pass by unnoticed.

The service started with an introduction from Rob and then a period of worship with our church band, all of whom were close friends with our girls and have been around the family for quite some time.

If some people were expecting a somber, mournful service, they were in for a surprise. For the next twenty minutes or so, many of us celebrated the victory of Jesus with loud, energetic songs of praise and then quieter worship. Next was a collection of photos that I had put together to be displayed as a slide show on the large screen and accompanied by music. Then it was time for tributes and I listened as best friends, Abi, Amy, Chris, Lauren and Matt spoke through their tears and grief. What really struck me was the constant testimony to the goodness of Jesus. Except for Chris, these were people still in their teenage years. I wondered at what they must be going through as they fought back the tears in their determination to speak.

I decided to say something after they had finished and acknowledged the support of the local community and the good friendships that Claire and Jen had enjoyed. I then spoke about God's love to us as a family and that it was this and not death that had broken me. "Once you've been broken by God's love, once you've met him in person, there's nothing else that can break you. I'm not scared of death… I'm scared of pain, but not death."

Mike spoke again afterwards, as Claire and Jenny had wanted in their 'death' conversation. It was poignant to think back to the two girls sat in the back of the car and discussing their funerals. No boring songs, lots of fun things and most definitely Mike!

I am sure they would have been most approving of his message on what happens when we die and why we need to come to Jesus. I hope no one left that service without understanding the reason for my hope and that God does not abandon his children in their hour of need. He loves us far too dearly to leave us to cope with such sorrow on our own.

God's people

Like moonlight shining pale in the darkness
Is the world as it tries to bring its comfort
As if a monster television on my wall
Or a holiday in the sun
Could do anything at all.

I've never really put my trust in toothpaste
Despite all the advertising claims
As if a tiny bit of fluoride on a brush
Could ever make me sparkle
Could ever do that much.

In the dark of night you're longing for the sun
You only stay alive because you know it's going to come
There's a vicious battle raging on in my mind
Sometimes I'm falling over but rising every time.

A crowd of people gathered on our doorstep
Weeping tears, being there for us
But though their kindness was certainly a comfort
They couldn't help me fix my eyes
Upon the God I trust.

When you're forced to stare into the eyes of death
With every passing moment you feel its icy breath
You get desperate for the people of God
They are the only ones who can help you to hang on.

The ones that suffer hurt but don't let go
No tragedy can change the truth they know
Light just seems to shine out from within
And seeing them makes my spirit jump
And death loses its sting.

What power can it hold over those who cannot die
Who have knelt before their Saviour
and received eternal life?
Death becomes a door from place to place
To walk through with my head held high
Rejoicing in his grace.

Phil, aged 18 in 1980

2 *Whispers*

My story really begins in Birmingham where I was born in 1962. Raised with one sister, I like to think I had a relatively happy childhood, although I must say it was full of oddities. My earliest memories stretch back to infant school and one day slipping away from the teachers to turn up at home in the middle of the afternoon. I didn't want to be there, so I came home. I don't

know why or how, but I seemed to have a problem with authority from an early age.

In junior school, I was outraged to hear of my removal from the top set. Mrs Salt informed me of the demotion in front of the class and I replied I wouldn't go! "Pardon?" I remember her exclaiming into the silence. "I'm NOT going down a set", I said. For moments that seemed to stretch out forever, there was an impasse, a silence until the crack of thunder, "YOU WILL do as I say". I swallowed, now embarrassed and replied meekly, "I'm sorry Mrs Salt".

Erdington, a few miles north of the city centre, was quite a rough area to grow up in. I was bullied at times and regularly chased by the gang from Tyburn Road. On one afternoon, we were playing at 'knock and run' when we ran into this gang led by the invincible bruiser 'Billy Boot'. "We just got told off by the geezers whose house you knocked on", they said. It was a lie – I doubt the house-owners would have dared, but we knew what was coming. Accompanied by a girl either side and a mottled crew of scruffs behind him, he first punched our big guy, Russ Scott, in the face. Russ had a wicked temper and was quite a good fighter but he just accepted the blow and walked on, spitting the blood out of his mouth. Billy head-butted my mate Stephen Grigg and then called me over. No way was I going to go anywhere near him but there was also no way I could outrun him. I was paralysed at the prospect of the punishment awaiting when fortunately my sister, Barbara, appeared with our dog, Danny. "What's going on?" she asked as one with authority. She looked Billy Boot square in the eye and off he went with his entire gang beside him. We had been rescued by my older sister by two years. Oh the relief but oh the embarrassment!

Further squirming awaited me when towards the end of junior school I seized the opportunity to relieve the school of a box of Walkers Crisps. An open window, a quick foray and I was out holding my booty. Most disappointingly, Neil a hard nut in my year who didn't seem to feel pain, saw me do it. I smiled at him in acknowledgement, surely he wouldn't tell on me, but you know what kids are like, they tell on each other all the time. Sure enough while I was stashing the box away in the wardrobe of my sister's bedroom, he was busy informing the headmaster of what he had seen.

The next day I was hauled into the headmaster's study. Mr Jackson was a fearsome chap but a fair one and he knew how to smile - but he wasn't smiling now. To my shame, a natural cowardice was betrayed as I blamed the theft on a wild lad named Andrew Hogg who lived nearby. Next day, I was called back into the study to see 'Hoggy' standing there. I don't remember exactly how it happened but I do recall that for some bizarre reason he confessed to the crime. I was safe and I didn't know why he did it, although I do remember him looking at me as if to say, "I'm taking this for you".

To this day it is a mystery to me and I find it scary. A wild boy modelled what, I was to discover in later years Jesus did on the cross for me. It is a memory that has never left, that someone for no reason could take another person's punishment.

However, there turned out to be a twist in the tale. More evidence came forward and the Hogg ended up being acquitted while I was brought back to the headmaster's study to bear the full brunt of his verbal anger at my lies and cowardice. My punishment was to be a caning in front of the entire school at the age of ten. I could think of nothing else as the day drew nearer and when it finally came I was shaking with fear. Everything else was a blur as I sat there cross-legged during the morning assembly, waiting for the moment to arrive. All the teachers, the children, the entire world and their dogs it seemed were in that hall.

Mr Jackson went through some minor points and then his tone changed and became heavy. He started to tell the school that there was someone here who was a thief and a liar and how shameful it was. My heart was thumping, any moment now and I would be named. A number of people knew it was me anyway but how was I going to take the pain up on the stage, caned in front of the school? Worse, there were girls I liked – Caroline and Joy – generally recognised as the prettiest girls in our year and they were about to see me squirm and probably cry.

The ultimate embarrassment drew close and then… reprieve! Mrs Reece – sweet and adorable lady – stopped the headmaster in full flow and said something like, "We request that the person concerned is not named or punished". I remember that she spoke for the other teachers and that she was serious and that it halted the headmaster. I remember the relief, my heart thumping and the incredible urge to whoop for joy. It was over, I had escaped but at the end Mr Jackson approached and took me back to his office. I was lectured, warned about expulsion if I did any further wrong, but not caned.

I was too young to question these events but looking back at them now, I wonder if the whole thing was staged. Perhaps it was all a wonderful conspiracy between Mr Jackson, Mrs Reece and Andrew Hogg. I do not know, but there are to be found here uncanny insights into Jesus and judgement. Mr Jackson, the judge, the rightful punisher of the guilty. The awful exposure of sin and cowardice to the great assembly is surely an insight into Judgement Day itself where the evil deeds of all men will be exposed. And then the glorious intercessor, Mrs Reece. Combine her with Andrew Hogg and we have Jesus taking mans' punishment on himself and interceding before God for us. Judge for yourself the oddity of these events but for me they are part of the pathway that led to being found by Jesus.

Handsworth

The next clearly definable part of my life was the starting of secondary school. Back then we had to sit what was known as the 'Eleven Plus' exam and I passed and was given a place at Handsworth Grammar School for boys. As I lived in Erdington, this meant an hour journey using two buses, one into the city centre and one out into Handsworth. Not many people lived this far away and as school started at 8.10am, it meant having to get up very early and hoping at least that one of the other five or so boys would be on the same bus. It wasn't that I really got on with any of them, it was just wanting company, particularly for the bit where you had to change buses. I must say though that I am grateful to one of those boys called Alex who was a year older than me. One of the hard nuts who lived in another part of the city but shared the same bus for some of the journey decided to pick on me and steal my bag. I had no chance of getting it back and it was being chucked up and down the bus. Alex intervened and demanded that the hard nut give it back. He did, although the next day in school he searched me out and tried to punch my face into a pulp. Fortunately he was caught before the world was deprived of such beauty.

I spent four mostly unhappy years at Handsworth. It was a rough environment for one who had no skill or heart for fighting. I hated watching fights and would do anything possible to avoid being caught up in one. But I loved playing football and a number of acquaintances on the football pitch were fighters and influenced me to stand up for myself when I had to. Two particularly bad memories stand out; the first was a fight with my friend Patrick. He was a bit of a hero to me, an Irish lad who played centre-forward and took no stick from anyone. One day we were messing around and he caught me accidentally in the face and made me bleed. The crowd egged me on to call for a fight after school. "After all", they assured me so vehemently, "it's a matter of pride. If you let him do it to you once, he'll do it again".

The vultures organised the event exceptionally well to take place in a street outside our sports ground. They circled around us and pressed me to hit him. Patrick, meanwhile, had said he wasn't fighting unless I hit him. So after more baiting from the crowd I did it; a weedy half-hearted punch aimed at the face. He easily ducked and spent the next few minutes trying to land pile-drivers on me, but my reach was too long and it was quite easy to hold him off. He resorted to trying some kung-fu kicks but I warded them off as well. The whole thing started to become a fiasco and the crowd drifted away leaving our friendship broken. Patrick regarded himself as the moral victor and the code at the school was once you had defeated your opponent in battle, you would from that point on treat him as an inferior unworthy of any respect. The truth was I had no heart for the fight. I wasn't scared, just disinterested, but I had lost one of my few friends.

The second memory is of two bullies. One was a Chinese sixth form student called Charlie. In my first year he walked up to me and grabbed my throat. I was too weak to resist and started to choke. His angry face full of hatred gave me the impression he wasn't going to stop and soon I was choking. He finally let me go and I recovered coughing and fallen on my knees while everyone around just watched. The second bully was also a

sixth former who decided he didn't like the way I looked.
I heard him say to a mate, "look at him, I just hate that kid." I had
to go out of my way to avoid him for if I was seen and could
be reached, he would kick or punch me. Fortunately I had the
pleasure of one day coming across a fight in which he was
involved. I later learned he had picked on another sixth former
who turned out to be a rather good fighter. He won really
easily and at the end superbly removed a shoe from the foot of
my bully and flung it onto the school roof. Yes!

Towards the end of the fourth year (Year 10 in modern language)
my parents announced that we were moving house to Solihull
on the other side of the city. My dad had secured a job at the
Rover Car Assembly Plant and I was asked whether I would like
to stay at Handsworth or move to a local mixed high school.

They should never have given me the choice. Stay at the
nightmare boys school where being tough was all that
mattered or move to a school a ten minute bus ride away
that had girls in it? Who cared about education? Living was
what mattered, so I pressed hard for a move even though the
Handsworth teachers advised against it. Back in those days, the
syllabuses being offered were very different to each other and
to change in the final year of normal school was a dangerous
thing to do. I realise now my parents were aware of this but I
was determined to leave.

Solihull

It was great, the answer to a dream. In September 1978 I swapped
the black and gold of Handsworth for the green of Tudor Grange
School, Solihull. My greatest memory of that school concerns a
boy called Stephen Seville or "Sev" as everyone knew him. On
the first day I was alone in the playground, displaying a 'skinhead'
haircut trying to look 'hard' so that no one would pick on me. I was
bewildered by all these new faces and really didn't know what
to do with myself when this boy approached and introduced
himself. He was smiling and had a deep voice and was able to

grow whiskers! We got chatting and he introduced me to his friends, Wedge, Dev and Fish. Strange nicknames but all were simplifications of their surnames.

Sev was kind and popular throughout my year group. People liked and respected him and although I was to fall in with a rough gang of lads in the months ahead, neither he nor his friends ever withdrew their friendship to me. This meant a lot because at the time I was a bit of an oddity. My home life had been deteriorating and my mum and dad were moving away from each other. I was too selfish at the time, too wrapped up in my own affairs to be of any help to them and eventually they got divorced.

I was also growing more insecure about myself, losing confidence, thinking that I was good for nothing and having little to offer the world. My haircut was a 'front' to stand out to people, to get noticed and my behaviour started to follow suit. I became angry and sometimes rude at school and remember on one occasion being sent to the headmaster's study. Within his four walls I lost control and started kicking out at his furniture and smashing things. He looked on in shock as I did it but wisely made no attempt to stop me. He wasn't to know that I was quite harmless; my temper was always vented at myself and things to smash, never at other people in a physical way, although my tongue could be pretty mean. After I had calmed down I became awash with tears. Somehow I had become desperately sad and unhappy and I didn't really know why.

The era of Punk Rock was made for people like me. It was the late seventies and the Sex Pistols, the Clash and Sham 69 had hit the scene. The tight white glitter men of the seventies were being despised by teenagers everywhere. No one wanted love anthems anymore, we wanted something energetic and aggressive and Punk did not disappoint. My clothing became tatty rags, red pvc trousers, tie-dyed shirts and chains around my neck and safety-pinned to my clothes. Sev and co were 'rockers' with denim and leather and motorbikes.

In Solihull the punks and the rockers quite liked each other. Our music had similarities, an element of wildness, although their music was more melodic. But much of it was too 'neat' for me and too predictable. They would rave about Deep Purple and Led Zeppelin and I admit they were good but punk went that little bit further. Not only did it take on the hated empires of disco and soppy love songs, it also took on music itself. It was a statement against everything that was established and accepted and that suited me just fine. Like the unhappiness that had grown within me, I don't know how or why this rejection of normal society came about, I just know that it did so that I lost all concern whatsoever for gaining qualifications at school or preparing for a career.

I left Tudor Grange with nothing and gained some part-time employment washing dishes in a hotel. Sev and his friends meanwhile were now at Solihull Sixth Form College. He had a Triumph motorbike and sometimes I would go over and see them and chat in the common room. I had failed my exams, I was getting into trouble but still their friendship remained. Admittedly invitations to join them in social exploits were rapidly declining but I had plenty of other things to do, so that wasn't an issue to me. It was just nice to see them on an ad hoc basis.

Solihull youngsters were very different from the youth I had experienced in Erdington or Handsworth. Erdington people were generally rough but honest folk who held no fancy dreams for their future and thought more about their immediate surroundings and the people they knew. At least that's how they appeared to me, while the Handsworth boys were arrogant and cruel, quick to hurt each other both verbally and physically. With them it was all about one-upmanship, being the best and I hated them for it.

In Solihull, the teenagers seemed much more friendly and with high hopes for the future. Their parents were often wealthy, with high expectations and large houses. They expected nothing less from their sons and daughters than the success they themselves had achieved. Many of the teenagers lived in rebellion against their parents and it was not uncommon for wild parties to be held while the parents were out. We drove their cars, we raided their fridges and camped in their bedrooms and many a son or daughter suffered furious parental wrath on the morning after.

It was within this hugely anarchistic and reckless setting that one day I received a piece of news that was both startling and unnerving: Sev had become a Christian. At the time, it didn't matter much to me why he had done this strange thing. What bothered me was that he was a part of the same enjoyable and adventurous scene as I was. There was so much going for us as young people in Solihull. We had places to go, lots of attractive and stimulating people to interact with and plenty of time to do it. Yet he for some unknown reason was not content with all of this. It was as if he had brought into question our way of life. He had dared to suggest there was something more than reckless fun-loving and self-seeking.

I cared nothing for what he had chosen to believe. The fact that he did it at all was what bothered me. I detected a change In him and the way people treated him. I saw that he struggled to maintain some of his friendships, perhaps because of the suspicion he had aroused in them. I also noted that his close friends Wedge, Dev and company stuck with him. Like them, I appreciated the person that was Sev far too much to think worse of him simply because he had become a Christian.

At the time, I simply regarded God and church as part of the establishment of life. Like school and social security and work, they existed to pin me down, to force out a perfectly acceptable social existence, but I didn't want to give in to it and so I was in rebellion against them all. Logic and reason didn't count, it was them against me.

A short time later, Sev was killed on the motorbike he had built his image around. There were a lot of bikers at the funeral held at the Solihull church. One of his favourite songs was 'Freebird' by Lynnard Skynnard and it was played as I stood there amongst the congregation, staring at the coffin, unable to make the slightest sense of death whatsoever. Sev's body now lies in St Alphege Church and sometimes when in Solihull I will visit the tombstone and look at the white bird and the inscription and remember the days of my youth and the kindness of a fifteen year old boy who left this world far too early.

I didn't know then what I know now. I remember hearing at some point that Sev's family and in particular, his younger sister Jane whom I knew, were Christians. I do remember that I thought she coped amazingly well with what happened. Although I saw her cry on more than one occasion I also remember amongst her friendship group an under-current of talk about God. One of those friends, called Nicky, became a girlfriend of mine for a while and maybe I was further exposed to Christianity by her blatant refusal to indulge in any of the 'unspeakable' stuff which teenage boys are so desperate to discover. Perhaps God was playing a significant part in my lack of progress!

It is amazing to think that one day I am going to meet Sev in Heaven. He was possibly my first exposure to the idea of God as a living, personal being and I wonder now if he will be one of the first people I meet on arrival? Perhaps just like that first day in Tudor Grange when I was standing alone in the playground, he may be the first one. It would not surprise me at all to find that within the warmth and generosity of the living God, there is a place for welcome from those that have contributed to my being born into his kingdom.

3 *Disillusion*

I suppose it is only natural that the death of a friend should cause a shaking to occur. I never considered that I could die, not really, the tragedies always happened to other people but now someone near and the same age had gone. Around that time, my much-respected Grandad Lawrence had a stroke and spent the remainder of his days on earth at my mum's house. I remember one day having to carry him to the toilet and being appalled that old age and illness could do such damage to someone so wonderful. He always treated me well and I think his death had a profound effect upon my life, although I did not recognise it then.

During my teenage years and early twenties I saw death take Grandad, Sev and a couple of dogs. One was Danny, who I loved but for some reason shed no tears over when he died from kidney failure. My parents meanwhile divorced in the last year of high school and I lived for a short time with my dad in Solihull and later with mum in Edgbaston. It was while staying with my dad and probably at somewhere approaching the heights of a mountain of insecurity that I met Amanda.

One night I was slouched over a chair at my local drinking hole with a few friends. None were proving inspiring enough to hold my attention and so my eyes wandered over to a young lady who was sitting with a few girls I knew well enough at least to say hello to. Perhaps it was the beer that drew me in. Whatever, I could not keep my eyes away from her and I became lost to her beauty. The conversations around me became like distant voices, similar to when you are lying in bed and can hear the talk from the lounge below.

This girl was alive and like a sudden and exhilarating burst of cold air, she blew refreshment into my being. So merry with her friends, smiling and laughing, it was as though there was an aura of happiness upon her and the sense of it mesmerised me. It was as if something that had been forgotten was being re-kindled within.

I could not take my eyes away and it did not go unnoticed. Once, then once more her eyes left her friends to meet with mine and twinkle with glorious acknowledgement. She must have laughed with her friends about the weirdo, the strange spikey blue-haired punk rocker that kept looking her way. I guess they would have told her who I was and possibly that I was reasonably safe to know.

Suddenly I rose and left my friends to talk to her. Memories become vague after this but I remember a few nights spent afterwards, sitting alone with her in the pub, inseparable and doing all the things people laugh at when couples express affection in public. I thought I loved this girl so much that when she left Solihull to become a nurse, I followed her to Plymouth. One of my close friends, nicknamed Spade, had moved down there previously to serve in the Navy and he agreed to take me in. Within weeks the affair was over. I had grown too clingy, too stifling for a young lady who still wanted to live and enjoy her new found friends.

I returned to Solihull with no desire to be there any more. My tail was between my legs, I had been rejected and all that remained was the faithful and deep insecurity that had just grown a huge chunk larger. Ironically, it was insecurity that characterised the relationship from start to finish, let alone the aftermath. It was the deep sense of loneliness, of not being loved by anyone that caused me to fawn so ridiculously over this girl. I do not blame anyone for this, least of all my parents who loved me as best they could. In my mind I was ultimately alone.

What I saw in the pub that night was not a girl, it was an ideal. It was as if I saw in her a happiness I could not have. I guess she would have had her own insecurities and perhaps was flattered initially by the attention, but all I wanted was to be loved and in such a way that was impossible for a girl in her late teens to give, whether she wanted to or not.

Relationships before Amanda were like the games that children play. There was nothing serious within them, just games of dares and don'ts and being seen to be with someone cool. But the experience that ended in Plymouth polarised my thoughts and determinations into one field alone: escape. Whatever was to happen with my life, Birmingham would not play host, for all that could be offered there was institutionalised drudgery. If people wanted to get jobs and get married and settle down and have kids, well let them. Let them continue the great and meaningless shambles of life. I wanted none of it, I wanted escape.

It is at this point that I introduce some of my diary entries. They are worth including because they speak so vividly of a young man aged twenty who can make no sense of life. They are honest and full of musings on a world that has no God and therefore no reason to spin at all, as it does at an extraordinary speed within a blackness of unknown proportions that is aptly called Space.

October 1983 *First entry*

My life is ticking away. Greetings. You and me are ultimately alike for we have no meaning. We are alike as we are alone in accepting the great depression that is death. Love is only a consolation. All living beauty has destiny in the ugliness of death. No one can love ugliness. I conclude then that love ultimately turns to pity for the one you love. If you want to avoid being pitied then kill yourself while you're still young. I will never kill myself. I am an island, untouchable. I can function without love but love is the greatest thing I know. I feel inhuman, trying to sacrifice loving because it is not worth it. But it is hard and if love really ends in pity what is there to live for?

November 1983 *Meaninglessness*

Autumn leaves, sweeping in circles on the spongy earth
At the whim of the wind and in perfect disarray.
I stand firm on jelly ground
Watching the clouds so grey and dull
And when the wind is lost, I become part of the lull.

All to do now is comprehend the silence
Its unholy significance
Once again the wind rises and fades
Like human generations
I feel as though I am nothing.

For an immeasurable time, I have no mind.
Just the sight of racing clouds
Of every shade of grey and every size and shape
There are a thousand, thousand forms to make
When the wind blows so hard and fast.

I turn my brain, cause crashing waves
A billion thoughts on the tide
All the faces I've known and know
Each with their own story to tell
Like a cloud or a wave.

What meaning these people?
What have they to say
That can change the game, the sham, the shame
Why don't they see it my way?

I become lost like the wind that created the lull
Impossible to understand are clouds and earth.
I understand nothing at all
There is no meaning, no point, no reason
To anything, anyone I see.

I am lost then, so shout and cry
Wreak havoc on the silence
As a maniac stab it in frenzy
The very fabric of quiet.

Wednesday 14 December 1983 *Birthday*

I was born 21 years ago today and I wonder what the good of it was. No significant contribution yet to be made to the world. Nobody helped, nothing changed by me. I am wasting away my life. There is nothing, no concern, no positive movement towards a satisfied and coherent existence. I feel a waste of humanity but it is only because of what others do. Why should I judge myself by others? How perfectly right to leave the whole game to them and have nothing of it myself. Oh but I would die in permanent loneliness. I am damned to this sham and it is a terrible insult to one's pride.

Thursday 22 December *Fighting nature*

How despicable people are in crowds. How undignified to be another aimless nothing in the great mass of life. I dig my self-importance – better to be an egotist than a snivelling jackal neutralist. With my dog and as a fellow animal I have been fighting nature tonight in the thicket and bramble. Gloriously vicious to smash through the vegetation and dare to tread the swampy bog beneath. Nelson the dog fell into the stream and I stung my arm but it was worth it, just to be inhuman for a while. I chased him and he chased me and it was better than being with people.

Wednesday 4 January 1984 *Sex and fulfilment*

I stayed the night at my girlfriends house and slept in her brother's bed, pleased by an electric blanket, bemused by pictures of the Nolan sisters on the wall (what sort of closet case is he?) and taunted by nude women on his calendar. Sex is fulfilment. Oh no it isn't, why kid myself? It is as beautiful in itself as any pleasure but still it fails. Sex comes and goes like snow or rain, but still gives no answers to life's riddle.

So I am walking with my girl into the countryside, stopping in at a bakery for cakes and holding each others hands. And I am accepting life's fulfilment as being a girl's hand in mine because what else is there? We stop at a pub for fresh, sweet cider and then enter a forest in which we lose ourselves. I lie on my back and stare up and up, through the trees and into the sky. The world has become silent and I no longer care for why I live. It isn't important, I am here and I am happy.

What am I recording my life for, what does it matter and who cares? If someone actually cared enough to read this book would that make it matter? We return to the pub and the 'bikers' are in there. Bikers are always in uniform you know. They want everyone to know they ride bikes and smoke hash. No, no, that's not the truth of it: I'm just letting the apathy get to me again. Better stop writing.

Thursday 12 January *Antipathy*

> I cycle home, neither fast nor slow
> What is fast to a snail is slow to a crow
> So how can one man ever know
> If he cycles fast or he cycles slow?
> You strawhead.

Dusk is a mockery of its summer glory. It goes before it comes and then there is the blackness – the philosopher's palace. As I walk my dog with thoughts on visiting continents abroad, the idea comes that there will be no escape from the twisted walkway of life. I can only withdraw upon myself and have as little to do with my fellow creatures as possible.

It isn't really living that bugs me, it is social life making me race and contend when I don't care for it. Oh don't I indeed! What a façade my brain paints for me. I don't really know whether I care or not. It's either a ruthless form of self-defence to help me justify laziness or a grim reality. I'm terribly indecisive but at least I've decided that.

But as for this social life, well it's an antipathy between me and them: they lie to me and I sing back to them likewise.

We are just going through the motions. Society lies because it strives to give purpose when there is no purpose, at least not ultimately. How can there be when death takes you whatever you do? I could justify happiness if there was ultimate happiness. Instead there is only decay. No one survives it and I go round smiling and laughing while it all happens.

Tuesday 17 January *Wags*

One gets it together to cycle to maths with headphone music to deaden the graft. One squats in the abyss of the noise-ridden college canteen and becomes like a frog, gawking at the girls who are squawking at the world their unquestioned importance. Hah! I spit on you wags with your make-up and need to impress. Suckers and slaves to fashion and men.

So with the scene bottled and labelled, one lifts and lowers the knees to reach the snug, smug library of toy-town Solihull. One tries to read a book on jobs in Europe but one's eyes have already travelled. They rove upon the old folk reading the news, so comfy and warm. They become immersed in a skirt bumpy and torn and airing its views. I know what you're saying to me lady. No one is really reading at all. Eye contact is the game but how oppressive is this hot sticky embarrassment of silence!

Thursday 26 January *The walkway*

I learn about Marx in Sociology, the old son of a bitch who thought he could create a perfect system without taking squalid human nature into account. I cycle home and argue most of the day with Ma over a 'job' offer from the Scientology centre in Moseley. The training is in Sussex and although I don't trust the guy I spoke to, I'm pampered by the thrill, the irresistible smell of adventure. I contemplate it while drifting up the Harbourne Walkway with my dog in the vivid enchantment of black and white which is night and snow.

This is weird and unreal; everything seems to be hung in a suspense that is heavy upon me, almost tangible and thick like treacle. This is fascinating, this is frozen beauty, this might be death staring at me from every point of focus. My steps are delicate and gingerly trod within this foreboding gloom. The black branches are the spinster hands of old bony hags. Their black bodies frown down from above like solid blocks of evil as I follow the silver way of ice with my dog running free from imagination and therefore oblivious to the danger.

I reach the soft, gurgling stream, bulging and fast after its meal of snow. I gather reeds from the bank and make words on the whiteness while an ominous electric sound hisses on. There is nature and there is me. There is nothing between us, no friendship and no compromise. I am reduced to a wide-eyed child. I want to believe my imagination and go wild and scream out my presence to the unseen spirit of the wood as a strong gesture of defiance. I can believe it's there if I want to, thick and stifling, calm and cold and with the formidable assurance of a spider, whose victim struggles helplessly in silvery thread, it moves closer.

Thursday 5 July *Pollution*

The days are passing quicker now and change is almost upon me. I've made up my mind that this year must be the one for moving out of home. I've taken to reading 'The Lord of the Rings' again to help me through these days of waiting. I bought some headphones last week and how sweet it is to walk and cycle with selected melodies again. I would enjoy it more if the sights were not so foul. Birmingham is the devil's garden and its people the devil. No that's untrue. I don't know who to blame but all I see is filth and all I smell is pollution. So what's going on, why is it this way? No one cares enough perhaps. The results are that natural beauty has been replaced by cold concrete clothed with fish and chip wrappers. If only one could restore the sanity of shrubs without crisp bags caught in their thorns. I only know the answer to all this filth must lie in the individual.

4 Travelling

Tuesday 17 July 1984 *Stalled*

I'm sitting between a few bushes between a park and a road in Kent. Nothing has gone right but I'm not freaked out yet. Yesterday I called on Ian who was to come with me on this journey abroad but at the last moment he pulled out on me. I can't say I congratulated the guy on the matter. So I set off alone and hitched a ride to Stratford in a Mercedes. The driver was an African and he told me the people of Libya all but worshipped Colonel Gadaffi – weird!

Next I caught a bus to Oxford for £1.50 because too many other people were hitch-hiking. Here, I changed my mind and decided to catch a ferry at Dover rather than Portsmouth. This meant getting to London and I managed it via a van and another Mercedes. London in the sticky heat with a heavy rucksack was horrible, especially the tube and buses, but walking was the worst and I've now got a huge blister on my foot.

Somewhere in Kent, while trying to hitch on the A2 to Dover, I lost my prized leather bag within which were my money, passport, travellers cheques and a small amount of hash. It's terrible and so hard to take. If it's handed in I could get done for possession, and do I even dare report the loss? I decide I have to and fill in a report at the local police station and telephone my mum and the travel agent to get my travellers cheques cancelled. Night is settled in now and I've made a bed in a thicket but am not getting much sleep.

Wednesday 8 August *Grounded*

Back in Solihull I can report that the postman has changed his hair-style. I sign on today at the dole office and encounter a socialist trying to sell his newspapers about the miners strike.

He told me the revolution was just around the corner. So I went looking for it but only found a few crisp bags, a bending woman and a burning fag.

At long last my new passport has been delivered and now I can get my act together and hop across the channel. My friends Gaz and Andy have already gone on ahead and the idea is that I'll meet them at the Isle of Noirmoutier in France.

The idea of not going now is unacceptable. There has to be change or I will go mad with frustration. It isn't me I see at fault, I will come through and live normally but in the right situation and with the right purpose. This city is pollution, litter and grime and it is hard to have purpose here, but elsewhere who knows?

I have no respect for myself but I also have little respect for others. We're all dreadfully wrong and do so little about it. Our values are misplaced, self profit rules over communal gain, the individual matters more than the people. This is wrong, I know it's wrong so why should I have anything to do with it? How can I make the effort for serious living when I feel like this? By accepting it like a wimp I suppose.

Saturday 25 August *Up and running*

I settled down on the Birmingham to London train and talked astrology with a black lady while constantly aware of an intense buzz inside, making me on edge about what she was saying. The train from London to Newhaven was palatable though as I relaxed to the hum of foreign wags around me. I was seated next to an Italian temptress who told me of her rather sad life in London.

I paced the decks of the ferry as England drifted further and further away. You will be enlightened to know that ferries do not move at all, the countries do. Yup, all the time drifting here and there, all in relation to the ferry you happen to be on.

I smoked hash with a Spaniard who I could only communicate with in French. As the effect grew upon me, I began to fear the

French customs officials and so purchased two litres of wine to ease the alarm. As Dieppe drifted nearer I became more and more out of my head and floated through customs to catch a train to Paris.

It was in the early hours of the morning when on a crowded carriage, and next to some rather snobbish French dames, I was violently sick. The whole compartment just emptied and I spent the rest of the journey blissfully alone. But worn out and ill was not the way to navigate through Paris with a heavy rucksack. Somehow I caught the right tube-trains and managed not to pay on the longest journey.

Some kind soul bought me a coffee and soon I was on the outskirts of the city trying to thumb a lift, but no one would oblige so in my illness and fatigue I caught a bus back to the centre, helped by a black man. With the uplift of a few 'joints' I caught a fast and comfy train to Nantes and from there caught a coach to Noirmoutier to meet my friends.

The island, halfway down the west coast of France is much larger than they had implied on the telephone. I'm meant to meet them at the gates of the main municipal campsite but there's a few of these campsites on the island. So I make it to the one by the main town and crash out with a joint underneath a hedge of small fern trees.

Sunday 26 August *Alone*

I opened my eyes to little kiddies playing on slides and swings. The day is lovely and warm and I lie carelessly on the beach eyeing the scantily clad wags. The sea sparkles like a thousand emeralds as I swim effortlessly.

After a chew on bread and pate and a slurp of milk I hitch quite easily to the south of the island and reach the nearest campsite to the mainland, but come 6pm Gaz and Andy aren't there either. Fools and imbeciles, where are they?

It's somewhere near 8pm now as I lie here in the back garden of someone's windmill house. Ah the liberties I take; my towel is drying on their washing line and there's a fire made, ready to wage war with the darkness. If only someone was with me I would be having a good time. Come evening and things change as I'm befriended by about eight 14-16 year olds and doss with them by the beach for ages.

At the end of the night I light my fire and stare out at a mass of uncountable stars and think how small I am. Look at them, what could I ever do to change the heavens? Look at me, I'm insignificant. I have come and I will go and nothing will have changed out there. How marvellous, surely it is a license to go crazy. How utterly ridiculous to think my life means anything. No matter what I do, my only judges will be my fellow meaningless humans.

Life only has meaning within humanity but people are fickle, constantly changing their minds and bending truth to suit their desires and needs. Who tells the truth if it will get them into trouble? Who will not lie when desperate and who will not steal in the perfect situation? Life only has meaning within humanity and humanity lies. It is terrible. What more excuse can there be not to bother with the effort at serious life?

So here I am looking for friendship and love while believing the real articles don't even exist. Everything falls short of what it is meant to be. I cannot justify anything I do for there is no justification. All I have is my beautiful escape, the knowledge that nothing matters ultimately. So I have a choice, smile and get on with it or sink underneath the knowledge. So I smile and say, "What matters? Mad hatters. All that matters are mad hatters.

Monday 27 August *On the road*

I dismissed the idea of meeting the goons, Gaz and Andy, the bold buffoons and hitched away from the Island of Noirmoutier. A teacher lady brought me to the mainland but had me sitting in the back because she trusted me not. Can't blame the lass though; one can only pity the wag for missing out on the unbelievable opportunity of my wonderful presence.

Two Parisian wags saw to my journey next but then I had to walk for half an hour until a lonesome lad in a comfy, fast car took me for a hundred miles or so to Le Mans. The next stop was a place called Alencon which virtually puked out agriculture. It's so classical rustic French countryside around here. The final lift was 250 miles to Dunkirk with a male nurse which was quite good because his broken English and my petit French complemented well. The night grew cold and the fog came down, so I opted for a rented room. The nearest one cost a hundred francs! I took it because I'm so tired. I had a shower and smoked a joint, almost ecstatic in the luxury.

Wednesday 29 August *Amsterdam*

Tsk, tsk, 'tis much better to talk French in Amsterdam than boring old English. After shaving in Dunkirk I've been exercising my thumb all day, but it's such a drag to give details. Travelling through Belgium was short and puny lifts although fast and quick. The most notable included meeting a middle-aged director of car exhausts who seemed to share my brain. How amazing to meet an enemy capitalist pig and find out he isn't one. Into the outskirts of Amsterdam, a dude with his own television show picked me up. How annoying to be a captive audience, listening to his success as his car telephone beeped and burped out his importance. But at least his freaky threads provided some compensation.

I caught a tram into the middle of the city. No one asked me for any money so I didn't pay any; in fact no one got hassled for fares. With utter disbelief rampant in my head I stepped off thinking this truly is double-dutch! I found a room to rent smack bang in the middle of the Red Light District. It's a Christian Youth Hostel – a place of propaganda. They play Christian songs at breakfast like supermarkets play background music to make a man spend more. And, what's more, I've got to be in by midnight because that is when they lock the doors. But it's only £4 a night and that includes breakfast.

I dump my rucksack – hoorah, hooray and go out for beer and to secure some hash. The deals cause me mirth, the way they're pressed and wrapped like bars of candy. While smoking a joint I meet with a lad who's become so bored of beer and hash that he no longer bothers. He sat and then walked with me into the night, straight as a stick, while the whole town freaked out.

Sex shops were a dime a dozen, except they've gone a stage further here: they just stick wags in the windows who smile and try to seduce me. I get about as seduced as a fly in a cobweb. This night, this town with its apparent lack of law has me on some exotic erotic fantasy. The town itself turns me on more than the prostitutes ever could. I return to my base and smoke more joints in the dormitory corridor, though no one notices.

In the morning, breakfast is pretty slim to say the least. I go to the Heinekin lager factory with Bertrand, a French student who's staying at the same place, and smoke hash throughout. The guided tour costs a guilder, around 25 pence, but I regard it as small payment for getting smashed on the free samples. Sadly I have to endure a screening of the great Heinekin history. But they make up for it after and I repay them by having a joint in their toilet. It's 3pm now but I feel like the end of the night.

At the real end of the night I end up with a Yugoslavian whom I watch get ripped off for some hash in quite an unusual way. A dealer from a café offered him some blow, took the money and then said it wasn't enough. The Yugoslav tried to give the hash back only for the dealer to hit him with a life-story of his problems and his boss. And in the end he bullied more money out of his victim.

Thursday 30 August to Saturday 1 September *Ostende*

Getting out of Amsterdam this morning is no easy task. I walk south to the outskirts and then spend an hour or two walking the motorway because there's so many other hitchers. The reward is a very long lift to Ghent in Belgium off an ex-Hells Angel who's a chain smoker – yuk. I eventually end up in Ostende, though there's nothing eventful about it. It's 5pm now and I'm in a furnished box which costs me around £6.50 including breakfast. Out of the window is a rather irritating sight of a ferry bound for England. So where shall I go next? My planning has been totally erratic so far – up, down, there and around. Maybe the south of France.

Tonight I saw a good live band jamming in the street while I screwed up on chocolate in my stoned haze. Ostende is a crummy place but good for pollution – many variations of filth and rich in lead. If I only hadn't paid for this room I could be exercising my thumb again. One thing I have over my fellow thumb-bums is that they're generally lazy and unemotive. My body and facial expressions are well-trained now so that they always get some sort of response.

The next day, it took a long and weary walk to leave Slimesville and then quite a few other lengthy plods before achieving the crummy distance of Chalon-Sur-Marne which is a southy bit east of Paris. I met up with a couple of Scottish guys who fitted their reputation perfectly by being lazy and huge wine consumers. We got drunk in town on the night and smoked a few joints but then suffered a really cold night as we slept beneath the starry black sky.

Sunday 2 September *Packet food*

I'm in a great place now, a town called Annecy which is smack on the French-Swiss border and right by the Alps. There are some huge mountains here but the main attraction is a great lake of rain water which people laze around in the hazy summer heat. I swam in it today and stared nonchalantly at the topless wags. The cost of things round here just aren't to be laughed at. It's around fifty pence for half a pint of lager and I'm addicted to it in the heat and with the hash.

I've just cooked a meal over some sticks, a mix of packet foods and I dread to think of the unsavoury chemicals in there. Surprisingly, the taste was delicious although I burnt my tongue. The guy who drove me to Annecy is well worth a mention as he was quite a cool dude and drove me for 130 miles. He was a doctor who fed me cheese and beer and also paid for me to go with him into a replica village of ancient France around the Roman times.

Monday 3 September *The middle of nowhere*

I've come 30km south to Aix Les Bains and encountered the first rain while hitching. So I'm sat in a café watching it fall against the mountainous background. Last night I smoked the last of the blow and had a few beers. One place tried to charge me around a pound for half a pint so I sipped it slowly and then slyly slipped away before the waiter came. So many cafes in France don't take the bill immediately.

I walked around the lake watching the multi-coloured fountains, thinking how entrancing they are, breaking out into a thousand shimmering darts of light. A girl walked past me and then suddenly dived into the lake with all her clothes on. More amazingly she then swam over and started talking to me in French. I surveyed her pretty face and knew she found me attractive. But I muffed it because I was more stoned than drunk and I just can't handle wags when I'm stoned. In the end she became bored of me and it serves me right I suppose.

I had quite a good sleep near the lake, very warm and dry and woke in the morning to make a fire and cook chicken soup with corn, instant mash and vegetables. Not exactly what I'm used to eating in the early sunrise. When the clouds came in I decided to leave Annecy.

Another 100 miles or so have gone by and I'm now somewhere past Valence in the middle of nowhere. It's very dark and I'm sat in a nowhere café supping another expensive beer after cooking another dried food meal over a fire. I've got to hand it to these dried foods; the very thought of them injures the brain but they certainly do no harm to my stomach. All around me are farmers fields and I've been sampling their pears and filling my pockets with them. But I've also burnt my tongue again.

After Aix Les Bains I had a succession of small lifts, one being on an unrestricted moped without a helmet which was fun. I had two long lifts and the first guy went twenty miles or so out of his way to drop me off at a good position. The second guy was a lorry driver and his cab was really spacious. 'Twas grand to perch myself so high and look down on the passing cars as we trucked to Valence. From there to here, the middle of nowhere, came the misfortune of a lift off an aged homosexual. I had to constantly manipulate my arm positioning to counter the movement of his arm towards my waist. When he realised he'd be getting nowhere, he just stopped the car and told me a spoof that it was good here for hitchers. I doubted him but didn't want to continue the journey anyway. The middle of nowhere had become suddenly attractive!

Tuesday 4 September 1984 *Kindness unlooked for*

Strolling along last night in the tangible darkness a guy actually saw me and stopped his car. I'd just been picking a few more big juicy pears and walking on with no lights on the road, hardly able to see. The light from his car was almost blinding but what on earth made him stop I'll never know. He did is all that matters and then I was on my way down south. We later picked up a German guy and zoomed for a few hours through the rest of the night to Agde on the south coast of France. I crashed out with the German on the beach in my bag of comfort on a plastic under-sheet so that its cleanliness would remain unchallenged.

Once the sun was up I swam in the sea and shaved and quickly learned that salt-water and soap just don't mix. Without much thought I automatically got to hitching again for motion has become my habit these lonely days. This time it was 150 miles or so northwards through some great scenery, especially a town called Milleau which had its houses on the slopes of a great valley. The southern central part of France is beautiful.

The best lift was off an author called Rene and his younger buddy Jean-Francois. Apart from supplying me with beer and wine and an invitation to stay at his, he bought me a five-course meal in a posh hotel in a town called St Flour where our journey ended. The first course was mackerel, potatoes and some spicy vegetables. Next came chicken with mixed herbs and chips. Then, get this, vegetable and prune pate! Fourth course was cheese and bread and finally, ice-cream. Far out.

After the "Au Revoirs", I stuck my thumb out and immediately was offered a lift. But the guy was a queer – he offered me a lift and food in return for sex. So I walked away into the dark night and met up with a couple of hungry hitchers from Oxford.

I cooked them soya meat and mash and left them to their tent on the roadside. I opted finally for a petrol station because it was undercover and it felt like rain was coming. Instead, the night grew colder and colder but strangely not older. I put all my jumpers and trousers on and snuggled up to a petrol pump but it was just too cold in this mountainous area. I had to keep getting up to dance and jig and in desperation tried one of the show-car doors. To my enormous relief it opened and I crashed the rest of the night away in the back seat.

Wednesday 5 September *Hitching up with God?*

Brrr!!! on a cold and early morning of yucky mountain wetness with my entire wardrobe of clothes necessarily on. At 7am or so, the first thumb stick-out produced a warm car. How pleasing and fitting to get an immediate lift. The day warms up and the second lift is for 150 miles or so off yet another generous guy who feeds me. But I've left my map in his car, damn it. I was really getting attached to that map – one of those entirely plutonic relationships you hear that other people have.

It's now evening and pouring down with rain so I'm sheltering in a disused petrol station. Maybe after all there is a guardian angel looking after me for my luck has been amazing at times. The final lift is from St Dizier for 200 miles off a young frog and his wag all the way to Dieppe. And even then, at journeys end, I'm offered a bed for the night at the lads house. Naturellement I take it, along with a good meal and plenty of giggles.

There is no stability in fate, no pattern can be made out of what happens to me. One moment I'm shivering and hungry, the next I'm in a double bed, drunk on wine and sherry, with a tummy full and fat. These past two days have been very difficult with regard to spending money. I feel really cared for and it gives me the creeps at times. Oh I've no hope in anything spiritual really, it's just that the concept considerably brightens things up. How delightful, how infinitely attractive to forget life's ultimate pointlessness and loneliness, how comforting to lapse out and believe in a spiritual host or something like that. It would do me the power of good I reckon to just throw my lot in with God and become religious.

I could escape myself then. My life is surrounded by hypocrisy anyway, why don't I just start believing in God? I could do it; after all I deny my conscience when I do bad things by simply detaching myself and focussing on something else. I could do it and what would it matter? If there is God then I would be justified, if not then it wouldn't matter anyway.

No, that's not the answer. All I can do is take this life I'm in with as little seriousness as possible. But damn it, even laughs don't last. Nothing lasts, everything wastes away. Damn it! What's the point in doing anything if everything wastes away? The only answer is to satisfy the 'here and now'. The past is dead, the future never comes, I am in the here and now. So why do I bother writing a diary then? Pah!

Thursday 6 September *Homeward bound*

After an enormous breakfast, my hosts show me the sights of Dieppe. It's a dump. Then comes a ferry ride across to England in the pouring rain. On this slow and dreary boat, I'm brightened up by once again meeting Jean-Pierre who was on the ferry when I crossed over a couple of weeks ago.

The guards at Customs can give you a real guilt complex. If I'd have been stoned, they'd have sussed it. I manage to ride the train from Newhaven to London for free but have to pay the £12 for a crummy rail fare to Birmingham. The boat ticket was loads as well – 218 francs. I've been really ripped off for travel prices today. So here I am back in Birmingham, back in the old and stale carbon monoxide – you don't even get it fresh here.

5 Re-born

Me, me , me?

Me, me, me! Woke up when I wanted
Heard a noise downstairs and am calling for a drink.
Hmmm, what am I doing today?
"Ssshh, don't talk, I need to focus.
WHAT? Yes toast thank you, jam, anything you can find."

Now I'm at the grindstone again
Why oh why do I have to work?
Such a waste of my beautiful time
These people with their stupid problems.

Hooray, back at home but no one here to cook me tea
Think I'll not go out tonight; said I would
But that was then.

It's all about me, always was until that day
The day I met the man who travelled so far
To give the gift that cost most dear.

It hurt him much to give it
For the purchase price was death
Yet he gave it with such a thrill of anticipation
That I expected a blast of ecstasy.
So strange then that touching this precious thing
Could make me feel so unclean

Surely he had made a mistake
To give something like this to me.
It was a treasure of blood, ruby red
And held in my hands it burst and bled
Shattered thus it then reformed
To purest white to change no more.

Oh how tears fell, as dirt within me seeped away
Felt like leaving the night for a bright new day
But a new terror gripped me as I turned to the man
For he had eaten my dirt and died at my hand.

Silence, an awful silence
I had killed a perfect man
I didn't mean to, I didn't know
That my filth was this bad.

Why did he do it? The silence went on.
"I didn't ask you to"I cried
Then came a rumbling in the darkness
As though it couldn't hold the one who had died.

He appeared more beautiful than before
Though cruel scars were now upon him.
Strangely they made him stand out more
And great honour was now due him.

As I gazed upon his beauty
I knew life was not about me, but him.
All that mattered was knowing this man
And pleasing him.

He turned me round and I was startled to see
Many friends and enemies.
"Make them a drink, put shoes on their feet
By loving them you are loving me".

You, you, you! What can I do?

Returning from the trip abroad so soon was quite a blow. My
tail was between my legs for I had given the impression to my
friends and family that I would be away for a long time. I wasn't
sure how they regarded my return and now felt awkward in
familiar surroundings. It was as though home was no longer
here. To go away secure in the knowledge of a home to return
to is a great comfort but I don't think I ever had that feeling.
I felt I had to prove myself to the people who knew me that
I could make something of my life. I did make some effort
to find work in Birmingham but my heart was set on leaving
and when a temporary job as a waiter at a holiday camp in
Lowestoft became available, I decided to go.

Five days after my return I set out again on a train paid for by 'Social Security' and arrived at the camp village and a room to stay in, worthy of no mention save that it smelt far too strongly of apple and blackcurrant. The work was totally hectic after my lazy days abroad and required far too much brainwork. As the guests assembled for breakfast I was stuck with two pretty but unemotional 'wag' waitresses who could have been shop dummies masquerading as humans. After that first shift I was on my own. For dinner there were six tables and 23 people to be served all in a mad, mad rush. The kitchens were chaos or rather an ordered chaos for everything seemed to work. But if the guests had seen the conditions and shabby handling of their food, they would never have eaten it.

I continued to smoke hash and amazingly held myself together to get through the first week with no problems. Gaz and Andy then turned up to work here too and we got to share a bungalow that was not being used by guests. They had lasted a month in France and really enjoyed themselves. I guess I'd have stayed a lot longer too if I had had some company.

The holiday camp job ended on the last day of September but Gaz and I decided to stay in Lowestoft for a while. We had made friends with two waiters who were local, one was Phil who rather stupidly offered us a place to stay without really meaning it and the other was Joe an extraordinary Irishman. He had been brought up a catholic and moved to Lowestoft by himself a few years previously. Sometime during the last year he had attended a 'Billy Graham' evangelistic crusade at Norwich City Football Club and become a Christian.

Joe was an intense character who clearly didn't like the job. Yet he stuck at it and began to speak to us about God. It wasn't that he preached at us, it was more that his life was so full of what had happened to him, he could not really talk about anything serious without God entering his thoughts and jumping from his mouth. We learnt that he went to a local church and I was particularly fascinated by his conviction. I liked to discuss philosophical ideas with him and became rather zealous to win him to my way of thinking.

After a brief trip back to Birmingham to pick up a few things like my bicycle, we hitched back to Lowestoft and turned up at Phil's front door, a cute little flat on the seafront at Pakefield Cliffs. He was aghast! My heart sank at the time but looking back on it now it was hilarious. He had said we could stay and he knew he had said it but he hadn't told his wife about the two young 'druggies' he had befriended and we could see her lounged in a chair behind the door.

After a brief trip back to Birmingham to pick up a few things like my bicycle, we hitched back to Lowestoft and turned up at Phil's front door, a cute little flat on the seafront at Pakefield Cliffs. He was aghast! My heart sank at the time but looking back on it now it was hilarious. He had said we could stay and he knew he had said it but he hadn't told his wife about the two young 'druggies' he had befriended and we could see her lounged in a chair behind the door.

We managed a cup of tea out of him but that was all and so made our way to Joe's basement flat which was further into the town but also right by the sea. No luck here though, for Joe had gone away for a few days and that meant spending the night crashed out on a dirty old mattress under a stair by his front door.

We signed on for unemployment benefit in the morning and began looking for some accommodation. But nothing was doing and so we smoked some more hash and squatted in a disused flat for a few days before getting a place to stay. It was now the middle of October and I return now to my diary entries which record the immediate events that led to the most significant event of my life. I was six weeks short of my twenty-second birthday when it happened.

Wednesday 17 October 1984

I scored an ounce of home-made grass tonight! What a haze
no doubt lays ahead but so what? I'm bored with all this serious
living. There's nothing interesting, nothing to get my teeth into.
Even wags have lost their appeal because it means subjecting
myself to another person. I don't want to be answerable to
anyone, not in the name of anything, least of all love. So I haze
my brain out, taking comfort in singleness because it's all so
easy to do.

Thursday 18 October

Walked along the beach in acute abstractivity, stoned and taking
photographs. The sea has perfectly absorbed the greyness of
the sky and the stones on the beach are quite dazzling in the
contrast they offer. How attractive is a simple mind, how utterly
fruitless it is to wrench away at the framework of life the way
I do. Who cares how the frame is made, it's there, that's all that
matters. I'm here, the sea is there, the town is over there. It's not a
riddle, there are no answers and even if there are, well so what?
I must strive for a light mind, that's all, nothing else.

Sunday 28 October

This evening I took Gaz on the back of my bike to church to
check out Joe's fellow Christian cronies. What am I coming to,
going to church indeed! It's probably just another wild impulse
of mine. I tried to sing but wouldn't dare allow my voice to be
heard. Afterwards we sat in what was called the 'fellowship' room
with quite a large group of lads and lasses singing and talking
about Jesus. Hmmm, I don't quite know what's going on here.
I've never associated young people with Christianity before.

Monday 29 October

Just can't stop eating biscuits today – maybe because I'm
thinking so much. Over the years people have mentioned Jesus
to me and every now and then I've lashed out bitterly about

it – it's hypocrisy, it's escapism from real life. I've openly mocked and inwardly despised all people with religion. Yet here I am suddenly being hassled by my own conscience.

Suppose it's all real? Look how convicted Joe is, look how convicted people in his church are! Look at me; what am I doing to be of assistance to other people? Even if God is an illusion, at least the values of the church are not; love one another, respect one another, share with one another. Aren't these just the values written on my conscience anyhow? All that separates me from them is that they believe in God.

I believe in good and that's what I've been saying to Joe, but I'm not satisfied with this anymore. I'm intrigued by Joe and by his church – maybe like a moth to light or perhaps like a fool to illusion?

Tuesday 30 October

This afternoon Joe and I joined a Maths class at the local college and did some Alegbra. Further into the day Gaz and I joined with a French class. Normal living was resumed in the evening when we climbed onto a garage roof and watched Lowestoft Town lose a football match.

The concept of God is like Lord of the Rings – so attractive but nevertheless a fairy-tale. God is a contradiction to my brain, but what does my brain have to say about creation? I just don't know. There's as much chance that there is God as that there isn't. I've spent so much time avoiding the issue that I've never really given him the chance I suppose. Why don't I take that chance? Why not deny all the confusion in my brain? Why not just take the step and see what happens? I want to, I actually want to. There is no joy in existentialism but how its champions would mock me if I did it.

Wednesday 31 October *Re-born*

Tonight I went with Joe to see a couple I guessed to be in their thirties. I'd come to argue with them about Christianity but when I was there I didn't want to argue at all. I think I knew at the back of my mind that the time for words was over and all that was left to do was to take the step and see where I'd stepped to. So, filled with this incredible urge, I tried to sit there patiently, trying to remember all the questions that puzzled me. I most miserably failed to be patient but finally the conversation reached the point where all that was left to do was take action. So I did.

John and Maria and Joe stood over me and prayed to God on my behalf. Then I asked Jesus to be my Lord and Saviour and I handed all kinds of past sin over to him. I said sorry for it and turned my back on living like that. I didn't feel any different afterwards except for a relief that the prayer was over and also a feeling of euphoria. I was stepping into a new stage of life.

Sunday 18 November *Baptism*

The last few weeks have seen some changes, me and Gaz ended up not bothering to go to French and that's the end of that I suppose; another event started but not finished. A while back I went to Colin the Pastor's house for what was called a nurture group. So now I go to Gunton Baptist Church but it's going to take quite an effort to sing sincerely. I still don't feel altogether sincere about all this. There are just some aspects of church that I am completely alien to. Oh well I'll just plod on I suppose. Maths is still happening and we've just done Percentages and Simple Interest. Jesus Christ certainly isn't a simple interest and, according to Joe, he wants 100%

At another meeting at Colin's house one evening, some people started talking in tongues; the Holy Spirit's personal message to God or something like that. They were praying for healing when a girl started screaming out. They said it was an evil spirit and cast it out of her. It was quite scary because she was violent and it was all rather weird but it certainly strengthened my faith.

I've also bought a keyboard for £100 and in between playing on it, have been working out what to say at my baptism. This testimony to Jesus I have to give to a church audience is becoming quite a worry. I keep telling myself that he will help me through it and he probably will but still I'm bothered about it.

Today is finally the big day. After the morning service, Pete Warnes cooks seven of us a three-course blinder. The main attraction was turkey and vegetables closely followed by a bottle of wine for each course. Scrumptious were the multitudes of desserts but bulging were the intestines close to my heart. Is not eating an intercourse between tastebuds and the belly? I can't be totally full though because there's still room for the butterflies to twitter in my stomach due to that dratted testimony I have to give tonight.

Soon I was there, sat on the front row of the church, underneath its horrible public lighting and resigned to my fate. And when I was stood up in front of that packed congregation I could barely keep my balance, let alone talk. But I did and then, along with Vicki, Waddy, Shona, Paul and Dave Keeble I got fully dunked in a pool. Baptism is a public confession that you have given yourself to accepting Jesus as your Lord.

Monday 3 December *Asking Heather out*

Last night, after weeks of pondering over whether to ask out Heather Warnes, I suddenly just do it. I wasn't particularly expecting to do so, although I knew I should. I was still in the stage of wondering how I'd do it when she walked into the room where I was sat, fiddling on my keyboards. 'Alone', I thought, 'we're alone, this is it', this is the perfect time to lay on with the corny words.

I winced as I asked her out for I felt incredibly corny and hopeless and like a lump of jelly. She wasn't exactly prepared either and neither did she give me an answer. It's strange; I've been quite bullied into the entire situation by constant ribbing from those around although I can't say I'm complaining. I hardly know this girl but that's no reason to delay and so I haven't.

Even though I don't know her that well, I can't say I'll be performing cartwheels if she says 'no' but I will boot Paul Ward and the other cronies for hassling me to ask her out so quick. It feels strange to be asking her out. Others do it because they're in love and I'm definitely not in love but she definitely looks loveable.

Tonight we all scootled to a party at John and Maria Deals and Sarah became a Christian. She walked half-way with us with the intention of seeing a friend but as she went off she just stopped, turned around and came with us. Heather was supposed to give me an answer tonight but didn't. Rat. Admittedly there was no opportunity for us to be alone and I did not attempt to make one. Fortunately I had managed to immunise myself against the situation by expecting a negative response. If one expects the worst then nothing is lost, that's what I say. Expect the worst in all you do… then nothing new can get to you.

Phil and Heather. Autumn 1985

6 Mission

Tuesday 4 December 1984 *Yes*

> Heather Warnes said YES to me
> One evening while I sat gingerly
> Playing keyboards, sipping tea
> She walked in so unexpectedly
> And turned the night to day.

Heather and Church

There were around twenty young people at Gunton Baptist Church when I joined. They met as a group after church services and also in houses in midweek. Much of the energy came from two youth leaders Erika and Heather, vibrant in their late twenties and both sporting loosely-permed long hair which suggested a sort of wildness about them.

Erika was wild in more respects than her hair. She packed a mighty punch when goaded, bantered exceptionally well in pubs, drank pints and was also a biker. Along with her soon-to-be husband Tony, she ran an evangelistic group called the Christian Motorcyclist Association (CMA) that went to rallies across the country. The CMA mixed with dodgy characters that freely moved on the wrong side of the law and this meant having to rely much on wits, charm and God to protect them. For they didn't hide what they stood for and it seemed some of these dubious characters respected them for it.

Ironically, Erika was quite similar to the people she was trying to reach. She too was balanced precariously on the edge of society, except her society was church where the biking culture didn't really fit in. Nevertheless, she regularly wore her 'Sunday-best' for a service, the standard uniform of leather and denim, and I guess this helped to lessen the focus upon the 'undesirables' that accompanied her and Tony from time to time.

Not that our church was against such people, for most of our congregation were warm and generous and made the effort to be welcoming to everybody, no matter what clothes they wore.

Tragically, Tony was to die in a motorbike accident a few years later and the memory of Erika's pain is still vivid in my mind. The funeral reminded me of the one I had attended for my friend Sev back in Solihull. Once again a mass of bikers filled the pews to pay their respects to yet another life lost on the road. Only now can I come close to realising the agony that Erika experienced, bereft of her husband and with two young children still to care for.

Did she lose her faith? Not at all, for her relationship with God proved true. The reality of her suffering was not sufficient to drive her away from the one she loved. Today she is re-married and still following her saviour.

Heather meanwhile seemed actually quite tame in comparison to Erika. Brought up in the way of the Brethren, where women were discouraged from taking leadership roles, she was accustomed to taking second stage in church matters. Most annoying to her was that as a female she had to wear a head-covering in case she participated publicly during services, but was forbidden to speak anyway. Other perceived outrages included no instruments being allowed to accompany singing and an accumulation of prohibitive rules loosely based on obscure Bible verses that could never be fully justified. Things might have been different if some of the 'fairer' folk of the congregation had stood up to the dominant few who were responsible for making services seem so burdensome.

However, she also learnt many good traits from some of these people, a number of whom were close family. In particular, her parents and Aunt Mary have been outstanding servants of God ever since I have known them. To this day they set the highest of standards, showing good stewardship of money and possessions and an outstanding commitment to hospitality. Also they have placed great store on the Bible as the word of God and have been keen to share the good news with others.

After university in Manchester, Heather returned to Lowestoft and the Brethren but soon joined Gunton. I guess this church had many of the things she had missed out on. They sang a mixture of modern songs and hymns and had musical instruments. The leaders there were hungry for a more charismatic experience of God, where the gifts of the Spirit could be practiced and used with freedom.

It was within this context that Heather became a key player in the growth of young people across the town being informed of the good news of Jesus Christ. Shortly before I arrived on the scene, she had become part of a small team of 'revolutionaries' from different churches that wanted to break the status quo of small and struggling youth groups and do something significant. From the simple beginnings of combining resources and doing some special events, the team became part of a national youth organisation and adopted the name Lowestoft Youth For Christ (LYFC).

Youth For Christ (YFC)

Things were now happening. Christian rock bands and drama groups from across the nation were brought in to play at church halls and even perform in schools. Visiting speakers would bring powerful messages and many young people who otherwise would not hear about God, did hear, because the context was culturally relevant to them. There was no holding back on any area of the gospel and no denominational traditions or religious trappings to stifle its meaning.

Lowestoft Youth For Christ will always be best remembered for organising a mission that was designed to reach youth and adults alike. It was called "Down to Earth" and most of the local churches were brought on board to support it. Big-name speakers of the time spoke to packed audiences at the central Marina Theatre. It was big news and many people became Christians. Even today it is possible to bump into people who say that "I became a Christian" or "my life changed" because of Down to Earth.

As the work grew, so did the mission field. LYFC became Waveney Youth For Christ to reflect what was going on in the surrounding areas. Churches in other towns began to give and receive support so that they too could gain access to resources that were previously denied to them. By sharing expenses, a band performing a concert at Lowestoft would perhaps go on to play at Beccles and then Bungay. A drama group coming in to visit one school could do likewise.

After a few months of finding my feet as a Christian, I became a part of the WYFC team. Perhaps it was just a cynical way of spending more time with Heather, but whatever my true motive, it was often incredibly exciting, good fun and deeply satisfying.

Lowestoft beach missions were now the flagship event of the organisation. For two weeks every year during the summer, we gained permission from the town council to park a double-decker bus on some land by the seafront and where you couldn't wish for a more public position. The bus came with a team from East Anglia Youth For Christ (EAYFC), led by ex-policeman Danny Pritchard. As volunteers they worked full-time as a resource for centres such as ours.

Using a marquee next to the bus we ran children's activities in the day-time which became so popular that as the years passed, some parents actually started to book a holiday to Lowestoft to coincide with our mission. But the real excitement, at least for me, was in the evening. The main function of the EAYFC team was to reach out to teenagers and twenties. They had become experienced in sharing the gospel on the streets and they trained us how to do likewise.

Each night brought an adventure of some sort; at the worst I'd be trying to make a sharp exit from a dangerous situation but at the best would be making friends with desperate people and sharing my faith where appropriate. I learnt a lot in those evenings. What really impressed me was the way people were treated with dignity and respect. There was no 'numbers' game being played, it wasn't about finding willing victims and shoving gospel medicine down their throats. It was about being genuine and honest and telling good news for the sake of the person you were talking to, not because of any need on your part to feel important.

I now return to some diary entries covering that period to show how much my thought life was changing and also how my relationship with Heather was growing more serious.

Thursday 6 December 1984 *Relationships*

The colours were really bright today as Sarah and I cycled to visit the Denes High School Christian club. Danny the driver of the YFC bus took the meeting and talked about relationships and sex before marriage. He drove home how incompatible it is for a Christian to be with an unbeliever. The Christian, is first and foremost committed to God while the unbeliever, at best, will see the relationship itself as most important. At some stage disharmony will occur as the values of one conflict with those of the other. Sex before marriage is usually where the conflict will start and in later years there comes the issues of living for comfort alone and giving money away to those in need. Of course, it is possible for an unbeliever to share similar values but even if that is the case, how can the Christian be really known intimately and enjoyed by the unbeliever who lives in rejection of the very one deeply loved by the other?

Sunday 9 December *Standards*

I walk this afternoon along the beach far into the enchanting twilight. How happy I am today to find such beauty in what I see of nature. I look at the drab grey buildings of man and am contented to know that I am no longer on the ugly road of this world. Instead I am alive to God and what he has created. It is no hardship for me to realise that what I previously thought to be true was not. I used to think nothing mattered but now I find the opposite to be true. There is justice because there is a judge. There are standards to live to because there is a standard-bearer – Jesus Christ. We have purpose and therefore have meaning, we all end up before God.

Saturday 15 December *Witness*

The morning after my twenty-second birthday sees Heather driving Paul and me to the Bethel church for a briefing on today's plan of action. At around lunchtime, I'm hovering by a huge YFC banner and a worship band, talking to people about Jesus in the town centre. I start with a bad experience as this lady who goes to the Spiritualist Church gets really angry about what I have to say about Jesus. Good! So she should be, the Bible expressly forbids calling upon spirits from the dead, so if my words were like a bar of soap, well all the better. By the day's end I'm really into this street witnessing, it's felt really worthwhile.

Evening is spent in a chair in a school hall listening to a Christian band called Rema. We were inviting folk to go when we were in the town and as I sit there I feel God's Spirit upon me like wave after wave. The words come into my head, 'trust God, don't doubt him, don't doubt that he's going to do great things in your life. Be happy, focus on him fully, give everything to him'.

Sunday 23 December *Love*

Today has been non-stop: church, lunch at Colin's, a carol service, turkey dinner at John and Maria's and an evening youth meeting. It was a really heavy talk on relationships which scared me because it threatened Heather and I being together. It made me question my motives and left a bad taste in my mouth. I wasn't pleased.

But that's just tough and it won't be that talk which decides our future. God has got to be boss in all areas. As we sat together tonight watching a film I became aware how different being in love is as a Christian compared to anything I knew before. Our relationship has something of God's love about it, it is more wholesome because it is subject to him and he teaches us not to put ourselves first. Of course, I'm having to learn this as I go along, but at least I have a standard, a guideline to go by. I seem to know straight away when I am going wrong. Also, a few nights back I accepted that God comes first whatever. If he wants us to separate then so we must, even though it would be so painful to do it now. But so it is and so must it continue to be.

Friday 4 January 1985 *Failure*

Bad day. I'm back in Birmingham with Gaz, seeing my friends. It started off quite well a few nights ago in the Masons Arms where I told them all I had become a Christian. Despite their amusement I stayed strong before them, even on the following night when they were smoking hash.

Today, I left Gaz behind and went with Benson to see some of her friends and got stoned. I had plenty of opportunity not to do it, but I wasn't prepared not to. It was as if there was nothing else for it. My conscience hassled me all the time but I wouldn't listen. But the moment I did it, the moments I took smoking a joint, I became creased up with guilt.

How Satan must have laughed, how Jesus must have winced. A few moments later, someone started questioning me about Jesus and there I was, stoned. What could I say, what right did I have to say anything? I became desperate and found a room where I could be alone. I don't know what the people there must have thought of me. I started praying and saying sorry to God. Weariness came upon me and all that was enjoyable about hash just disappeared. It was as if I'd just time-warped forward a few hours to the tiring after-effects of the drug. I know now that whatever I have inside me that distinguishes me as a Christian will not tolerate drugs. There can only be one master, there is no room for two. Ironically when I get back to Solihull I find that Gaz – who hasn't become a Christian yet – has spent the evening at a house where hash had been smoked constantly and he hasn't touched any of it.

Saturday January 19 *Pride*

I'm sat on my bed, pondering over the situation. I love: it's great but it is also a burden. Material things screw me up; there is her with career sorted and financially stable and there is me with nothing definite or substantial. It shouldn't alter things, yet it assaults my pride and scares me too. With the social farce as it is, with all this emphasis on what one has rather than what one is, I can't help thinking I'm sitting on a time-bomb. At some point, surely there will be an explosion, either my pride or her worldly self will cause it. I feel quite angry about what is expected of me. I detest ownership and it's all a lie anyway. No one really owns anything. All is God's and we are caretakers at the most. I mention it to Heather and she tells me she knows full well that all things belong to God. Yet I take no comfort in her reply.

I find it hard to trust her or myself in this. How sordid it is that this materialistic stuff has to be so influential. I just have to be patient I suppose and keep trying to make something happen. I turn to the Bible and open it at Psalm 4."Remember that the Lord has chosen the righteous for his own and he hears me when I call to him. Tremble with fear and stop sinning, think deeply about this when you lie in silence on your beds. Offer the right sacrifices to the Lord and put your trust in him."

Thursday 7 February *No time to scribe*

It's very hard nowadays to maintain much interest in scribing my life. Each day passes and I get more absorbed in proper Christian living which means my conduct is under constant examination and challenge. Christ is no game; this isn't something I can just leave when I feel like it. This is a life's dedication to life and death, I can't leave it like everything else I've just given up on, by just shrugging my shoulders and saying it doesn't matter ultimately. It does matter. I am called upon by God to carry out the tasks he has appointed me to: saving people from Hell, using my life as an example to lead people to life under God's authority. And yet like a fool I persist in holding on to my ways and what I deem appropriate and right. There is no time for this, I must submit all to God. I know what I must do and yet I don't do it!

Saturday 23 March *Thinking about marriage*

Late last night at Heather's place, after a driving lesson in her dark blue miracle machine (how is it still on the road?) I became wary and untrusting in our relationship. "Pray about us", I told her, "make sure about me."

It's because as we get closer together I become more and more unable to handle the here-nor-there state which is before marriage. I can't handle this sitting on the wall, I must be either on one side or the other, either getting married or not – and therefore ending it.

I leave her house feeling quite ridiculous for patience has deserted me and I have jumped into a ridiculous situation. I want to confront her about where we stand and are heading but I know she will avoid it. And because I know it - perhaps she is right to do so at this stage – I am bitter. Yet it is all to do with my lack of patience and trust in God to sort things out in his time. I think I want what I have to be bottled up and sealed where it can't be touched or lost and marriage is the way to do it.

Come the morning and I'm still in a mood at this horrible drawn-out process of waiting, of being subject to another person's acceptance or rejection. This is where relationships can be so bad, there's nothing you can do alone unless you force it. If I seek to impose what I want, then I swap the relationship of love for one of possession.

This is it: that which is patient in me, those aspects within which treat our relationship in a loving way are those which are the 'Jesus' within me. And that which wants to bully and confront is a personal darkness, caressed by Satan. What a fool I am! When I confront or force decisions upon Heather out of so called love, then it is a lie. The true love which comes through knowing Jesus will move us on together. He hasn't moved me on at a crazy speed-driven distance ahead of her. When the time is right to marry we will know it together.

Good. I have become wise to myself and Satan now. It is not Jesus' love that compels me to confront, it is insecurity and perhaps possessiveness: all stemming from my dark side.

Tony and Erika got married today and the service was really fun. The worship was full and 'hearty' like worship should be and their non-Christian biker buddies were quite amazed at the sight of our tambourine-bashing pastor. Heather was the chief bridesmaid and looked quite indescribably beautiful in the purple flowery dress which Erika demanded she wore. The reception was a laugh as well, particularly as I teased Heather a few days back that chief bridesmaids had to give speeches. I jokingly mentioned to Erika what I had said and to my utmost glee, Erika carried it through and made her do it!

Sunday 24 March *Experiencing Jesus*

Tonight, after a Bible study sat with Heather on Pete's brown beanbag, I had to question the reality of my relationship with Jesus. Do I merely know about Jesus or do I actually experience him? Knowledge of him comes in bundles, in fact mountains of it. I've seen him powerfully at work in other people and I know that I have changed a lot, but where is my actual experience, what can I pin down and say that is most definitely Jesus?

I can only think that I experience Jesus through my conscience and emotions. There is experience in that there is this incredible sense of peace that is mine to draw upon. So what is this experience which comes upon me, what substance has it? Can I continuously draw upon it, how can its presence be increased within me?

This is something no lesser in wonder than creation itself. I have no answers to what it is and what it is made of, I only know that it is there and that I need it constantly for Christian living. At the moment, if I'm honest, God's Spirit seems only to come upon me in spurts and there is no real consistency in my life. Yet I know through God's word that his Spirit is consistently available to me. So if I am to believe that, then it is me who is responsible for the flow or restriction of his peace and power upon me.

Tuesday 21 May *The Reps*

I've had it with trying to copy up diary notes from a month behind, that's it, kaput! Today I release myself from the dreary drudge. Suffice to say, that over Easter about thirty of us travelled down in cars to Spring Harvest, a Christian festival in Prestatyn, North Wales.

I wasted the event and spent a week that should have been full of teaching and worship, caught up with myself! While God's Spirit was pouring out on others, I was bound up and ineffective. But it wasn't a total waste as I think I've learnt a valuable lesson: Satan will use anything weak in my life to keep me from being useful for God.

One of my friends called Sean came down from Solihull a few weeks ago. He was pretty messed up but all through the first week, God was strongly upon him, showing him the misery and fear in things he thought were good. He became convicted about many things he had done wrong in the past and also said he had a real fear of actually meeting the devil. He became a Christian on Tuesday 14 May and decided to stay down here with us. So now, from Birmingham there are me, Gaz and Sean and we've all just moved into a little cottage on the outskirts of Lowestoft.

Heather, as part of WYFC, has organised this Christian band called The Reps to be in Lowestoft for the week. They're going to take school lessons and assemblies and perform evening concerts. They're a nice enough bunch, six of them and each one with brightly dyed hair. They came to the Trinity Coffee Bar that we run, last night and interviewed themselves. I think the teenagers there were interested enough. Tonight they played at Kirkley High School and surprised me with their music – I wasn't expecting it to be good. Also a few people became Christians which sort of makes it all worth it.

Thursday 23 May *The flesh*

Today I've been fasting and while praying God directed me towards verses in Philippians where we are urged to forget what is behind and press on towards the prize of Heaven. I also considered, "there are many whose lives make them enemies of the cross of Christ." They are going to end up in Hell because their god is their "bodily desires".

I'm finding it very difficult to not be a servant of my 'bodily desires'. It is the greatest struggle of all and I seem to walk one step forward and then two backwards. It hinders my pressing on towards the prize and I'm wondering what can I do to defeat myself?

I cannot do it but Jesus has done it, he defeated my 'darkness' at the cross. Now it is left for me to claim that victory which is his and put it into practice. But how do I do it, how do I claim victory and live against myself? It is up to me to fix my eyes on Jesus and his nature, I have to gain a true perspective of the treasures of Heaven, for then will earthly desires seem pale and ugly.

Sean and I cycled to house-group at Colin's tonight. The teaching was on what qualities people need to have to be leaders. I know I am far away, yet I can't justify standing around waiting for those who do have the qualities to get their acts together and lead us out onto the streets.

Monday 27 May *What to do with myself*

Oh, the irritation of finding something to do, a wee bit tipsy and alone at night-time. Don't want to sew my coat, can't do anything concerning God because it doesn't work when I'm tipsy – which is hardly ever nowadays. Can't do any Maths and I haven't for ages and the exam's in two weeks and I've given it zero commitment. Can't telephone anyone because it's too late and don't want to anyhow. Also the hot water doesn't work so I can't wash my clothes but lo, I hear the sound of Paul, Gaz and Sean, YES, REPRIEVE!!!

Monday 3 June *Inertia*

Inertia, the state of sleepy inertia. What can I do? Maths exam in ten days and I have the book in front of me but I'm sleepy and cannot concentrate. Inertia. I can ride my bike into the countryside but I can't be bothered. In fact I can do any one of a dozen things but none of them attract. There is nothing I want to do yet I don't want to do nothing!

Inertia. Only the ultimate things attract. Jesus. Now the idea of meeting Jesus in prayer becomes attractive. Oh but I'm incapable, too tired to focus and my mind is wondering all over the place. Heather and I returned from seeing her brother Bernard in Bath last night, but that's all inertia will let me say.

It's not just inertia, it's frustration as well. My life is meandering instead of flowing smoothly towards specific goals. Actually that's too positive a thing to say, rather my life is a stagnant muckpool where movement only occurs when stones of other people's lives are tossed in to cause ripples in mine. No wonder I feel sick with nausea, it's perfectly correct to feel nothing other than nauseous with my life and what's more, I shouldn't even allow myself the luxury of feeling sorry for myself – that will only lead to bitterness.

Thursday 18 July *Tiredness*

I've moved out of Carlton Colville and am staying with a friend and doing some temporary work before the beach mission starts. I'm constantly tired since beginning this job, clearing tables, serving food and washing up. I've talked about Jesus a lot to my fellow workers although spiritually I'm clinging on to Jesus by my teeth.

I have to keep depending on his grace so much but nevertheless, I'm still being used. I felt him with me when I talked to two girls at work. Heather's constantly knackered as well but I still see her most nights, although hardly ever for more than an hour before she needs to crash out. It should get better for she breaks up for the school holiday tomorrow. Yet with the beach mission approaching and lasting two weeks I don't see our situation improving.

I've left the Monday night outreach coffee bar and am doing a similar thing on a Friday instead at Gunton. But I'm hassled about it and argued with Colin for an hour last night over various things. I might end up resigning, I feel like doing so, I've got so many strained relationships at the moment, in fact everything I do seems to be strained.

Thursday 25 July *Billy the Goat*

I finished the job at Pleasurewood Hills today. Hooray! That place was doing me in. A girl called Sarah came to work in my last week and I talked to her loads about Jesus. She seemed to be really interested and read in the Bible about being filled with God's Spirit. Last Saturday, Mark brought her along with another girl called Emily to the annual celebration of Norwich YFC. But they left early because they hit us with boring talks about Danny's bus and their accounts. I spent the whole day there with Heather and Eveline and heard some good talks about church and hospitality. The beach mission is almost here, we had a meeting on Tuesday night for prayer, worship and practical things. We've come up with a working theme of cowboys and Indians for the younger ones and I'm going to be 'Billy the Goat'. I have to act so thick that I'm not even sure whether I'm a cowboy or an Indian! Waveney YFC has been whittled down over the past few weeks. Someone from the national team came and helped us to do a general execution of the bulging committee – now there's only Heather, Eveline and Rob Clarke left.

Thursday 29 August *Beach Mission*

The number of kids coming to our daytime club increased everyday in the first week. There were almost sixty of them by the third day and even more by the end. Getting among them went reasonably well, at first I didn't speak to any of them at an individual level about Jesus but I did about other things. Strange thing this year is that most of them are local, which is good because we might get more time to spend with them than just the two weeks.

Although we were all constantly tired, spirits were high and it was obvious that God was with us because the fellowship we had overcame all the niggly things that tiredness brings. I missed church one Sunday morning because I was so exhausted. The night-times were also quite exciting and a few people became Christians on the last Friday, including Richard who is Vicki's brother.

At the end, about fifty people made commitments to Christ but how many of them will last is another matter. We had an amazing baptismal service on one Sunday evening where people we had met from the evenings got baptised. There were some amazing stories, like Tom and Donna. Tom was on probation and waiting another court case when we met him. They were living together and, without being told by any of us, became convicted that this was wrong. So they got married just a week later. Then Tom's court case came up and he was let off with a suspended sentence which totally amazed the local journalist who reported the event. One guy, a down and out alcoholic, gave his life to Jesus and another guy was healed of some deformity.

On the kids' side, virtually all of them ended up making some form of commitment. So we've started up a 'Double Decker Workshop' running for six weeks on a Saturday morning. It's a sort of follow-on to help the kids fit into existing church youth groups. It was great bringing people to Jesus, I loved it.

After the mission I took off for France with Heather, Eveline and Paul and we spent a few days on the Island of Noirmoutier. This was the place where I was supposed to have met Gaz and Andy last year. It's strange to think back to how I was a year ago, so much has changed.

Monday 21 October *Yes*

A couple of weeks ago, Heather and I decided to get married. Wheeee I'm excited! The date set is January 1st at Gunton Baptist Church – our church – at 2pm to be followed by a reception at Gunton Hall and then an evening buffet. So how do I feel? I dunno, things happen so fast nowadays, I don't get much time to stop and think about them. I'm just happy I guess.

Sunday 27 October *Lifestyle choices*

I am now almost a year old in Christ, so how much have I grown? Well smoking and drugs are totally alien to me now. I still dabble in alcohol but nothing like before. Pubs and clubs have gone, although the occasional pub outing still occurs. It's not that I'm saying not going to pubs means I'm growing, it's just that I mean the old attractions have gone and made way for something more attractive: the positive life in Christ.

The change is that purpose once sought has now been found. My purpose is simply that God is allowed to carry out his perfect plan for me. There is nothing I can do to attain a greater sense of self-value than this, for in Christ I am accepted by God as perfect. In fact the nearer I seem to get to Christ, the further away I get from my self. The classic search for one's self is over.
I found myself before his cross and when I did I was frankly quite disgusted. So now I'm trying to lose myself and the more I do of it the more contented I become.

I went with Heather on Friday on WYFC business to chat with one of the 'sisters' at the convent. It was going quite nicely until the sister started talking about praying to Mary. I stayed as quiet as I could about it, just a little groan, but I was uneasy. I was just about to say something to her when instead I decided to just shut up. This woman had probably lived a life of devotion to God whereas I was not even a year old. What right had I to speak?
I did have the right because the Bible is the ultimate authority, not someone's lifestyle and praying to Mary is questionable. But there is also respect and kindness. Will God really block out someone from Heaven because they got it wrong over the Mary thing? She also believed in Jesus' work on the cross. But what is her duty to, a saviour or a tradition? I don't really know I suppose, but I do know I don't like these big, traditional church buildings with their obscure services of woe. In the evening back at our church this bloke had an evil spirit commanded out of him, it was horrible.

Monday 4 November *A Wimber meeting*

The weekend was quite an amazing experience as about thirty folk from our church went off to Diss to a John Wimber* meeting. God was really working through him and his team and everyone was full of expectancy that healings were going to happen. Not everyone was touched by the event though;

the cynics as usual were left out. I had this sort of strain removed from the base of my spine; two friends were released from something with really hideous screaming from both of them. Jacko had a fit of uncontrollable laughter, he just wasn't stopping and Shona's mum was healed of something and laid flat out on her back.

People fell down like a pack of cards as waves of God's Spirit fell upon us. This guy at the front had said, "The Holy Spirit is now going to come and rest on people". He prayed with his eyes open and it just happened. Nobody who was praying for anyone had their eyes closed and the authority and power on show was amazing. Heather and I asked for prayer and this sense of peace came upon me while Heather just collapsed to the ground and lay there.

* John Wimber (1934-1997) was leader of the Vineyard movement
Source: www.crvineyard.org/wimber.htm

Easter 1998 in Lincoln

7 Family

Saturday January 1 1986 *The wedding*

I don't recall too much about my wedding day, just a few things stand out. It was the last time I can remember that my immediate family and friends from Solihull were gathered together. It was nice to have photos and enjoy conversations with my parents and sister. My mum and dad had divorced and re-married quite a few years ago but just being with them as we went through the formalities reminded me of times gone by and stirred something sad inside.

As for my friends, I think they were quite blown away by the experience of charismatic Christians getting married. It must have been quite something to see two people come before God who actually believed the Bible and that they really were making their vows before him. Also there would have been the songs, a mixture of hymns and shorter choruses that were all in plain English and sung by many within the packed congregation who clearly meant what they were singing.

But that would have been nothing to what was coming next for them. Heather's parents had contributed much to the wedding arrangements and out of respect to them there was no alcohol at the reception. Most people in the Lowestoft Brethren Church to which they belonged had a very negative view of alcohol. I understood their reasons why, although didn't really agree with them. Their view is that alcohol can only lead to ruin and there are many examples they can give of destroyed lives. Therefore drinking should not be encouraged and Christians should set the example that a happy life can be led without alcohol.

I am of the opinion that while nothing should be your master, all things can be enjoyed in moderation and within the law. I think this is a fair approach as either school of Christian thought could refer to verses in the Bible to add weight to their argument. At a wedding Jesus turned gallons of water into wine yet also rebuked gluttony and addictions many times.

I like having a drink. It is not something I am proud of or feel superior about. I was brought up in a drinking culture and to some extent I still live in a drinking culture. Church as I have known it has always been full of Christians who drink responsibly and simply do not see it as an issue. However, if I find myself to be with a person who struggles with alcohol, I will gladly not drink in his presence if that is what is needed. It's people who matter, not regulations.

One thing I am strongly against is drugs. The difference between drink and drugs is immense in my experience. Even the 'soft' drug Cannabis is a league apart in terms of effect. It produced an effect in me that was so intense that there is no way I can condone it. I was never in control of myself when I took it. However, there were times when I took it so often that it became quite boring.

Although there was no alcohol to be had at Gunton Hall, that wasn't quite the case in the car-park within my friend Jim's car. Deprived as Jim was of a drink, he remembered his stash in the boot and bid me forth. I was feeling so nervous about my next speech that I was quite pleased to nip away and calm the nerves while pleasantries were being exchanged elsewhere.

Fear of wedding day speeches had been steadily growing. Bad memories of mumbling during my baptism testimony kept coming to mind and the approaching stage of the service was even bigger. It was going to be such a strange mix of people in the congregation. There would be the formal suits and hats of the Brethrenites, ready to call Heather's parents to task for any wanton displays of charismatic behaviour. Then there would be my folk and friends from Birmingham; how were they going to take being among Christians and this new life I had embarked upon? Finally, there would be my new friends, many of whom would be grinning profusely at the prospect of the juicy mix ahead.

I wasn't used to public speaking; I didn't like the sound of my voice and found it difficult to concentrate on what to say. My mind would often go blank as I burned in embarrassment while staring at a sea of faces. So really it was no surprise looking back on it, that young as I was in the things of God, I turned to a stiff drink rather than prayer as the best preparation. Readily I gathered my courage in the car and had a laugh, especially when Jim told me that for all the weirdo's there, at least my wife was the "best looking wag". Of course it didn't occur to him how strange he must have looked with his round glasses, grey suit, red kicker shoes and bleached white hair!

Bad move. By the time we had emerged from the car, the proceedings had started and a barn dance had begun. I was greeted by everyone laughing at me because there had been no groom to lead the bride into the first dance. Heather was now whizzing through an archway of many arms with some unknown stand-in.

For our honeymoon we had a few days in Paris planned for us which meant leaving the reception relatively early in the evening, driving to a hotel and arising early in the morning to catch a plane from Stansted Airport. Heather had predicted that her brothers would be decorating our car and that this would in no way assist our schedule. So we parked it a mile or so away and arranged for someone to take us to it and get their car all messed up instead. But it didn't work. Somehow, brother Bernard had infiltrated our plans and our car was a disaster. What's more, when we set off for the hotel, a number of them followed us to ensure our first night together was made more memorable. We shook them all off, except Bernard's car and it wasn't until later in the night that he was finally satisfied with his performance and left me to mine.

1986-90 *Two children*

Almost two years passed by since getting married at the age of twenty-three (Heather was twenty-six). We lived in a little bungalow built by Heather's dad and named our first baby Claire. She was born on the 1st October 1987 and I busied myself by gaining a diploma in Graphic Design and then doing some freelance work. It wasn't much but at least something I enjoyed and when Heather returned to teaching, I helped to look after Claire. Three years later, we had moved a hundred yards or so to a new house, again with help from Heather's dad.

Jenny was born on the 12th October and it is perhaps not surprising that there are no diary entries for this period of time as the demands of toddlers lead to much tiredness. Also, we were both still heavily involved in church and Waveney YFC. However, memories of these early years are extremely happy and full of lots of people around our house and fun and friendship with God.

1991 *A repeating vision*

Diary writing re-surfaced again from May 1991 to April 1992 and I was particularly pleased to find some entries that tell of events that significantly impacted my life. I saw for the first time a heavenly vision that has since presented itself on many occasions, to the point that it has become part of my spiritual 'furniture' - rather like the gift of tongues, those strange words I can utter to God that have never changed over many years of use. The ability to speak in tongues has been such a comfort to me in the later years of bereavement. They are my first port of call in times of desperation for they lighten my spirit and help me to focus on Jesus. The first use of the gift of tongues can be found in the Bible in the book of Acts.

The vision came at a meeting when someone prayed over me. In my mind I was suddenly seated on a vivid green, grassy hill in rolling meadows, watching a powerful river surging down from somewhere above. It twinkled as it surged, giving an appearance of enchantment. I had the strong impression that it was the River of Life as recorded in the book of Revelation, described as being crystal clear and originating from the throne of God. I also felt it represented the activity of the Holy Spirit and was flowing in obedience to the will of God.

For some reason, I was frustrated that I couldn't enter the river and the vision just melted away to leave me depressed and frustrated. I went to another meeting three days later and the same vision came again. I was sitting on the grassy bank but this time Jesus was sitting next to me. I asked "why Lord, why can't I go in?"

He responded "No one is allowed into that river for it is the activity of the Holy Spirit and the work of the Father. The work belongs to the Father and the worker is the Spirit. Whoever steps into that river can do no more than obstruct or hinder. You have been trying to manipulate the Father's hand, to bend it to your will. Now, WATCH the river with me, I will show you where it goes and we will follow it. By being with me you are given eyes to see where the river is going, the work of the Father and the workings of the Spirit."

I was then reminded of John 5v19. "The Son can do nothing by himself; he can only do what he sees his Father doing, because whatever the Father does the Son also does. For the Father loves the Son and shows him all he does."

That evening I was filled with peace. No more striving, no more trying to force and squeeze out some sort of ministry or work of God. He would initiate and lead me as I looked to him and waited expectantly for direction. The same vision came a third time but this time, I flew with Jesus and followed a smaller river that broke away from the main river. This was a river for me, it was God's river but something about it was personal, it was as if there was a familiarity to it, a sense of belonging as if reserved for me to follow.

A short time later, I went with a few friends to a meeting where a lady spoke who had been healed of Parkinson's Disease as well as other illnesses. At the end I approached her and asked if she would pray for Sean and his bad leg. After praying for him, she wanted to pray for me and as she did she said my main influence would be upon hurting people, the neglected people of society. It wouldn't be in the spotlight of church life, but on an unglamorous path. I both accepted and struggled with this 'word'. What did it mean, tramps, drunks? Surely that wasn't me?

What I didn't know then was that there was indeed a time approaching far from the stage of normal church life. But first, a test of trust was coming that scared and humbled me to desperately call on God. During the Spring and Summer time of 1991 I fell foul of a series of headaches that affected my ability to concentrate and all I could do was lie down in bed until they wore off.

The '72' Project

At the same time, a number of YFC centres in East Anglia and 'Streetlife' (the team that helped us do beach missions and who owned the bus we used) were gearing up for a project called '72'. The idea was inspired by chapters 9 and 10 of Luke's Gospel where Jesus sent out his followers into towns and villages to tell the good news. They were told to take no purse, no bag, nor sandals but to trust God for their provision. The '72' returned with joy and said, "Lord, even the demons submit to us in your name."

So in August of that year, a team of young people were gathered together and organised into small teams to be sent out into the rural areas of Waveney, Stowmarket and Newmarket. We helped co-ordinate the Waveney teams and set up operations in the small town of Bungay. My headaches, meanwhile, were getting worse, so folk gathered around me and prayed and God filled me once again with peace and told me that all the responsibility for the work ahead lay with him.

While three or four small teams went out into the surrounding villages, around twelve of us remained to focus on a group of thirty or so people mainly aged between 16 and 25. They hung around the town centre and various other areas and it wasn't long before we had made friends with them, using the contacts we had from the local church who were supporting us. This church was being led by John and Maria Deal the very people who had led me to Christ some seven years ago. Their fellowship treated us so well, fed and housed us and prayed and worshipped with us.

On two occasions, the most bizarre thing happened, that to this day I cannot really explain, other than to say it must have been the work of God. I was sitting in the town centre eating sandwiches with the rest of the team when a ridiculous suggestion came into my head. It said something like, "go over to that bakery opposite you, tell them what you are doing and that the Lord has requested a cream cake for everyone of you, free of charge".

I dismissed the thought as obviously idiotic, but it wouldn't go away. I became more uncomfortable just like the times when God impresses upon me to share something with someone. Finally, I took a deep breath and told our friend Emma who must have been around sixteen at the time what I was about to do and would she come with me to help carry the cakes?

She went immensely deep purple, goggled at me in panic and said "ok". So in we went, I did exactly what I believed I had been told and the woman at the counter looked at us and without hesitation, asked us how many and then put the required number into little white boxes and handed them over without asking for money. Rather than just saying a thank you, I also said the Lord would bless her for what she had done. And that was it! We took the cakes over to the rest of our team and demolished them. I think it was the very next day when the same thing happened all over again, but this time it was a portion of chips for all of us. Again, I went with Emma and did exactly the same as before. Everyone was presented with hot chips and no money was used to buy them.

I wondered afterwards whether the lady in the bakery or the oriental man in the chip shop was intimidated by me. I can't see how they were, for we were not threatening in our behaviour. Far from it, we were nervous and embarrassed. For the lady it was broad daylight and it would have been easy for her to dismiss us as having a laugh. As for the oriental man in the chip shop, there were a number of men working there and it was unlikely that any of them had even spotted our group outside. I found out later that some of them were part of a notorious family in the area who were not people to be intimidated in such a way. But it was also the way these people just accepted my request, there was no questioning, they just did it.

I hold that it was God, that he has a sense of humour and that he wanted to teach us something. Not just that he would provide for his children or reward them with delights such as 'spiritual cakes', but also that he was in action, dynamically present and working in the hearts and lives of people who to us were just a backdrop to the event, nothing more than mere surroundings.

During the two weeks of '72' we saw God break into people lives and heard how people in the smaller teams on the road had also been provided for. It was indeed quite as reckless and adventurous as it sounds. There were some safeguards built in, for people who were known to be Christians in some of these villages were contacted beforehand, informed of what was happening and asked to show hospitality should a team come their way. The teams were aware of who these people were and there were also leaders who travelled around in 'support' cars to pick up on any problems. So we weren't being totally irresponsible!

September 1991 *Holiday and Hospital*

One morning while the '72' project was in full swing, we received a telephone call from Addenbrookes Hospital, insisting that we drive there immediately. So, leaving the children with Emma, we drove for an hour or so to Cambridge where we were met by a neuro-surgeon. Having analysed a CT brainscan sent from my local hospital he informed us I needed an operation to remove a blood clot from my head. Unfortunately we had booked a holiday in France and so I cheekily told him I was unavailable at the current time. He must have thought it wasn't imminently dangerous as he allowed us to go with the helpful advice that there were plenty of good neuro-surgeons in France.

I did get one headache while we were over there and I know I caused concern amongst the people we were travelling with but we made it back ok. A few days later I was due at the local hospital for another scan. I woke up that morning with a throbbing headache and feeling sick; I didn't eat all day. I went to the hospital mid afternoon where they discovered I was bleeding to the extent that immediate surgery was needed.

Soon, I was in the back of an ambulance and racing off to Addenbrookes. I was placed in a ward that accommodated dying people. I remember watching a man in a long-term coma who wasn't expected to re-surface. I watched his visitors, standing over him and talking as if he could still hear. I ate nothing at night-time and the next day was wheeled into the theatre by a man who turned out to be a Christian. "Our church has been praying for you" he told me. Someone from my church must have got in touch with him. That's the beauty of belonging to a church: when it matters, the people of God are there.

I remember lying there prior to the operation just after my head had been shaved on one side. I wondered why they didn't shave both sides for I must have looked quite odd. Perhaps they didn't expect me to make it? My thoughts became fixed on God. I wasn't scared, for there was a great peace upon me but I do remember saying to him that if my life was spared I would not mess about anymore that I would live utterly for him.

Who knows what must have been going through the mind of Heather? Strangely, the people I would be leaving behind weren't in my thoughts. It was just me and God at the end of all things as I knew them. This is what it all boiled down to in the end, me and him, everything else was diminished.

But I didn't die. They removed it successfully by drilling two opposite holes in my head and blowing out the clot rather like one would blow a pea from a pea-shooter. That's how it was described to me, although no reason was given as to what had caused it at all. Many people thought it had happened through playing football but I disagreed with that opinion because I wanted to play football again.

Recovery

Stuck in hospital for a week I was so relieved to leave that ward. It wasn't anything to do with the nurses, or even the food, it was to get away from drips in my arms, from the daily fear of being catheterised because my body had been so traumatised. They finally succumbed to the pressure I was exerting for an early release and I was allowed home to rest in my own bed.

One afternoon I was thinking about the beauty in people when you look at them in a positive light – something which I rarely did. Too often I took people for granted and saw them in terms of what they did for my life, as if their value was only found in the context of their contribution. No wonder I got so frustrated and felt empty. Jesus said that happiness comes from dying to self-seeking. I prayed, "Lord, please help me to pour out my life into you and people. I don't even own my life so help me to not be so concerned about it. I want to be known as someone who cares for others but I'm so weak. I don't want to build a platform for myself, I want to forget all about that and only do things as you lead. I'm only happy when I'm serving you, when I'm in the thick of things, sharing the gospel and seeing people respond to its truth. I thirst for you God, yet I can't seem to get it together to pray much or read the Bible. I know you don't forsake me, I've got nothing to pay my way, I'm not doing anything to deserve it and yet my life is in your hands."

Two days later I was back in hospital after another throbbing headache. Then it was back home, only to be hit by another throbbing disaster the next night. I was steeling myself to have to go back again and wondering how long this was going to continue. Words from the Bible came into my mind, "My grace is sufficient to meet all that you need". I knew God was with me and that he would give me enough grace to get through each day. I had no idea about what was going to happen tomorrow but if I was strengthened for today then I could be confident that I would also be given the strength for tomorrow.

Three more days followed of throbbing headaches and sickness but on the third night some folk came round and prayed for me and although the headaches persisted for a while longer, I no longer worried about them as life-threatening.

Days passed and Claire's fourth birthday arrived on October 1st. She received her first token of independence from us: a tape recorder. Now she could sit in her room and listen to music on her own. It was quite amusing to see her spending time alone but also sad, because in a way, we were already starting to lose her, for her own life was on the move.

Another near death

My headaches were continuing on a daily basis but the intensity of them started to lessen. I was signed off work until 30th

October and also had had to relinquish my driving licence. On the final day of this recuperation period another alarming event occurred but not before another vision of the river appeared. This time, while people were praying over me, I was with Jesus again flying over the smaller river that flowed from the larger one. I saw that it ended at a great city, a massive, important city with very tall buildings, like sky-scrapers.

In the evening, Claire fell ill with Croup (a wheezy constriction of the airways) to the point that she could hardly breathe. The doctor advised us to carry out the normal procedure of steaming her bedroom through regularly boiling a kettle in there, but for some reason we were not happy with the advice. Barely had we left the surgery and got home when her eyes rolled and she started staggering around the room. We decided to drive up to the local hospital as fast as we could. If we had not of done so she would have died, for five minutes into the journey she started to lose consciousness and on arrival, the doctors responded immediately to her predicament. I remember watching with the fear and trembling that only a parent can understand. We were praying throughout as they managed to get a tube through her nose and into her lungs just in time to save her life.

Three hours later she was all tubed up in the intensive care unit but breathing soundly. We were so thankful to God, it was the hunch that had saved us. Looking back, I still firmly believe that it was the Holy Spirit who caused our unease. This of course leads me to the inevitable question that if God wanted to save her then, why were we not warned in a similar way some fifteen years later when there was no one to save her?

It is no good asking such questions and one might as well expect an answer to "what is the mystery of the universe"? All I know is that my family belong to God, that he loves us deeply and that he is good. I will not hurl accusations at the man who hung on a cross for me nor question the wisdom of my creator.

The next day I wrote in my diary: "From this day forth I pledge my head to Heaven for the gospel (a quote from a Keith Green song). Although I'm weak and unable to carry it out humanly speaking, I pledge by the power of the Holy Spirit alive and at work in me, to live a life of thanksgiving and trust, of praise and worship of my heavenly father. It is my heart's desire to deal with people with love and kindness. I acknowledge the fragility of my life and, that with the twinkling of an eye, I might taste physical death and be transported to an appointment with the Most High God. I therefore pledge my life to live according to this knowledge, not following my own ambitions or seeking my own pleasure."

"If any man would come after me, he should deny himself, take up his cross and follow me." (Jesus Christ)

1993 *The Toronto Blessing*

The pledge to God was to be the last diary entry for fourteen years. Memories without diary entries to lean upon are not as clear as they should be because of my head injury. In July 1993 Amy was born to us and somewhere in the following year we ended our association with Youth for Christ and left Gunton Baptist Church. It is pleasing to say we left on good terms and that the church gathered around and sent us on our way with prayer and encouragement.

First and foremost many of these people were our friends, some of whom we still see to this day. So it was sad to leave them but the time was right and I think they recognised it as well. We had been growing rather stale in our walk with God. It wasn't that we were losing any passion, it was more that we had lost direction. We never have been the types to be content with just attending and this was becoming a growing danger.

After much prayer and talk with close friends we began attending a New Frontiers Church that met in a local high school. We knew a number of people there already so it proved quite easy to fit in, although Claire found it a bit difficult to begin with. We were well-known to the leadership, particularly as some of them were involved in setting up the Youth For Christ centre in Lowestoft. I think they were a bit cagey about us coming at first and I remember one of the elders saying he thought their church would be just a stopping-off place for us. Well, we're still there now, so even the wise get it wrong sometimes!

I think he thought the more rigid structure of leadership would not sit well with us who had had so much involvement with activities outside of normal church. But we had experienced first-hand the difficulties of working outside of the local church; the problems of integrating new Christians and having viable support structures.

In the first few months of our attending, the church underwent a dramatic change. What was known as the 'Toronto Blessing' arrived with the force of a mini-hurricane. Services that simply would have been regarded as highly charismatic became extraordinary. The Spirit of God just seemed to blow the formalities out of the window. Time after time, people would begin laughing in abandon or laying on the floor, oblivious to those around them as God poured out the knowledge of his love in wave after wave. Sometimes speakers would become unable to continue with their message. This was either because of the weight of God upon them or due to what was happening to the congregation. Sometimes the noise was like a crowded market-place.

Some people stopped attending during this time and I understand their reasons, although I believe they were the poorer for doing so. To this day, it is difficult to try and explain what happened and I am aware that God is a God of order. I also realise that some 'emotional' people were perhaps not experiencing anything of God at all. I saw some sights which I questioned and quite honestly annoyed me. I did not regard what was happening to them as authentic – judgemental fellow that I am.

But a lot of the people that were affected were genuine and stable people. They were not extroverts or the types that would welcome the attention. In some services we were quite strongly affected ourselves, although I admit to being jealous that Heather seemed to receive much more than I did. My personal assessment of this 'blessing' is that it blew formality out of the water and that has been a blessing in itself. Our church is not afraid of God turning up in a service and perhaps 'Toronto' was a big shove in the right direction.

The Day of Pentecost comes to mind when the believers were accused of being drunk, such was the power of the Holy Spirit upon them. They then proceeded to preach the gospel with much power and conviction. In the years that followed this out-pouring, my experience of church was a much greater focus on sharing the good news. Our services and activities became much more geared towards the two great callings of the Body of Christ: to love Jesus and to share his love.

Mocker comes to church

When you came to our church
What did you come to see?
Some people to giggle at,
Weirdos with flutes, wrinklies in suits?

Well some of them kept raising their hands
But there was nothing on the ceiling
A few of the nutters prayed out loud
Someone got hysterical, hands and voice trembling.

This bloke walked to the front,
Said"there's somebody here,
Who's eyes and ears are sealed up!"
What he said next was even more weird.

"You've walked into this person's house
And started laughing at his wife;
She trips over her words and sings out of tune,
Comes from the moon and doesn't dress right.

Well the church is Jesus' beautiful bride
And he's worked so hard to clothe her
For many a year he's been preparing a home
Where they both will live forever.

So go ahead, mock his bride
Wax your ears and seal your eyes.
Enjoy the stage, seize your day
Until his is here and he blows you away.

8 Claire and Jenny

Claire and education

I spent a lot of extra time with Claire during her first six years while I studied Graphic Design at Lowestoft College and a few years later obtained a degree in Business at Norwich. I also worked as a freelance designer but wasn't really very good at it. Towards the end of the degree, I found a much better job doing clerical work at CEFAS, a Fisheries Research Centre in Lowestoft. Heather meanwhile kept working as a teacher through various stages of part-time to full-time depending on the stage of her motherhood. I remember spending hours with Claire making up stories and reading through Enid Blyton classics.

As she grew older she developed many personality traits that were similar to mine. A Stoddart can be extremely headstrong and quick to flare up and pronounce critical judgements on the unfortunates around them. In our defence, we are also quick to forgive and forget: so once I've growled or yelled at you for some error, I want things back to normal and relationships restored.

Claire could be lethal at times in dealings with her friends and family. Towards the end of her teenage years, there were many times when Amy or Jenny had foolishly sneaked into her room to 'borrow' clothes or jewellery and had been discovered and brutally dealt with. Claire was also particularly good at dreaming up punishments for her sisters that would hurt them most. Rather than resorting to physical violence, she would verbally destroy them and then come out with a consequence for the offending action: usually the denial of access to something she had but the offender did not. Occasionally Heather or I would suffer a loud dressing-down for failing to discipline her siblings as she saw fit.

She also had a heart of gold. At some point Claire decided that the presents she gave out would be quality and costly to her. After her GCSEs she managed to obtain a part-time job as a call operator at Hoseasons, a leisure business, and became financially able to do this. It wasn't just buying presents she needed funding for, she had also developed a huge appetite for live music and building up a large CD collection.

As for school, Claire was more like Heather in her commitment. While I wasted much of my compulsory education in complete disinterest, Claire had a hunger for learning and succeeding academically. Her reports from junior to high school were excellent, she graced many a 'top' set and interacted well with teachers and friends, including a girl called Carla whose friendship lasted throughout their lives. It was a cruel irony that her first friend was also probably the last friend she talked to as they both sat in the front seats and died together in the car-crash of July 2006.

Working as hard as she did, it was no surprise that Claire achieved nine GCSEs with seven at grade A and two at grade B. She also managed a merit in GNVQ Information Technology worth four GCSEs, but I note from her records that she tended to keep this a bit quiet and I reckon that was because it wasn't a distinction. I knew from my degree days when I was working very hard that anything less than 1st class was a bit of an insult. It wasn't that I or Claire were snobby, it was just that was where our standards were set. The fact that it took me a meeting with Jesus and an extra 15 years of life to be like that is another issue!

Like me, Claire wasn't one to make academic judgments on others, it was a personal commitment. During her sixth form, I remember with glee the times she would come home complaining that this boy-genius had once again defeated her on some science task. Her chosen A Levels were Biology, Chemistry and English Literature and she applied herself to these with relish, all the time working at Hoseasons, a day at the weekend and a few evenings in the week.

At sixth form, Claire had two major complaints. The first was being forced to take an AS exam in her first year in Critical Thinking. She found the subject a chore and an unnecessary intrusion upon her education. She had set her mind on becoming a chemist and to study pharmacy. To be accepted to do this, she would need top grades in her chosen subjects and so this unwelcome imposter received the harshest of treatment. Somehow, after a host of missed lessons and virtually zero revision she gained a 'C' at the end of the year.

I know the school were unhappy with her attendance for this subject and there also had been a few issues over form registration and 'tutorials' - an hour of waste once a week in Claire's mind. Now employed as a teacher, I have been forced to conduct tutorials over a number of years and so she had my deepest sympathy. The girl was working extremely hard and there was no way I was going to object. Even Heather was silent over the issue.

The second complaint Claire had was over the issue of Education Maintenance Allowance (EMA). This complaint was what fuelled her disdain for the pastoral side of sixth form. While she spent much of her time working and studying, she watched others receiving this hand-out and not having to work like she had to. Our fourth and final child Thomas had been born to us in January 2000 and, even though we had by now one and a half times a teachers' salary coming into the house, it wasn't enough to be lavish. When EMA was introduced we found ourselves just outside the qualifying amount. Also EMA did not take into account the outgoings we had in looking after our other three children.

Claire was pretty mad about EMA. If the subject came up, she would launch into a furious discourse upon the injustice of it. Her way of striking back was to avoid form registrations and tutorials whenever she wanted to. A student in receipt of EMA must register on the system to ensure continued support. I remember once her being called to task about it and the angry retort she gave to the poor teacher who had no idea of her feelings.

Claire could be sharp with people. She wasn't an angel but she did have a humble heart. I know from her diary that like me, if she had offended someone badly enough it would bug her to the point that she would try and make up for it. Perhaps the next day, the teacher would receive an extra-friendly smile. Nevertheless, I know that when it came to EMA, her method of retaliation didn't lessen throughout the two years.

Towards the end of 2005 and start of 2006 I took Claire for interviews at three universities. I say "I took" but it could be argued she took me for she organised mostly everything. By now she had passed her driving test and we had two cars. The old blue Vauxhall Astra virtually became her car and she drove on some of the trips but not the first one in Manchester. We took Jenny with us and had a great day seeing the university while Claire was passing her interview and being offered a place. It seemed to me that it was somewhere around this point that the two girls started to become really close. Jenny was growing up and becoming more accepted amongst the older church youth and able to hold her own in the bull-ring of sparring conversations. They talked almost non-stop during that trip and a stranger would be forgiven for assuming them to be best friends rather than sisters with three years between them.

Claire loved the idea of studying at Manchester, but when the two of us went to Nottingham, she knew this was the place for her. In her diary she made the following entry:

Sunday 4 December 2005 *Can't appreciate the mountains without the valleys*

"Had cell-group on Tuesday, I was so so so scared about Nottingham (uni) – like almost in tears scared – so everyone prayed for me. Then I was awake all night worrying. On Wed morning I thought I was gonna hurl. It was really icy and the car for no apparent reason stopped working. Then the alarm went off and wouldn't stop and it's never done that before.

Dad was stressed and I was nearly in tears and was thinking of not going. Everything was going so badly and I was unreasonably petrified. I was ok for Manchester and for Nottingham I knew what to expect and already had an offer anyway so why worry?

I knew all that but still all I wanted was to not go, I was constantly close to tears. In the end my explanation was that it was God telling me not to go – I was sure of it, I even said to Dad I don't think I'll end up there before we even got close.

But everything went really well from then onwards. We found the place ridiculously easily. It was gorgeous – the campus was beautiful and I could really see myself there. The course was really good, the people nice and the interview went really well. Also I knew I loved the city from before from New Day! (Claire had gone into the city as part of a Christian outreach team from the national New Day youth event run by Newfrontiers).

I felt that it was where I was meant to be. So after that I started thinking about the earlier problems and thought if it's where I'm meant to be maybe it was the devil. Then it led to the obvious question of why did God let it happen? And I decided because of it I know it's where I want to be so much stronger and I proved that to myself by going. My faith was tested and I feel so much better for going. You can't appreciate the mountains without the valleys - I feel that now. My trust in God with this uni thing has just gone up so much."

Success

Shortly after the trip to Nottingham, Claire was offered a conditional place on a four-year MPharm course in Pharmacy. This included some time to be spent in a far-eastern country and to say the girl was excited was an understatement. Her interest in Chemistry and Biology spilled over into her social life and it wasn't uncommon to find her locked in a nerdy conversation with various interested people from school or church. The walls of her bedroom and even the ceiling became covered in revision notes. When I went to the bathroom, or sometimes even the kitchen, one or two scientific diagrams would stare down at me from the walls. She was going for it big-time.

Our final visit was perhaps the most enjoyable. On a sunny day in February the two of us drove down to Reading and we talked and joked through most of the trip. Claire had even sorted the music in the car so that it was acceptable to both of us! The university was a pleasant place but at the time had not been accredited by the professional Pharmacy body and so it wasn't first choice. But she needed a fall-back just in case she didn't get the grades that Manchester and Nottingham were demanding. Back at school in May, she received a certificate for 'outstanding achievement' in Biology. Sadly, Claire never got to find out that there was no need to go to Reading. On August 18th 2006 the Eastern Daily Press reported:

"Two teenagers killed in an horrific car crash this summer while celebrating the end of their A-level exams would have been the highest-achieving girls in their school. Claire Stoddart and Carla Took, both 18, were killed in an horrendous head-on collision on the A12 at Blythburgh, near Lowestoft, on 1 July. Yesterday, as thousands of students across the country opened their A-level results, smiles were tinged with sadness at Benjamin Britten High School in Lowestoft, as the thoughts of staff and fellow students turned to the two teenagers.

The girls emerged as the school's top two female students. Claire was awarded an A in English literature and Bs in Biology and Chemistry, which would have been enough to secure her place at Nottingham University, where she was hoping to study pharmacy. Carla gained three As in English Literature, Media and ICT and a C in History, which would have given her a place to study Media at Lincoln University. It was also revealed that Claire's 15-year-old sister Jenny, who was also killed in the crash, had achieved an exceptional B grade in her ICT AS-level, which she had taken two years early.

Claire and Jenny's father, Phil Stoddart, said: "This just confirms how hard Claire and Jenny both worked for all they wanted to achieve. I'm pleased the results show that. If Claire was here she would be excited she got her grades and got in at Nottingham, and she would be interested in everyone else's results and getting the whole group together celebrating. But she would have been disappointed she didn't get three A's, as she always strove for perfection.

I was not particularly looking forward to receiving the results in a way. To me, they are just pieces of paper. It was the way they lived their lives that mattered.

For many of the students collecting their results in the concourse yesterday, it was an emotional journey, as jubilation was mixed with grief for the friends they had lost."

Jenny takes charge

While Claire displayed many of my characteristics, Jenny was more like Heather. If someone asked me, "what stood out about her the most?" I would answer with no hesitation that it was caution and gentleness. Where Claire was headstrong, Jen was hesitant to step forward. She was very concerned about avoiding pain and wanted to be absolutely sure there was no danger facing her in the things she did.

It was most surprising to me when one day in her early years she came rushing into the house saying she had cut her leg. As it was Jenny, I was expecting to see a slight scratch, but she had been playing on a newly-constructed wall where the brick edges were sharp just to touch. She revealed a long, gaping wound on her shin that showed the ligaments inside.

It made my stomach turn and on the way to hospital my eyes swelled with tears at the look of terror upon her face. She knew whatever was coming her way was going to hurt badly.

The doctor did his best to keep her calm as he sewed up the damage in two stages, internal and then external. I remember him saying afterwards that she'd never be a model for the scar would always show. It had become her identifying mark.

Fortunately, modelling was not on her agenda. Although she loved to dress up with Amy and Lauren, their friend from across the road, her two main focuses were becoming art and sport. She would spend hours drawing and painting. Her sketches were often of groups of girls, all named and dressed up, with labels describing each item of clothing. On Saturday mornings she played tennis and developed both fore and backhand shots that could see off many a pretender. Sadly she never got round to sorting a good serve out. One of my last social activities with her was spent smashing balls at each other on a dodgy grass tennis court. "Hit it hard as you can" she would request of my serves. At school she became part of the netball team and did athletics and occasionally running.

Jenny also loved drama and many times set to writing and organising small plays and indulging in long karaoke sessions. In these she worked out dance routines and performed the popular songs of the time. At Christmas times before the teenage years of shyness set in, the girls did an annual play. Although Jenny nearly always wrote the production and gave each person their lines, Claire was the narrator and performance director. I guess this was due to her claiming 'big sister rights'. She wasn't going to show herself up by acting if she could help it.

Jenny would always have a sensible role, something dignified and authoritative. I got the impression that if she could not stop Claire from bagging the top managerial position, then she would make sure it was obvious to the audience who came next. Thus her characters would have a definite air of authority about them, while Amy would get the mad-cap roles (which admittedly she was never shy of). Amy had to sing the insane songs that had been invented and do any crazy pantomime stunts. Lauren would be drafted over on Christmas day to participate and in later years, cousin Jude was also roped in and dominated under Jenny's leadership.

For, although Jenny was gentle in spirit, she was still a leader. It was not in a loud and overbearing way, but rather she led by achieving a consensus. She was particularly adept at including people and coming up with ideas that would suit as many as possible. I remember the problems we had in arranging birthday parties for her; she didn't like leaving people out or offending anyone. Another outstanding quality of her nature was the softness of her heart.

By high school both Claire and Jenny were quite properly conducting separate social lives. Nevertheless, they still had plenty of things in common. Each had a large group of friends and both were highly prominent in organising things to do. Also, Jenny was receiving school reports that matched those of her older sister. She became part of a gifted and talented group and took an AS Level exam in ICT at the end of Year 10.

Just like Claire, she never got to know how she did. I've heard people say what a waste and how sad it is that high-achieving girls such as these should lose their lives. But I'm just proud that they gave so much to their education. I never had done until after becoming a Christian and so it was very refreshing for me to be exposed to such well-lived academic lives. I saw the hours they put in; sometimes I got annoyed at their workloads and agreed with their complaints about unfair amounts of homework. But it was good.

But for Jesus

If not for Jesus then perhaps I might agree with the people who talk of waste. If there was no God and the end of life really was dust and death, then fair comment. But there is God and because of this not one moment of their efforts have been a waste. Both of them came to a personal faith in Jesus and the Bible tells us that all deeds will be laid bare and judged accordingly.

As parents, we wanted to make sure our children developed a solid faith that would not be dependent on how good their church happened to be at any given time. They needed a discovery of a personal God who desired intimate relationship with them. We also wanted more of God ourselves, so in addition to church, we went each year to an Easter event called Spring Harvest where we could experience dynamic ministries from across the country and internationally. The kids had their own programmes including Bible-based seminars on lifestyle and worship that were relevant to their age and culture. There was loud and fun praise mixed in with soft heart-bearing worship songs. At these events they made friends and saw a bigger picture of church.

When we joined Lowestoft Community Church, we started going to the annual New Frontiers event which had moved to Stoneleigh in the Midlands. There was a children's program similar to that of Spring Harvest and it was here that Claire began a more personal walk towards knowing God. Due to the popularity of the event (the final year, 2001, attracted nearly 26,000 people) and perhaps the insensitivity of a 'jobsworth' organiser, all of Claire's friends went into an older age-group program than she was allowed to – even though one of them had a birthday within a month of hers!

This meant that each year she had to go on her own, which was quite an ordeal for a young girl during a five year period up to the age of thirteen. But Claire was independently-minded and stuck at it and I think she was richly rewarded. Away from the distraction of friends she listened carefully to what was being said and 'became' a Christian.

The only problem, we discovered, was that she 'became' a Christian every year! The organisers sent 'response' cards after the event to local churches to inform them of any commitments made by their young people. So it was quite funny to meet with an excited youth leader and hear the 'good' news. Claire told us afterwards, she just needed to be sure she really was a Christian.

What really mattered to us was the evidence for her life being recognisable as that of someone who had put their trust in Jesus. This is a difficult issue at any time. Anyone can say that they are a Christian but it is the fruit of the tree that shows clearly what it is.

I have always felt with my family that the hand of God rests on every one of us. It's not something that I can easily explain, but I believe Claire and Jenny knew Jesus before they even made their good confessions of faith. I know that faith has to be personal and that no one can say, "I am a Christian because my parents are", but it seems that some people just seem to grow up with a drip-fed revelation of Jesus that when they come to give their testimony, they find it difficult to say when their conversion happened! Perhaps Claire had this problem and just wanted to be able to pin it down to a day in her mind when she could say that was it.

Whatever the reality might be, whether Claire became a Christian at Stoneleigh or was already one, I am just so deeply thankful that all three of my daughters have displayed convincing evidence of the Holy Spirit at work within their lives. I cannot say when Jenny or Amy 'became' Christians but I have seen fruit and I still see Amy today and know there is a visible dynamic between her and God. As for Tom, who is not yet eight at the time of writing, I have the same confidence, the same unwavering belief that God is slowly wooing and drawing him in. Our family is so blessed.

Claire and Jenny visiting Manchester University, November 2005

9 Their own words

Further evidence of Claire and Jenny each having a personal relationship with Jesus can be found in the diaries they left behind. This chapter contains 'spiritual' extracts written in their final year but it is worth pointing out that many entries were not spiritual as such, but rather to do with the people and activities that formed their social lives. It should also be noted that Jenny was only fifteen when she died while Claire was eighteen and set on going to university.

Jenny: 25 -30 July 2005 New Day!!!

Went on a coach journey to a Christian camp for a week. In the evening we went to the meeting and I wish I'd taken notes because it was really good and inspiring. After the morning meeting we went on a coach together into Nottingham to do outreach. We were mainly just thrusting leaflets to people about the Christian event at Notts County Football Club. We were not really talking to them about it, which probably wasn't the best way to deal with this evangelism. To be honest though, I thought me and Amy Willis worked better without the others but it was probably me just thinking that as an excuse.

On Wednesday PJ Smythe preached and was excellent! Really funny and great how he related to you. We did outreach again, clearing up huge junk like mattresses, old tv's, wheels etc that had been dumped in the woods. My hair was really curly, it had rained and I was dirty all over. We were late home for dinner, but it was really satisfying.

On Thursday night we went to the stadium and Adrian Holloway spoke. This was my best evening here because I was with close friends who I feel comfortable around and the music was great and we went mad! Loads of people became

Christians – Bex and PJ too (Yay!). Also lots of people got healed, including a girl who had a bad allergy to rubber, latex, nuts and fruit. She was instantly healed and ate a fruit and wore a rubber band without needing to go to the hospital!

On Saturday we went to morning worship and a seminar on being filled with the Holy Spirit everyday, which was good. Then it was outreach and giving out leaflets for the stadium event. We talked to:

2 black guys, middle aged, one said he was a Christian and seemed interested!

2 middle aged guys, who didn't believe in anything, but gave us their time. We challenged them with questions making them think and they were very interested.

3 skaters, one man interested in the subject, but the others just flirting! We got them thinking though, especially the one with a lip ring, he was nicest.

A teenage boy, who was a Roman Catholic, said he wasn't sure of difference, but was enthusiastic + said he'd like to come to the concert. Quite fit too!

17-18 tall Gothic boy, polite, said he'd like to come, but then his friend took him away!

Just as we were going I talked to these really nice guys, about my age. One said he used to sometimes go to church, but he hadn't gone for a while; seemed interested though.

I'm hoping they'll get involved. I'd prayed for confidence/ boldness from God and got it definitely. We went to the stadium in the evening and after the preach we went down to the front and went crazy.

Claire: 11 Oct 2005 Content

Back writing, it's about time! I'm lying in bed listening to Jack Johnston, it's 11.20 but I haven't got school tomorrow so just feel calm, relaxed and content. Content is my general feeling at the moment… MAJOR REVELATION! That's what I prayed for at New Day! I took a faith step and kneeled on the ground and asked for contentment. Flipping Heck! What an answer to prayer. I wasn't even thinking about it but that's the word that describes me best (and it's an odd word). I can't express how much of a big deal this is! Nothing much has changed but I'm totally happy with it. What an awesome God!

On that note, I'll start by describing my relationship with God – it's amazing! I feel so close to him and can feel his presence in everything I do. Worship at church is awesome. I'm seeing so many answers to prayer and am really enjoying and getting a lot out of reading my bible. I'm just so overwhelmingly lucky. My relationship feels so personal – God's so close to me WHATEVER I do and I know that's why I'm feeling so happy with all other aspects of my life.

I wish everyone else had this feeling. I can't describe it and NEVER want to lose it. I'm in prayer for other Christians right now, Abi is having a hectic time at uni, good but hectic and she feels away from God. Jim says he struggling with his whole faith as he doesn't think it's fair that God tempts and tests us. So I'm praying he will come back and know God better. And Tim (sketchy details) I know is going through a rough patch at home, so just that God will be with him and he won't drift. Totally different circumstances but I am praying for all of them.

God's taught me a lesson another way too. I dunno why but this story embarrasses me, but it's a major thought-change and it should be here. On the way home from the sixth form party, Marv came on to me very strongly (details not needed!) and then was really funny with me at school. But God has given me two areas of contentment. First, I don't want any attention from drunk people. If they like me, I want to actually be really liked for me – and he was the total opposite. So I'm happy being single and waiting for the right person – which is a major step for me!

The second one was exampled in Adam – he got really angry at Marv for being like that and was really protective. It just made me realise what awesome friends I've got, especially Adam at that point, but all of them at school and church. I can completely trust them all and they all actually care for me! I've had so many fun things going on – Bloc Party, birthday meal + Chinese, Rachel's party and loads of other things big and small. Like hanging out with Sarah and Carla this afternoon or going to cell group tonight.

Well, better go to bed, Jenny's birthday tomorrow and I'm going to see the Coral in concert. Well, that's my general and main thoughts right now, the key word I think being contentment. But it's midnight so "Please close your eyes woman, please get some sleep".

Claire: 11 Oct 2005 I don't do failure

Just got back from Birmingham and off the phone from Abi. Had an hour-long moan, I miss her so much – she was listening to 'Bright Eyes' too, who else is like that! I feel just like I don't fit anymore and what makes everything worse, a few entries back I felt so sorted with God and until speaking to Abi I didn't think anything had changed, but now I realise it has. I'm never in the company of Christians and that has a major effect. I haven't read my bible, or listened to a worship CD forever. And my personal time with God, which used to be on-going, is now almost non-existent!

I don't think Erin knows how much I need her right now. I've just lost my best friend and she's drifting too, so I have no Christian best friends to talk to. Chris is still the same, he's so reliable. I've never appreciated him more – he doesn't change his friends with situation. If he stopped being around I don't know what I'd do. I wish Abi was here, I miss her so much, and Sam. I feel so ready to leave and it seems everyone is ready for me to leave and have classed me in the same group. This sucks, I feel so lonely. I need to get back to God which I guess means back to Christians. I guess I'll have to manage without Erin. It's so hard, it just seems so much easier to be with my school-friends, I've never had that before. I'll just have to pray and try. Chris will help.

Also I have decided to sort the situation out. It's not working for me and sitting here being bitter with people isn't exactly going to help my relationship with them. It will just make this leaving year worse and certainly isn't healthy. "I'm not sure how all of this got started but we're gonna make them God damn certain how it's gonna end"! (Road to Joy by Bright Eyes)

Now obviously the first step is to pray. I can't sort myself out alone, hence the 'we'! But I'm gonna have to take steps too eg bible reading and making an effort with people (I asked Erin if she was free Saturday instead). My bible verse to work on at the moment is "Don't hit back, discover beauty in everyone" Romans 12 v17. This includes non-Christians as well; enough with the bitching and I must MUST give George a chance. I'm gonna have to make such an effort at school as I have completely alienated him. There are gonna be setbacks of course as I have become cut off from several people but the important point is to keep trying.

Remember, "God hurts but he also bandages up" Job 15v18. How good are these verses – this is why reading my bible is so important. The key thing for me to remember is to do any of this I need to regain my strong relationship with God. Otherwise, where is the incentive, where is the power? "People without God can produce nothing" Job 15v34. I can't do this on my own. What I can do is take the physical steps, and I'm sure as hell gonna try. I don't do failure!

Jenny: 31 Oct 2005 They found out I'm a Christian

It was first day back at school today after half-term. Really all I want to write about today is something good that happened. I know I have prayed, ages ago, that people would know I was a Christian – without me needing to tell them in an embarrassing way. God answered my prayer today with Matty and Steven. They were saying at break that there was something they had found out, when I realised they were talking about me! I was worried it would be something mean. On the internet, Steven

*said "I didn't know you were a Christian", and that broke the ice.
I told him a bit about it and the church (the modern-ness etc)
and he was really cool and understanding about it. He said it
was interesting that I was a Christian. I pray that more of this
happens for me with other people.*

Claire: 21 Nov 2005. Making the effort

*I just feel like I'm waiting for university which isn't a good attitude to
have as I still have nine months here and that's a long time. Went to
Manchester last week; feel like I screwed up the interview, but loved
the uni. It was so traditional and the city was so cool with so much
happening. I'd like to go there if I get in but I haven't seen the others
yet so can't really judge. I wish Manchester would let me know.*

*My relationship with God is, well, I don't really know. Randomly
I feel touched and my beliefs are still strong but sometimes I seem to
just forget that whole side of me. Not purposely, I just do. I guess to
sort that out I should put more time and energy in. More time with
God I mean, keep my bible-reading regulated and listen to more
worship. That's an effort I'll just have to make no matter how busy
I seem to be. It's gotta come first, above everything. Above exams –
that is gonna be hard for me cos I really wanna do well so can go to
uni. Just have to trust God on that – sacrifice other things.*

Claire: 27 Nov 2005. Boys

*Spoke to Aaron, still dunno if I like him. He seems nice, chatted easily
enough and hates EMA* (always a good sign). But he's still a Kirkley
boy and then there's always the issue of liking him because he's
there – young, Christian NEW guy – good looking and friendly. Do
I think, "he fits, guess I'll like him"? I think I'll have to examine myself
on that one. I was ok with being single, content, so why ruin that for
someone I'm not sure I like, when God's got someone perfect for me?
I just have to be patient. I'll think and pray over it anyway.*
** EMA – Education Maintenance Allowance (pocket money grant from the
Government to sixth formers)*

Jenny: 29 Nov 2005 Answered prayer

Ok so I haven't written for a month but nothing very exciting has really happened to me. Fenny now knows I'm a Christian without me saying it – so God answers my prayer yet again! I spoke to James and Mo a bit today, the conversation got a bit religious and I uncharacteristically said, "yeh I'm a Christian" and started explaining how I went to church, that I liked it and had friends there etc without getting really embarrassed or anything. I think this is God answering my prayer yet again, as I don't know where else that confidence would have come from.

Jenny: 1 Jan 2006 Everything but God

God's been answering a lot of my prayers lately: I've got to hang out with someone I like lots, work's gone well, the parties were fun and a success and I've now got a decent phone. These are just some of the things that are a result of God; he's also given me more confidence to talk about Christianity to people.

I heard that at a party my school friends were at, this boy I know got really drunk and depressed and apparently that scared all of them a bit. I think he may have a problem, he is always drinking and needs God. I know he does. Nothing else is missing from his life. He has money, friends, a family, a personality, good school life, but not God. I want to speak to him about it.

Claire: 9 Jan 2006. The midweek meeting (Cell)

Feeling a little agitated, it's the annoyance as before and thinking about it, what can you do? It's always gonna be there, just have to work round it and get over it. Can't exactly ask for help at cell though: "please pray that I won't chuck this at your head!" Don't think it would go down too well. I guess I'm more opinionated than I thought and with Chris, Dan, Nathan and now Aaron I just can't get a word in so my views are never known and I do most definitely have them!

The structure just irritates the hell out of me; we never get the chance to talk and then, in the 'word' (bible study) when I can talk, I get interrupted as it's onto the next point. This is gonna sound brattish but to be honest I'm used to being listened to! At school I barely have to raise my voice and at church socials I can generally get an audience, and at work too. That's awful, really awful – so that's what it comes down to: I'm an under-cover attention seeker at heart – I always thought I hated that.

Ok so cell can teach me a lesson then, but it's still irritating not getting my opinion heard. I guess, with exams I'm stressed, as it is anything that can make me feel worse. Nathan and Aaron were amazed at how much I'm doing, but to me it's nowhere near enough. I need an 'A' and I'm not clever enough not to revise. Should be doing it now but am too stressed and really need a break. I just really want to go to Nottingham.

Gonna ask Sarah and Carla to Alpha. Think Carla will be ok but Sarah is having such a rough time right now, I doubt she'll react well. I'll do it tomorrow but for some reason am scared about it; she's my best friend so why ever am I? All she can do is say 'no'. As Mike said, it's all about putting your feet in the water, so it's what I'm gonna do. Hope God gives me the right words – have been praying.

Miss Abi already! Should be going to see her in February though; think I'll get my train ticket at the weekend. Is Aaron more annoying than Nathan? Hmmmm.

Jenny: 2 Feb 2006 Baptism?

A couple of Sundays ago, me, Amy and Bex went to 'Elevate' which was really good. They played older, good songs and Johnny gave his testimony, saying how he became a Christian. We then split off in groups to pray; me, Bex and Amy W went together and the prayer really helped. We prayed for our friends and each other being able to talk about Christianity, and about baptism which was really good.

Hopefully I'll be getting baptised soon. I hadn't really thought about it before, but Claire said, "why not?" and the only reason was that I hadn't got round to it. She said, "what if you die now and God asks why you haven't been baptised? You'll have to say you couldn't be bothered". That is a stupid reason, I agree with her. I just need a testimony. It will probably be quite hard to think of and quite dull.

Jenny: 10 Feb 2006 Drugs

It's Half-term now. YAY! I have to work quite a lot though. I finished reading this book Rozzy lent me and got a really good bible verse out of it. I'm going to try, every morning, to find a verse, and write it in my diary, and that verse may help me throughout the day. It's also a good way to read more of the Bible.

I can't wait till the summer; I can wear cool, colourful clothes, hang out at the beach, not be cold etc. Also New Day is something I'm really excited about, and I'm looking forward to spending more time with Jack, there's just something about him. I like everything about him, his personality, no other boy is anywhere near him!

Some of the girls at school have been talking about having a 'Weed' night, which is really stupid! I thought they were just joking and was like "yer, I'll go," but Jez is really serious and knows someone who can get hold of it! Now I think about it, there's no way I'm going, it would mean doing drugs, not just messing about. I want to have a clean slate when it comes to that.

Jenny: 9 March 2006

On Sunday me and Amy W went to talk to Rob about getting baptised and he was obviously really great about it, saying he'd try sort it out for April sometime. Me and Amy were so nervous about saying it and she did most of the talking. I feel she knows more about it and explained it better than I would have done.

It's good how she's confident like that. She's got really trendy at the moment, wearing cool stuff, making her hair rock-ish etc which is a good look for her: go Amy!!

Claire: 19 March 2006. Alpha

We had Alpha tonight and I was a little apprehensive. It's the Holy Spirit day so I didn't know what to expect and didn't want to scare my friends off. At one point we had to write out our questions to God and put them on a cross and I basically said, 'I've stepped out in faith so why is nothing happening?' If anything, the situation felt like it was getting worse. But then on the way home they asked loads of questions about the Holy Spirit and prayer; really in-depth questions and we talked about 'tongues' and things – really amazing.

One of them said, that after seeing people in tears she believed there must be something when she didn't before. I thought it was a mistake to ask them but again God proved me wrong. My faith needs improving I know, but that's happening more and more – I mean I got them there, that's a massive step for me. I keep doubting God when I know he can do ANYTHING and it's really important I get that.

It's weird speaking to Aaron because he's talking about people converting ASAP, but I'm amazed they are even considering it. I need to think bigger I know, even with faith the size of a mustard seed, I shouldn't discount God from doing things in my life because of my small faith. I've got such a good relationship with them, I must have shown some faith inviting them. God can even work in rubbish weak people like me.

Jenny: 22 March 2006 Leaflets

I did kids club today and again got to have lots of good conversations with Nathan, which was really good. I enjoy just hanging out with him and feel I can be myself totally. It's probably because he's a Christian and very laid-back. He gave me a huge stack of leaflets to give out today though, which I'm a bit wary of. They're for 'Reverb', where bands are invited to play at our church.

He has the gift of being a 'people' person as he's very social and outgoing. I can be social, but in a different way to him and am quite shy. I feel quite under pressure now, as he expects me to get loads of people at my school to go. Hopefully I can give some to people like Andrew Spooner to give some to other Year 11s.

I put "Come to Reverb" on my MSN name and then James came on. He'd obviously blocked me ages before, seen that, and then decided to talk to me. I really hope him and Matt go with the others. He talked for ages and then seemed pretty interested in me being a Christian and said he should go to church one time. That would be great!!

Jenny: 26 Mar 2006 Sin and sex

1 week left until holidays! I gave out some of the Reverb leaflets, but have loads left to give out this week. I don't know if James etc will come, they probably won't; oh well, their loss. Hopefully Emily and her friends will go. Most of my friends are going, including Ellen and Dionne. I need to get Jenni, Katy etc to go and Joe and his friends, but I'm a bit worried about giving them to him.

The service at Church today was really good. We're going through Romans and Mike did a sermon about 'Spiralling downwards'. It let us see how sinful humans are and so how great God is in forgiving us. Also, sexual sin is one of the worst types, as you're not only sinning against others, and God, but your own body. I never want to have sex outside marriage, I'd feel so dirty.

Aaron pulled my hair out but I thought it was Nathan so I hit him and blamed him and wouldn't believe him. When I found out it was Aaron, I was too up on myself and proud to admit

I was wrong. I don't like that characteristic, I owe Nathan an apology. Goodnight, wish me luck with Reverb leaflets!

Jenny: 6 Apr 2006 Reverb

After about 45 mins of persuading I got Steven and Matt to come to Reverb but I don't think they enjoyed it to say the least. I hung out with Sam a lot and we got on really well. Me and him just walked around talking, just like good friends. I didn't actually pay as much attention to my school-friends as I should have done, but I wanted to take advantage of speaking to people who I don't have as much chance to hang out with.

In general Reverb was really successful as there were loads of people there, mostly emo, but that's cool. The band's weren't too good but I didn't pay too much attention to them anyway.

I just want to thank God for the success of Reverb and safety. Also that he got Steven and Matt there, and that he let me hang out with great people.

Jenny: 16 Apr 2006 Interview

Mike Betts asked me to be interviewed at Church in the service and I worryingly accepted. I don't feel I'm too good in front of lots of people, but I asked God to give me courage and to give replies that made sense and were not foolish. The interview went fine and I didn't really say much anyway!

Jenny: 21 Apr 2006 The difference

To be honest I haven't had a very good last two days. Sean has been especially annoying and called me some stuff in drama. He said he was joking but I think otherwise as it would be a very harsh joke. Everyone's been nasty to Lizzy because of a bad rumour. Can't everyone see it's just a rumour; I mean it has been people who didn't like her before that has been spreading it. Are people this stupid or just determined to put others down?

When I look around I just see mankind filled with hate, deceit and cruelty which can often over-shadow all the good things like love and kindness. I compare the Christians I know with other people and see the huge difference. They are just nice. Though people like Claire and Laura are nice too. I get very disappointed when my own friends turn nasty and cannot see why they do it.

Jenny: 10 May 2006 Blunt

At school, I told Jack I was a Christian and went to Church etc. I think he was quite shocked but seemed pretty interested. When he asked, I was honest and said that, unfortunately, he was going to Hell. He may have been quite freaked out by this. Me and him got on well all lesson though, wow!

Jenny: 14 May 2006 Church

Church was really good today. I am proud to be a part of it and love going. The worship's full of life and passion and with Mike Betts talking, you can't go wrong. It means so much and he's funny too. I went to 'Elevate' (youth event) in the evening; there were a lot of people there and the worship was great. I brought Phoebe and was a bit worried it would be too much for her as she kept looking round. But I decided, in worship (with a nudge from God) to just go for it. In result she enjoyed the whole night and is interested in coming to church.

Claire: 19 June 2006 Nottingham

Again writing when I shouldn't! Even more in the middle of exams than before. Have got two tomorrow, Biology and English. Am still feeling calm about the whole thing. Had Biochem and think it went ok. I think God is really with me, giving this amazing sense of peace and exams have not really been too bad, although the worst are still to come. I think keeping up reading my bible even when I've been busy (like tonight!) is really important. I really think God wants me in Nottingham, the city is really on my heart and if God wants me there, that's where I'll be.

I mean really it wasn't the easy option at all, surely that would be Bath, and there's so many problems but I guess that's why God wants me there, it will be such a challenge. Have found out Ed is gonna be there too which is really cool, someone to navigate the new church with and seems like a nice guy. I'm so bored with revision, having to drink something alcoholic so I'm over the limit and won't go out!

Claire: 25 June 25 2006 Chilli Peppers should be awesome

Well, should be my last encounter with boredom! Last exam tomorrow but it's Chemistry and has the potential to go either way. Will just have to stay calm and really think about the questions. On the plus side, at least I can take my text book and data book in which I have discovered have a lot more detail than I first expected. My week's mapped out afterwards though. Working tomorrow 1:30 to 5:30, a bit annoying, but I well need the money, because me and Sarah are going to Norwich to do holiday clothes shopping. Tuesday night have this thing at the Depot for Cell and am not really sure what that will be like. We're dressing up as Ents from Lord of the Rings, so will look like such geeks but never mind. At least no one can say it's boring!

Working all day on Wednesday, much needed money again, and then having a 'holiday meeting' round here which should get us all very excited! Me and Carla are gonna waste a day in town on Thursday because we can. Then we both have work and after are going for Joe's leaving thing and will hopefully meet some people from school in town. Friday is Chilli's! Should be awesome but I'm a little scared as am driving, it's just the parking which gets me really. Saturday is work, football and am going out for Hannah's birthday. Then Sunday church and work ready to go away Tuesday. So busy week!

Jenny: June 25 2006 Baptism again

I've had a pretty nice day today, I just needed sleep. I talked most to Aaron R and Sam today at church and at the BBQ. Me and Claire stalled Chris well because it was a surprise for his 30th. We distracted him with a werewolf information sheet and it totally worked. It shows how well we know him; we planned it out and everything!

Me and Amy W are meeting Sue and Rob on Wednesday about being baptised which is good but a little scary. Claire said it's like 18th July when baptisms are on, which is really soon. I don't feel prepared and am so scared. I want to invite lots of my friends but I don't know which ones would go; Roxy and Bex definitely. Hopefully Lauren, Sophie etc but it's a good chance to get other people to church like Steven, Jack, Joe etc. I need to be brave.

Claire: June 26 2006 Weekend

This weekend's been so dull in comparison from what's ahead. Exam on Friday went fairly well again, amazing! Worked in the evening, was sick on Saturday which was horrible, felt so bad, but got a full day of Chemistry done, so feel ready for tomorrow which is cool because I didn't really have much time today. Carla came round in the evening and it was nice to catch up with her. Today's been busy; church, which was good. Finally got to know some of Nathan's friends which I think is vital for them if they're gonna get involved, not me personally, just meeting other church members!

Had a surprise BBQ round ours for Chris which went well. Me and Jenny had to distract him so we went for a big werewolf thing which he totally fell for! We all watched the football too; England actually won which was quite a big surprise for everyone. Aaron helped me with my Chemistry in a totally un-annoying way so that's cool. Oh, God also answered my prayer and gave me all the time off work I need and more, awesome!

Jenny: June 27 2006 Ents

I dressed up as a tree today, to be precise, an Ent. I must say it's one of the stupidest things I've ever done! We thought it was a good idea, but the end result was just me, Claire and Roxy with a few big branches and leaves sellotaped to us. We had a bundle of long grass strapped to the back of our legs, we had a bit of face-paint on and back-combed our hair to make it wild.

None of it really worked. The car ride to the Depot (church) where the film-night was happening was really funny as we realised what idiots we looked and how embarrassing it would be. We kept shrieking and everything, we were like "let's turn back", seriously! It was that bad.

It was very embarrassing when we got there. There was like only fifteen people there and not many of them had made much effort – just cave-girls etc, so we looked really stupid. When we got out of the car I was laughing so much, and so embarrassed that I nearly threw up and was properly crying, I tell you it was quite an experience, one I'm not likely to forget!

Claire: June 28 2006 Final Entry

Exam's over! Wooooo! Been so busy though and haven't had time to relax. It's my own stupid fault I know but I'll chill out over the weekend so that will be good. Chemistry went surprisingly ok on Monday. I knew what to write for all of them and think I could have actually done ok. Strangely, Aaron said he thought it was really nasty but Nathan thought it was ok: my only worry is that I'm missing something!

Went to Norwich Tuesday with Sarah and spent way too much, like a couple of hundred pounds, bad right! Got so many holiday things though which I totally needed. Then Tuesday night, Ents from Lord of the Rings. What were we thinking, the most embarrassing thing I think I've ever done, why?! We looked like ridiculous tree people, so stupid; at least we didn't go with the nets. The evening as a whole was ok, everyone else dressed up normally, seriously why!? We lost the tree outfits pretty quickly. Had the girls over for a holiday talk: so soon, can't wait. Shopping, work and going out tomorrow – I need a break!

Jenny: June 28 2006 Who to baptise me?

Me and Amy W had our meeting about being baptised today. It was fine and laid-back but gave us more information about it. Andrew's getting baptised on the same day which is really cool, as it means it won't be just me and Amy alone! I don't know who to get to baptise me. The elder will be Ben and then we get to choose someone. I'm thinking maybe Erin, Chris or Dan but I don't know if they'd want to do it. It's on the 16th July – pretty close. I'm hoping to start inviting some friends from tomorrow, I hope they come.

Jenny: June 29 2006 Final entry

I told Claire, Lauren and Sophie about me getting baptised and invited them to come. Lauren may be working but they all seemed really keen and said they would. Claire and Sophie were excited for me and asking questions about it. Claire said "Are you allowed to go if you're not part of the church?" I was like: Yer!! I also told them about dressing casual as I think Claire is thinking of an old-fashioned traditional church, which it really isn't!

It means a lot to me that they're coming; Bex and Roxy are too of course. I want to ask people from youth club – James C definitely, Waddy, Johnny, Sam T maybe, Dionne, Abi, Jazzy etc. I also would like Taryn and Lydia to come. I don't think Mary wants to so I won't push her, I wish she would though. Maybe Ellen too. I'd love Steven to go and Matty but I'm worried they'd laugh. I want to ask Chris to baptise me; he's really influenced me, but I don't think he will. I hope he does, a lot. RED HOT CHILLI PEPPERS tomorrow. Can't wait! Yay!! Bye xxx

10 NEWS www.EDP24.co.uk/news

Eastern Daily Press, Tuesday, July 18, 2006

Picture: BILL DARNELL

FATHER'S TRIBUTE: Phil Stoddart talks about his daughters Claire and Jenny at their memorial service, which was held at Lowestoft Community Church yesterday.

Tears for tragic sisters

By LYNETTE ALCOCK

One of two teenage sisters, whose memorial service was held at a Lowestoft church yesterday, had been due to be baptised there the day before.

Claire and Jenny Stoddart, 18 and 16, were both killed in a horrific crash on the A12 near Blythburgh on July 1, which also claimed the lives of two other people.

They had been travelling home from a pop concert in Ipswich, organised to celebrate the end of their exams.

On Sunday, friends and family had planned to attend Lowestoft Community Church for Jenny's baptism.

Instead, yesterday, the church was holding a thanksgiving memorial service for both sisters.

More than 500 people, including friends, family and teachers filled the seats, lined the aisles, and poured into the courtyard to pay their respects. A video link was set up in the hall neighbouring the church.

But although they had been brought together by tragedy, and united in their grief, they chose to remember with songs, laughter, and pictures of two sisters who "shone like stars".

At the service, Jenny's best friend Amy Willis, who had been due to be baptised with Jenny, spoke emotionally of the day they had planned.

She said: "Yesterday me and Jen were supposed to be getting baptised together.

"She was so excited about it in the weeks before the accident, talking and planning what we were going to wear.

"She was my best mate, the person

I could tell everything, and I trusted her wholeheartedly."

The last diary entries of both girls were published in an order of service, Jenny's revealing her enthusiasm about the baptism, and poignantly ending with how excited she was about going to the concert.

"Red Hot Chili Peppers 2morrow. Can't wait. Yay!! xbyex."

Friends of both girls paid tribute to not only Claire and Jenny, but the whole Stoddart family for welcoming them in.

But even in the moments of greatest sadness, as they were

GREAT LOSS: Jenny, (left), and Claire Stoddart who were both killed in a terrible crash on the A12 near Blythburgh.

choking back tears and fighting for composure, they retained their humour. One friend Chris Clarke, laughed as he struggled to speak.

"I look like such a wuss," he said. "If they were looking at me from up there they would be having such a laugh at me."

Another friend recalled family holidays with the Stoddarts telling how the girl's father Phil had once taken them to a nudist beach.

Mr Stoddart spoke about his faith in Christianity and took time to thank all the people who had stood by the family over the past two

weeks. He said: "I must say a very big thank you on behalf of myself, Heather, Amy and Tom, we have been overwhelmed with the support.

"Thank you for showing concern for us."

But even on such a sad occasion, he was still able to laugh and joke with Claire and Jenny's friends, adding: "I didn't knowingly lead the kids to a nudist beach – just for the record."

Paying tribute, community pastor Rob Clarke, who led the service, said: "There was such life in those girls, such ordinary teenage girls

UNITED IN GRIEF: Above left, friends arrive for the service at Lowestoft Community Church; above, tears in the crowd outside the church and left, Chris Clarke, (with microphone), son of community pastor Rob Clarke, (on the left of the picture), fires up with other friends to pay tribute to the girls.

but with a profound faith. Many people were touched by them while they were alive, and many more have been touched through their deaths."

■ Police are still appealing for witnesses to the crash which also claimed the lives of 18-year-old Carla Took from Lowestoft, and 40-year-old Simon Bonner from Yoxford.

Anyone with information should call Halesworth Roads Policing on 01473 613500.

■ A memorial service for Carla Took will be held at St Michael's Church, Oulton Broad at 1.30pm on Thursday.

Eastern Daily Press.18 July 2006

10 Aftermath

Tired

How much more can I take?
There is no sleep in the house
All I keep seeing are their faces
I'm tired and I want to rest.

A little boy keeps waking up
Wailing, a sort of deep inconsolable mourning
Cuddling may soothe the sobbing
But nothing can touch the void within.

A mother's eyes keep sparkling
Barely containing the well beneath
Happy memories have turned to water
They used to surface as laughter but no more.

A sister's heart is carefully guarded
Storing up sorrows in locked away places
But when the night comes, doors are unlocked
And wounds are revealed but not dressed.

How much more can I take?
What can be done to end it
I will gather my remaining strength
And enter the house of my Lord.

I will eat and drink at his table
Though my mouth is dry and barely able
I will taste of his goodness and declare He is faithful
Until strength flows within me once more.

Weak body, weak mind
Driven by emotion, tormented by loss.
What hope can there be for one such as me
Unless it be that cruel cross?

Where he cried out to God in the deepest of pain
"Why am I forsaken, when I need you so much?"
Darkness fell and paraded hell
Heaven was silent and hope seemed lost.

Then a tearing in the darkness and the coming of dawn
Resurrection from death and a new day born
For all who will trust him and receive him as Lord
And I come running, renewed and restored.

Media

As might be expected from a crash that had killed five people,
media interest was inevitable. Even on the day it happened
reporters from two different newspapers had arrived at our
door only to be turned away by our friends. Apparently they
had also called on our neighbours but had been sent packing.
As mentioned before, our policeman warned us about the
press and in particular to watch out for those representing the
national papers. In truth, apart from the thoughtlessness of
those initial reporters, we found them to be alright. Most of our
dealings were with regional television, radio and newspaper
staff and I think we surprised each other. I was impressed with
the sensitive way they handled us and I think they found us to
be a most unusual family.

They had discovered people who weren't bitter and angry
about what had happened. For me, it was simply the fruit of
our Christian lives being on display. Also I remember Jesus
clearly telling me not to question him on what had happened
or to blame myself or anyone else. I knew it was important
to obey him and allow no malicious thoughts to set in. It was
to be essential for my healing that I walked in unconditional
acceptance and forgiveness. Anything less than this would
compromise my relationship with him and this I could not afford
to do. Even now I reject any regrets that rise to attack me. Sure,

I could have been a better dad and I could have offered to drive them to the concert myself. Such thoughts are poisonous and not for those who are justified by the blood of Jesus.

"Aren't you angry with the young man who drove the other car?" they asked us almost incredulously. I didn't lie then and I am still not speaking falsely when I say it is a room we refuse to enter. We who have known forgiveness for our crimes at the cross will not dare to rise in judgement against another law-breaker. That is a matter for Jesus and for the legal system. Also we are filled with the Holy Spirit and I do not think we are even capable of acting against the new nature that has been built in us over the years we have known Jesus.

Blogging

I don't particularly know why I started doing it, but shortly after the funeral I started to write diary entries again. A few months earlier I had created a 'MySpace' site on the internet as a bit of a tease to Claire and Jen. I remember coming across a message from Claire to Jen saying something like "Oh no Miss Bennett, our father has acquired 'MySpace'. We are undone!" (They were going through a phase of pretending to be sisters from Pride and Prejudice.)

The site gave a facility for users to write 'blogs' for others to see and, encouraged as I was by the presence of God, I became inclined to share my experience of dealing with grief as a Christian. What particularly bothered me was that many who knew Claire and Jenny were unaware of just how significant knowing Jesus was in this horrible death situation. I wanted them to know how much it mattered that the girls had died as Christians and 'MySpace' provided that opportunity.

The entries start towards the end of July and are honest accounts of both grief and blessing. They form the majority of the remainder of this book and are sometimes written as poems and songs.

Tuesday 25 July 2006 *First entry*

I was praying this morning and once again found myself sitting
with Jesus by a small river in strong daylight. But this time he
allowed me to see further on and a group of people having a
real laugh. Jen and Claire were there, giggling and carefree.
I was absorbed by the image. When I started to focus back on
normal life I opened my eyes and they were streaming but
these were tears of joy.

Next morning's prayer time was short but powerful again.
I started thinking about how Jesus looks now and as usual the
face was sort of obscure but the clothes were gleaming white,
pure, brilliant, dazzling. The idea dawned on me that when
I really come before him, I am not going to be able to stand in
his presence.

Why? Because as I gazed, the power of his love just hit me
and I trembled and cried. Only because this awesome person
became a man and gave up his life on the cross can I stand
before him clean and accepted. If there was no cross, Claire and
Jenny would not be with him, safe and happy. This is no small
matter for me. All who have put their trust in him will not be
disappointed.

Thursday 27 July *Car Crash Survivor*

My wife and I went to the hospital four weeks after the
accident to see Sarah for the first time. We had to prepare
ourselves beforehand because one seat either side and it could
have been Jenny in that bed. Also if Claire or Jen had stayed
this side of life we'd see what it would have been like for them.

Well when we saw her we were amazed at how good she
looked, bright and well patched up and exceptionally pretty!
I am so pleased she's made it through. But metal plates and
wires and a dodgy spine mean it'll be a hard road back. She
had many fractures and I remember in the days after the crash

we had been responsible for keeping our church informed
so that they could pray for her. Being a part of the large and
growing New Frontiers family of churches meant that Sarah
was prayed for in churches across this nation and also by some
in Europe.

The condition she was in was not good. There were times
when her life hung by a thread. Neither she nor I will ever know
whether the prayers of so many added time to her life.
I was compelled to pray. I was trusting God for everything then.
My daughters had not died without giving their lives to him
previously and I fully trusted that they were now with Jesus.
Death had not driven me away from God; rather it had brought
me closer to him.

I gazed upon her skinny and smashed up body and thank God
that she survived. It is no good to question God on such things,
why one lives and another dies. He is good – of that I know.
Apart from the spiritual stuff, it brought a smile to my face to see
the signatures and messages of all the people who have been
visiting on her plastered leg and also the home-made cards.

It is strange how death brings people together. Something
inside us, whether God fearing or not makes us want to stand
together, united against the dark enemy who stands over us all.
But Jesus told us to not be afraid of death, rather to fear the One
who can destroy both body and soul. I am so glad I did. So glad
that before this dreadful day, I had knelt at the cross of Christ.

Friday 28 July *Sorting Jenny's room*

Today turned out to be quite a hard day but God and friends
were here to help. In the morning my prayer time turned yet
again to the river and the vividly coloured countryside rather
like the Yorkshire Dales with Jesus at my side. This time he
allowed me a more panoramic view of the surroundings and
for the first time I saw it: his city in the distance. It was gleaming
and looked utterly awesome; the sight filled me with wild

excitement. It had gates that were open and people were free to pass through them. I knew I couldn't go in but wondered if Claire and Jen could. I got the impression they were free to go wherever they wished but chose not to go into the city just yet because it was still being prepared.

I also sensed that everyone there was filled with knowledge – Claire and Jen didn't go in because it didn't seem time to go in. It was not a hassle to them, they were perfectly at peace. The thing about being in the presence of Jesus is that there is a simple acceptance that his ways are perfect. The idea of questioning them is ridiculous because in your being you just know he is in charge and he is right. It was a short but incredibly uplifting experience.

Then it was time to do more sorting. Debbie and Eveline came round and helped Heather to totally sort Jenny's room in preparation for maybe having someone to stay for a year in September. The room is now empty of Jenny's stuff. Some of it went into the now spare room which we are setting up as like a memento chill-out room but other bits were binned. My stomach churned as I dealt with some of the girls personal stuff like ID cards and their wallets which were still scarred and mashed from the accident. It felt really bad to throw things away but after a game of tennis with Pete it was alright. I can't say just how important it is to have friends round at times like these.

Saturday 29 July *Suicide?*

If I could choose to die, how would I do it? I guess a car accident is as good as any. One moment they're talking freely, maybe listening to music, the next they're no longer here. If I could choose to go, would I go now? I mean I'd be with them and I'd be changed. I'd be with Jesus, face to face but there would be a fear of heart-breaking rebuke. "Why did you do it?" he would surely ask. "Why didn't you trust me enough? I was giving you enough strength to live and to live well. Why have you left your family when they needed you? I had so much for you. I was going to use you to bring people to me. I am so desperate to see people come to know me. I am in anguish that any should perish. Your children are safe with me. Could you not have had the faith the size of a mustard seed?"

No, no, no!!! Even if the button were there and I could just press it and be with Claire and Jen. NO!! Heaven and Hell are no games for it is vital that people know there is only one way to God. Wake up! God is real. Can I really deny God? If I have any doubt about where they are, then my whole faith is a sham. They are not safe, I am not safe, no one I know is safe, just one big waste of time. To deny all I've experienced of God, to look all my friends who know God in the face and say "you are fools" is ridiculous. They are not fools and I am no fool either. Twenty-two years of knowing Jesus with no contradictions: he's been the same throughout. I stand on the rock and let everything else fall down in distress, but I know my God is real. I know he loves me, I have met him, my kids are with him, I have work to do here and I will do it joyfully.

Monday 31 July *Like get moving!!*

A friend from church came round this morning and asked how I was getting on. I talked about how dynamic praying was nowadays. I start by acknowledging God for who he is and what he's done but often I still get drawn to that picture of sitting by the river. I become aware of Jesus being close by and he's been quite content to just sit with me and bring comfort with his presence.

Lately I've become aware of how active he is; you could almost say restless. It's like he's saying I'll sit with you as long as you want but there's so much to do. Come on get up, there are places I want you to go, people for you to meet.

He has a sense of urgency about him. He's comforted me with assurance of where Claire and Jen are. Now he's aware that time is getting short and there's so many people who need to hear about him. He has full knowledge of life and death and his chief purpose is moving about his church, directing his people so that more might come in and participate in all he offers.

His desire is almost consuming. He wants none to perish without knowing him. He knows what awaits people when they die. Grieve briefly for your dead then move on. He says: "As long as it is day we must do the work of him who sent me. Night is coming, when no one can work." (John 9:4)

Tomorrow is the Youth Festival NEW DAY. I'm away there for a week with about 50 others from our church.

Tuesday August 1 *Meeting Christ*

Johnny Pike said today the last month has been like becoming a Christian again. That's so true. I remember it now when I first became a Christian, I've got it recorded in a diary somewhere. I just get so excited about God sometimes, its like waves, suddenly a big one crashes on me and I sense his presence and it's just too awesome to handle. My eyes fill up with tears, even now I can barely type because his presence is on me, my eyes are streaming!!!

I so love God. I was praying the other day and I realised there's no way I'll be able to stand in his presence when I meet him The sheer force of his love will just blow me over. No wonder it says the folk in Heaven just keep falling down and worship him. You see him and his presence just melts you. You perceive his goodness and it's just too much too handle. Words are insufficient and this is BEFORE I even start thinking about what he did on the cross for me and my family and for everyone. When I see him now it is only in part, that's what the Bible says. One day I will see him in full and already I know the joy will be indescribable. Meeting loved ones will be one thing, but meeting him will just be MEGA. No words, no need, you just perceive.

Thursday August 3 *Worshipping God*

I am finding lately that when I'm focussing on Jesus that Claire and Jen are usually involved in some way. I gaze upon him and sense that they're gazing upon him too and thus we are still together.

I am utterly convinced that there is no such thing as death for people who belong to Jesus. They passed through from this strange land we call earth into their home. I do not belong to earth. I am most at home when I am joined in with the multitudes worshipping him. I wish to be there but must stay until he allows me to crossover.

I really don't want to stay here because I've glimpsed there; a distant country that I know is my home. It's a better place, there is such joy there, such a deep love for Jesus. All people there love him and he moves around at will and people love it when he's around them but are ok when he moves on because that's him; you can't put clampers on Jesus.

I see it now as like a spacious land inhabited by him and people who have passed through from this world. It's like they're camping because I get the distinct impression that the people there, that even Claire and Jen, are waiting for something even though they're already having such a fantastic carefree time.

They're waiting for the gleaming city to be made ready. The gates are already open. I've seen that previously and there are no guards so they could go in but none of them do because they're happy to wait for his call. They're waiting for him to finish it. It's his place and he's still preparing it even as he is still moving amongst those who have passed through and amongst those of us who are still left on earth in the foreign land. This is nothing to do with his finished work on the cross; this is something to do with the final judgement.

I am now in such a hard place. I no longer want to be here, I want to go home. My house is no longer a home, nor is it Heathers or Amy's or Tom's. Even my body is not a home it's a house, nothing more. My main purpose here is as an ambassador of Christ and his Kingdom.

The vision of Heaven has ruined me. I am restless yet I have peace in him. Have I had these visions to heal me, to help me get through the passing through of Claire and Jen? Are all visions of Heaven given to people to help them to cope with something beyond normal day-to-day living?

Two of my children pass through and I have visions. Paul the apostle had amazing visions: were they given to help him fulfil his calling? Did Stephen see Christ at the right hand of God to enable him to coping with dying as a martyr? Am I being prepared for something beyond just coping with the passing through of Claire and Jen?

Sunday 6 August Jesus enters the heavenly city.

Today in the main meeting at New Day we were singing 'Be Lifted Up'. I closed my eyes to worship and saw again the gleaming city. This time there was a multitude of people within. The place was packed, a massive congregation making a mass of noise. There was an intense buzz of excitement as they waited in anticipation... and then he came.

I was reminded that there was an earthly portrayal of this when Jesus came riding into Jerusalem humble on a donkey and the people cried 'Hosanna', excited at his coming. But I was seeing the real thing; the King coming in to take his place, the wedding feast imminent.

As he came, I was amongst them; I was shouting his name, anything I could think of, "JESUS, REDEEMER, SAVIOUR, LORD"! Everyone was in awe of him and I was no different. We were filled with an indescribable desperation to worship and the noise was incredible. I reached out as he passed by just to touch him; my entire being was desperate for him. I was hysterical. "Even the rocks will cry out in praise of him" the Bible says. My very being was struggling dismally to cope with the need to worship him.

Then came the crunch. I've been saying to God lately, 'I've seen Heaven, I've been in your presence. All I want now is to be there with you. How can I focus on things of the earth anymore? I am totally ruined. I need a commission or I need to come home. Your home is my home.

Well the joy of those celebrating in the golden streets of the city is greater for those who have participated in the work of populating the city. The wedding feast will be more enjoyed by the workers because their toil has made them hungry. When he came into the city, yes he accepted the wild worship, but he also looked across the masses and his gaze said something like, "my brothers and sisters, my co-workers, my friends!!"

This is another reason why he's so great: he's shared his glory!! It's been his work but we've been allowed to share in it. We have a co-ownership of the city. This increases the wildness of the celebration. We took part in populating Heaven. But it doesn't matter in a selfish way; we're not joyous for us, we're joyous for him. We cast heavenly crowns into the air because they are worn for him. The joy is indescribable.

Mon 7 August *The fake piper*

Today's motion picture was uncomfortable to the point that I actually despised it. Walking to the meeting I told my wife how difficult it was to have any motivation for living. I felt worn out, tired, weary, just so uninterested in the fag of having to live.

This was in spite of all God's been showing me and yes I know so incredibly selfish. Well Heather did her usual job of smoothly chiding me to "just get on with it". So we went into the meeting and listened to someone teaching on being active amongst the lost. And then it came:

I became part of this happy, dancing troupe of people who were jigging their way on a dirt road through a crowded camp. First thing I noticed was that this troupe I had joined were not dancing like God's people do, which is like a wild, joyous celebration, but rather they were dancing in a forced, controlled, perhaps even rehearsed manner and it was done for the benefit of the crowd they were passing through.

Next I saw the leader of the troupe. He was pretending to be Jesus but it wasn't him; he was a fake. He played a flute or pipe and did the same fake, forced dance as he led them. Both he and the troupe ignored the crowd, they didn't even look at them. The fake Jesus' eyes were glazed and he was horrible to look at.

Then I started to look at the crowd through whom they were marching. These were desperate people. Their arms were bound with handcuffs with chains leading downwards, to their feet. They cried out in their pain to the fake Jesus and his troupe but they ignored them and danced on unconcerned.

I was disgusted but then I broke away from them and started moving among the crowd. I came up close to a distressed young child who instantly cried out to me, trying to raise her arms to be hugged and comforted. All around was this terrible wailing and then something happened.

I sensed it rather than saw it. There came the sound of a violent, rushing wind unsettling the leaves in the trees overhead. The real Jesus and his real church were about to break onto the people. It was dark and I had the impression he had been waiting silently with his commando army for the troupe to pass by.

But now they were on the move, swift and silent they suddenly appeared in no small number. They were like thieves invading an enemy's camp. They had come to do a job as quickly as they could and then move out. Their weapon was surprise.

I became one of them, an urgent thief having to move while there was time. I became empowered to break the manacles that were binding the captives. I was now just like him and his army. I broke strong manacles, hard forged gold coloured steel with my bare hands. I was jubilant with what I was able to do; there was a thrill upon me but also urgency. No time to waste, move, move, move.

What a strange vision this was, yet it made some sort of sense. The Bible refers many times to our world being under the domain of Satan because in rejecting God, mankind has effectively elected to serve him, the chief rejector of God. The fake 'Jesus' was Satan masquerading as a do-gooder, as he does, appearing through world systems and leaders to be caring for mankind when he is really dragging people into hell.

As for the real Jesus and his 'commando' army, he says himself in Luke 12:39, "But understand this: If the owner of the house had known at what hour the thief was coming, he would not have let his house be broken into." Being a Christian means being part of a commando army operating in enemy territory!

Tuesday August 8 *NEW DAY*

I'm just back from New Day a youth event run by the New Frontiers churches in the UK. It's been going three years and growing all the time. This year there were between five and six thousand people including around fifty from our church in Lowestoft.

People became Christians. I don't know how many, but it was over two hundred because at least that many responded on one night after Adrian Holloway, author of 'Shock of your Life' spoke about what Jesus had done for us.

Well we worshipped wildly through the week. Sometimes it was crazy, particularly one night when I got caught up with this immense heavenly congregation and just couldn't stop shouting his name and titles. After I regained awareness of my surroundings there was a big space around me! People must have thought I was a nutter, but I didn't care, why should I? There is nothing like the heavenly party. Other people from our group were also a bit crazy, so many of them got caught up with the wonders of God. A girl (not from our group) who was severely dyslexic was healed and read fluently from the Bible. She said she had a reading age of 6 and just couldn't make out written words. Then she took up her Bible and read ever so clearly a psalm, 'Sing to the Lord a new song'. Her healing happened during the meeting and I saw her afterwards outside the big top tent getting some air with her friends. They were jigging with joy, so excited about what had happened to her. It was so moving.

Oh and we camped and there were mega problems with the loos. Sometimes they were closed completely. To get a shower was a strategy in itself; you had to plan when you were going to get one and where and how you would handle the shower itself. They looked like the TARDIS from the outside and felt like being within a LETTUCE on the inside; insipid soggy stuff around your feet as slimy green walls hemmed you in. But I wouldn't have missed it for anything.

What do you do with photos?

What do you do with photos?
You have to put them up
Yet you want to take them down.
They demand you stop and stare
Yet it hurts to dwell upon them.

There are a horde of photo albums
Gathering dust on shelves
Sometimes I stare at them, wonder if I dare to look.
I have to decide whether the strength is there
To walk in the memories of their lives.

It's really a no-win situation
I dread losing my memories
Sometimes they seem my only connection.
Like a student I revise them
And remember the things that defined them.

Claire had a strange birthmark on her back
Like a patch of sun tan.
Jenny had a triangular scar on her shin
From when she fell off the garden wall.
In some photos I can remember what they were thinking.

Yet revision brings pain
A sort of stabbing in my stomach
And my mind can't seem to cope
And shudders like a cold engine
I have to come away.

It's really a no-win situation
I dread losing my memories
And yet I can't face re-living them
What shall I do with photos?
I cannot love them or leave them.

Oh God, may I never lose sight of Heaven
These days when you seem so distant
They destroy me.
Grief and despair and the accusations
Creep out from the darkness.

"Never to see them again while on earth"
So points the finger of Grief
"Never to know them as they were" adds Despair
Accusation smiles and wonders why
I didn't drive them to and from the concert?

Well, I remember Jesus plainly telling me
To accept no accusations.
I remember the amazing insights as I prayed
Of the girls in paradise
Of the Lord of Life shining so bright.

I remember my tears of joy
And as I do they begin once more.
Darkness crept in but now flies away
The radiance of the Lord Jesus is enough
And the photos can stay up.

Heather, Margaret and Walter. Golden wedding anniversary, August 2006

11 Grief and joy

Saturday 12 August 2006 *True perspectives*

Heather and I prayed together this morning. We do this pretty regularly because we know we have to continually draw strength from God in order to get through this ordeal. Also, it is not just about us; there are people young and old who are watching. I know some are silently asking the question 'is God really there for you, is he there for me, will he be there when I really need him?'

Well Jesus was already prepared for us; like a dad who gets up early, prepares the day and is ready for when his children wake up and stumble sleepily onto his lap and ask "what we doing today dad?" It doesn't really matter, for they trust him so much that whatever they do, it isn't really an issue.

Well after a while he starts to speak. Today is Heather's parents golden wedding anniversary. We consider them and the first blast of Heaven is an insight into how Jesus sees them. Not frail and old but as children, fresh and vibrant, dressed in robes of righteousness because they too love Jesus. They appear bright eyed and competent and in the prime of their being. The body is just a tent, soon to be left behind and its frailties must be endured. The important thing about handling the weakness of the body is to do so with the joy of Jesus inside you. Unbelievers cannot comprehend it and believers find it hard to describe, but the joy of Jesus is a treasure. I feel his presence so strongly once again as I write this, tears once again falling freely.

Next I feel the need to declare where we stand in Jesus. As we pray I speak it out; we do not grieve as those without hope, we are raised up with Christ. We know Jenny and Claire are with him in this beautiful land which has almost become familiar. We know their joy is without measure. If I can barely contain the joy that wells up within me whenever his presence comes upon me, how much more those who are experiencing him in full? This earthly vessel which I call my body is woefully inadequate to contain even a sip from his cup. We are ambassadors for Christ, I feel like running and dancing amongst unbelievers, shouting 'wake up, wake up, he's alive, come meet him, come join in.' Oh Jesus, you are ruining me.

Monday August 14 *What's He Like?*

Well you've got to understand first that no one can describe Jesus fully. How could an insect describe a human, what words would it use? It would have to become human to really describe a human. Strange thing is, Jesus loves being with people. I don't know why and I don't think why is even relevant. Why does a mother love her child - is that a necessary question? Anyhow, he reveals aspects of himself as he sees fit I guess. I just want to say how I see him now, sort of best I can.

Well firstly, he's incredibly friendly. He's one of these people who could sit with me for ages and not get bored. It's not anything particularly special about me, for we all are special; it's more about him and his appetite for enjoying people. What I make of it (and the Bible backs up this impression) is that I'm his reward. It cost him a horrific crucifixion to have me as his child and I am a treasure, a reward that he holds dearly. Secondly, he has no desire to consider the bad things about me in terms of punishment. It almost irritates him that I should draw back from him because I know I'm not worthy of him. He hates accusations. Again, I just know this deeply upsets him and the Bible tells us that all punishment due to believers was placed on him. Therefore, when I act like I can't be in his presence it's actually an insult to the cross.

Thirdly, he draws me in. I perceive something of his strength and determination and joy and I just want to be where he is, doing the things that he does and pleasing him in any way I can. He's a hero, a leader, a man amongst men. Everything that is pleasing and desirable in terms of kindness and loyalty is in him. He's the sort of person you see suddenly and realise that you've got to go and be with him. Whatever else you're doing at the time just becomes irrelevant. Aw!! You've got to just meet him for yourself!

Thursday 17 August *Parallel roads*

Today was A-Level Results day. Claire got an A in English Language and two Bs in Chemistry and Biology. I was sitting on top of a rather large hill in the Lake District when my mobile phone rang. It was a lady from the Eastern Daily Press (EDP) newspaper who'd arranged to speak to us to hear what we had to say. Well Claire achieved the grades she needed to get onto her Pharmacy course in Nottingham and Jenny had taken an AS-Level qualification a year early and passed with a B.

Well of course I was proud, but the greatest thing that the girls achieved in life was that they met Jesus for themselves and followed him. So when their time came to leave this world they were ready. They were found to be fully prepared for the most amazing meeting of their existence: an audience with their maker and judge. Any other achievements of theirs were secondary and also heavily influenced by that one major decision they made. They would have trod different paths if that decision had not been made. Their academic results turned out merely to be contributory indicators of lives well lived. They worked hard, they enjoyed people. They loved concerts and movies and organised countless excursions into merriment.

None of this dented their passion for Jesus. They were never that interested in alcohol, they were too high on life. I remember the volume they sometimes generated at night as they stayed up late in either of their bedrooms. They had grown so close to each other, it was almost as if they had been travelling on parallel roads that had now converged. On 1 July 2006 they were travelling together on one road: it turned out to be a narrow one that led straight to Heaven.

Friday 18 August *How do you move on?*

I wake up each morning and find my first real thoughts are Claire and Jen and then I turn to Jesus. It's not automatic, but it is almost like a mental command. Doing this makes the day acceptable and I can take my place amongst the mass of humanity. I don't really see a time ahead when my thoughts will be free of what happened. I don't really want them to fade and I also have a strong experience of Jesus and Heaven and my church family which is fully mixed in.

On one hand I feel that I mustn't lose my memories of the girls but on the other I know that they are fully alive and have moved on themselves. When I see them again it won't be as the eighteen and fifteen year old teenagers I knew, it will be as fully mature people. I believe that I and they will retain full knowledge of our relationship and experiences together but our focus will be changed. What we knew as being in a family will have evolved into something better.

Therefore I must move on and fulfil the calling of Jesus upon my life. What matters is that I am fully engaged in the populating of Heaven. People need to know about the One who has paid the judgement price for them so that they can receive his forgiveness and all that follows.

This is so important. I have seen Jesus and sensed his hard work and desperation to bring in as many as possible before the day approaches and people can no longer be saved. The Bible says "let us work for as long as it is day, for the night approaches when no one can work". Day is the time we have left on earth, night is when all is done and it will be too late to enter in.

Friday 1 September *Do bubbles burst?*

We returned from two weeks away in the Lake District and Scotland to a home full of images which had been left behind. Memories of family times with the girls flooded back and then the next day we spent three hours recounting the day of the accident and beyond to our solicitor. It was hard, to say the least, and we were both left with headaches at the end. With this and the pressure of returning to teaching a few days away, it turned out to be a pretty bad week. It's like a honeymoon period that has ended. You just go back to being normal Joe Bloggs as if nothing ever happened and you think you're expected to just get on with things. Like you broke a leg and now it's healed.

Aren't we Christians who are supposed to be ok? After all we know where Claire and Jen are and we have experienced the presence of Jesus many times. We are fully convinced that he will strengthen us and bring us safely to his home where we will one day see the girls again. That time will be riotous and to even consider it brings a rush of joy to my being.

The reality is that we are but human. In this life we suffer as he himself suffered. We are not exempt from pain and we will bear a scar for the rest of our lives. We have been struck a huge blow and are learning to cope with the damage caused. Sometimes we find our bodies are wracked with weakness to the point of not feeling able to stand up; there are dreams and images of car crashes, unwarranted fears, tears falling readily, surges in emotions and unexplained anger bursts. I expected none of this. But is our faith diminished? Not at all, we share in the sufferings of Christ and we remain faithful. He never guaranteed an easy life and is certainly not to blame for what happened. One day our trust in him, along with the trust that many other believers have shown, will shine in Heaven as a tribute to him who has enabled us to walk in his steps. It always comes back to him, and to know him is to love him.

Friday September 8 *So what happens when you die?*

Well I've read the Bible and accounts of Christians who have
died and come back. I have listened to Ian McKormack who
tells of meeting with Jesus while being pronounced clinically
dead from the stings of one of the most deadly jellyfish known
to man. His account is amazing and can be found on
www.aglimpseofeternity.org. I have also seen and sensed things
while praying sometimes, but still don't know much because
it's not for me to know. All I really have is the Bible as sure and
valid. Some people have spoken of a sense of moving through
a dim place like a tunnel until they encounter a bright light
which turns out to be emanating from Jesus. Others mention
angels escorting them to Jesus.

If a Christian dies before the day set aside by God for the dead
to rise and judgement, the Bible tells us that they still go to
be with Jesus. For such a person has already been judged
favourably by means of their faith in Christ.

Furthermore, the apostle Paul states that for believers to be
absent from the body means to be with the Lord (2 Corinthians
5:8). In the book of Philippians he talks of his desire to depart
and be with Christ. Also, Jesus indicates through his story
of the rich man and Lazarus, that dead people are alert and
active. There is a passage in the Gospel of Matthew that records
Moses and Elijah talking with Jesus. Since these men had
died many years before, they were plainly not in some sort of
soul-sleep waiting for their new bodies. Also while Jesus hung
dying on the cross, he assured the thief next to him that today
he would be with him in paradise. The implication is of being
conscious and not asleep.

On a number of times during prayer and worship, I have seen
Claire and Jen enjoying a bright and glorious land. It seems
they are also waiting for the day when they will celebrate the
massive victory parade of Jesus. He will enter into the heavenly

city amidst tremendous applause and celebration and the great feast spoken of in the Bible will begin. As Claire and Jen wait they are not impatient or held back - because the gates are open - they are filled with the knowledge of God - they will go in when they are called. They are incredibly happy.

Obviously I cannot be totally sure of what I see and it is not meant to be offered as any sort of proof of the life beyond death. What I have seen is something between Jesus and me. I do not believe my mind is capable of forming such images or that I am suffering from some sort of delusion as a mechanism to escape the reality of death. What if Jesus comforts me with such sights; surely the issue is really to do with whether he exists or not? If he does, then people should not have a problem with him meeting with his children in such ways. I am perfectly assured that he loves me dearly and therefore I have no reason to question the things I see. I take them at face value and do not find anything in the Bible to contradict them. If I did, I would reject them because the Bible is the only reference point we have in which to validate our experiences.

Another mystery is the day when Jesus returns to earth and the resurrection of those who have fallen asleep in Christ. Paul says in the book of 1 Thessalonians that "according to the Lord's own word ... the dead in Christ will arise first". From verses in Corinthians I know that this means they will receive new immortal bodies. Paul goes on to say that this will happen in the twinkling of an eye and at a trumpet blast. Then, as the Lord Jesus descends from Heaven, the dead will meet him in the clouds, along with those who are still alive on earth and belonging to Christ.

After this comes the final judgement spoken of by Jesus in the Gospels and also talked about in Revelation. All people whether alive or dead will assemble before Christ. Those who are dead and not belonging to him are currently in a wretched place the Bible calls Hades. Therefore there is not one person who has ever existed who is dead in terms of being deceased, for all people will be there.

Christians will be judged worthy of Heaven not because of their deeds or good lives but because they put their trust in Christ. He died on the cross to take our punishment on himself. There is no condemnation for those who are in Christ. Unbelievers will be condemned to Hell where there will be darkness and anger and frustration. They will live in torment because they will have missed out on Heaven. The devil and his demons will be there too.

As for those who never heard of Jesus. God will judge them fairly. No one will say God is unjust. He will be seen to do what is right. Therefore you and I should leave that to him. No one will be able to accuse him and I can only conclude there will be people in Heaven covered by the blood of Jesus who never knew of the cross. I believe this will include babies and young children as they have not developed a sense of right and wrong and have never rejected him. This last issue is difficult but should not be a stumbling block to anyone. We will all be judged on what we received and this will be personal between each individual and God. I pity any man who thinks he will successfully use intellectual accusations when he meets with God. The Bible says this: "For since the creation of the world God's invisible qualities – his eternal power and divine nature – have been clearly seen, being understood from what has been made, so that men are without excuse." (Romans 1: 20)

Monday 18 September *Fancy causing a party?*

How about getting all dressed up in clothes that make you look absolutely fantastic! I mean, these clothes are really tops, not your everyday stuff, you'll look pretty stunning to say the least. Once you're dressed it will cause a few things to happen. Word will spread like wildfire and there'll be whispering like leaves in the trees: "Hey, did you know ...?" Someone will gasp in response and a huge grin will spread across their face. "Wow, you don't say, I've just got to go tell someone; this means party-time!"

Others won't be whispering, they'll be shouting the news. They'll proclaim it at the top of their voices and a great crowd will stop in amazement. A huge thrill will come upon them. They know what this means... get ready everyone... it's PARTY-TIME!

Well do it. You will cause all this to happen when you finally open the door and answer the one who is knocking. Let him in. You will find out he comes carrying gifts. The most amazing one is forgiveness; everything you've ever done wrong will be forgiven. One parcel will contain these amazing party clothes. The colours shimmer so much that all you'll see is a dazzling white. Put them on. He has made it possible that once you are dressed you will be clean and acceptable to God. You will be ready for the party. How did he do it? By taking your punishment on himself, by dying on a cross. Another gift will be an expectant thrill buzzing inside you for the day of the party. It will come to dominate your thoughts so that you become focussed on meeting him face to face at his party. You'll want others there, your friends, your family, and yes... as you mature, you'll feel compassion for your enemies and want them there too.

When's the party? Well lots of them are already going on. Whenever anyone becomes a Christian, Heaven goes wild and angels go crazy celebrating one more person saved from Hell. They consider again what Jesus did on the cross and tears fill their eyes with wonderment and joy. And then, the party to end all parties, the wedding feast of the Lamb. HIS PARTY. All people rescued by him assembled in this huge city, going absolutely mad with joy. "We're here Jesus, JESUS, because of you, of YOU. You are amazing!!" Words fail from here on in.

Darkness and Light

Darkness, a black aura striking terror in the living
People who are made to walk in light dread to enter it
Thick and heavy, it can almost be touched,
It brims with menace, a merciless malice.

Darkness feeds on fears of the unknown
Death and beyond, pain and loss
It welcomes the foolish who are empty of God
It delights in distorting truth and destroying absolutes.

Light. When you suddenly feel like jumping for joy
When laughter and energy define you
It warms, it thrills, it grows, it builds
There's a party going on inside you.

People stop what they're doing to draw near
"Is this a long lost friend I've met again?"
They draw near for a warm embrace
Weary from travelling they are returning home.

I have met the One who is the source of light
He shines so bright I can barely look upon him
My eyes cannot contain the sight before me
My body fails, my senses reel.

I see the One who knows me
Who loves me completely
There are no limitations
Anything he desires of me I know is right.

Monday 25 September *Freaking out at school*

It finally happened. I think maybe it's been brimming away,
I certainly didn't expect it. I was teaching in the last lesson of
the day at school and was tired, waiting for the day to end.
There were about twenty minutes to go. Someone else was
also looking forward to the bell going and the welcoming

freedom of the weekend, but he wasn't doing any work, in fact he hadn't done anything all lesson. I knew it as a problem and had hassled him as much as I could because so much needed doing. His attitude was bad, basically "I don't care anyhow and I'm not prepared to do any work." So I pointed out what needed to be done, and where it needed to go and he said it was done, nothing more needed and "aint doing it".

In a flash I thought of Claire and Jen, motivated and giving their best and here was someone still alive, still here, just wasting his life away. Life is a gift, a privilege, yet I don't know why it's worth living when we could just be with Jesus all of the time. Why do we have to live here as mortals when we could be with him fully? Maybe by having lived, we have the opportunity to bring glory to him by choosing to live our lives how he wants us to. By making the sacrifice of not living to please ourselves might be the answer. One day maybe there'll be this fantastic celebration and we Christians will be so pleased because we demonstrated he was worth it.

Think about it, angels don't get this opportunity. They spend their time doing God's work and worshipping him, but they haven't had to cope with being human. Maybe our capacity to love him is heightened by the fact that we have to choose to love him? Only we will know the full extent of what Jesus did on the cross because he did it for us. The angels will never boast personal experience of being rescued, but we will. They celebrate us being saved, we celebrate ourselves being saved. This is why the gift of life is a privilege, because with it comes free choice and we chose him. You have to think of life without the good thing to fully appreciate life with the good thing. We can but the angels can't.

So back to this lad, I thought of my girls and freaked at his attitude. I yelled violently at him and told him to leave. He and the rest of the class had to put up with a sudden outburst of anger. Not good, I shouldn't lose control but something just snapped at the attitude. Too many people don't care and it makes me angry, but it's no excuse to lose my temper. Or maybe it is?

Tuesday 26 September *Dealing with dreams*

It was always going to be a problem. Late into the night, I dreamt Claire came down our stairs. I looked at her; she was dressed to go out. I said "you're here". She said "yes I've just been ill, I'm ok now, I'm just going off to university."

Well I was overjoyed, I hugged her so tight, so long and my tears wouldn't stop falling. She was crying as well. Everything was okay and then I woke up and it dawned on me that everything was not okay. I will never see her again while I'm alive on earth. The dawn was coming in. I turned over to look at my wife, but her face was Claire's. I kept staring at her but all I could see peacefully sleeping away was a grown-up Claire. What trick was this? I just kept staring at her, thinking this is how you'd have looked as a mother, an adult, peacefully sleeping away married and responsible.

This was too much. I got up, made a cup of tea and started to read my Bible. It's the only way. Read and focus. Pray, speak out truths. Remind myself to be with Christ is better by far. Call on him, utterly depend on him and trust for strength. Soon there were stirrings in the house. The ride is still bumpy but he will prove to be faithful. An easy life is not what I've been promised. I am learning to stand in a way I've never known. I will not submit to despair. He is my Lord and I am most welcome in his presence.

12 Birthdays

Where you are

Where you are is better by far
What you were is nothing to what you are
I thought you were both so beautiful
But now you surpass that so much more.

I was thumbing the skin of my Ipod
Pushing the rubber right down
I've lived for a year with the grime on the skin
But now I see the gleaming white beneath.

How is it the band performs so well?
You'd forgive them for being tense on the night
Being a bit less than what was expected
but I should have known not to doubt them
I should know not to doubt you.

Sorry God, I got lost in my loss
I wanted my girls back when I know I should not
I wanted what had gone before
But what they are now is so much more.

It shouldn't really change my life
If anything, it should spur me on
A guaranteed promise is something worth living for
It's always worth behaving for Christmas.

But let me tear the wrapper a bit
Just a peek inside
It would mean a lot to me now
If I could just see what they are like.

Are they as young as you are?
Wild and free, fresh morning breeze
Wise yet wide-eyed, satisfied but still hungry
Filled with your knowledge and peace?

It must be amazing to see you
Even in Heaven they still behold you in awe
Yet you remain their closest friend
Beside yet above them and they love you for it.

Must I stay here now that I've seen?
Nothing on earth compares with it
No answer is needed, I know your heart
Every lost soul is like a dagger in it.

The month of August had turned out to be mostly one of
respite and refreshment. After New Day and the fun of being
around young people, we spent a week in the Lake District
and then another week in Scotland with close friends from our
church. There were Abi, Erin, Chris, Sam and Dan, all of whom
had closely shared in the tragedy of the car crash. Our daughter
Amy particularly hit it off with the two girls and Tom had a
great time attacking all of us at random intervals.

On the first working day of September both Heather and
I returned to our teaching jobs. Some people had advised
against us doing this so soon, but Heather was adamant that
she was returning and I too felt it right to go back. I can't say
I wanted to do so, but felt the longer I left it the more difficult it
would become. Also I felt determined to meet the challenge of
bereavement head on. What was there for me at home anyway,
apart from photos and memories?

However, I didn't realise just how much of a battering my body
had taken. My emotions were delicate and it didn't take much
for tears to start falling. I also found myself lacking in energy
and tiring very quickly. Ironically, my form group were in the
same year as Jenny, as were a number of my subject groups.
Some of them knew her from the neighbourhood as the
schools are within walking distance of each other. It was hard
sometimes to not look on some of the girls and think of Jenny.

There was also the new intake of pupils and I found classes with them extremely difficult, because they needed discipline and that was hard to give. My heart had been cracked open and it was hard to be harsh without becoming over-emotional.

So perhaps I did return too early, but on the positive side my fellow teachers treated me as best they could and the year group that were Jenny's age were on the whole outstanding. It is something quite wonderful for an adult when a young person treats you well. They are in the midst of so many struggles as they try and work out their place in life. Their bodies are going crazy so that they walk into lamposts and trip up over their own feet. Their emotions are like roller-coasters and acceptance means everything to them. On occasions, tough lads refrained from doing things wrong just because I was around and girls went out of their way to cheer me up. There is so much violence and selfishness that can come out of young people but there is also so much good and there is something particularly beautiful about it when it happens.

As September ticked on, we began thinking about how best to mark the girls approaching birthdays. For Claire's we decided to take her best friends out for an Italian meal in Norwich and for Jenny's we did pretty much the same. The idea was to try and make sure that those who perhaps were missing them most were not left alone on these occasions. Birthdays are particularly poignant times for remembering and yearning and it is best to face them in the company of other people.

Sunday 1 October *Claire's Birthday*

So how will I be today, maybe a little muted, forlorn and defeated? My mind will insist on becoming lost in memories, so perhaps not the best of days today? Well I went to church this morning and was praising God, even though I didn't feel like it. My heart had ruled my head yesterday and I'd played a full 90 minutes football. Towards the end I had cramp in both feet and here I was in church absolutely exhausted. But how can I not praise God?

During a song I saw Jesus in the beautiful land that he has allowed me to see. His land, where the colours are so bright and there is an awesome sense of majesty and splendour pervading the very atmosphere. He was alone. No angels, no people, just him and the land he has created. He was shining again, such a peace and tranquillity about him. I think I've said before that when I see him I don't see just a person, I also seem to perceive his character – as if to look at him is to see many things at once – happiness, hilarity, energy, youthfulness, abandon and also sorrow. I sense he will always carry sorrow in a way that we never will, even beyond this life. I reflect that there are children of his who are lost to him. We are not capable and never will be of bearing the pain and loss that he carries. All these things and his love for life mean that I am wide-eyed in amazement just seeing what I see. No wonder my body shakes and tears fall just considering this man who is God.

Anyhow, he stooped to pick up a small bright purple flower with yellow inside. He looked at it, considered it carefully and then placed it back where it continued to grow. I realised that he was doing a last check and that his eyes were now watching towards the horizon. Suddenly he spoke "ALL IS READY, COME IN". The voice seemed to gather power and repeat itself until it filled everywhere. There was a stirring on the horizon and then I saw a multitude of people approaching, running and celebrating as they came, shouting wildly, none were jogging, all were sprinting. These were his people and he had been alone because he alone had paid the price for their entry: one man, one saviour. No angels alongside him, no heavenly creatures. Maybe they had been with the crowd, I don't know. But none should be beside him to share this moment.

As the multitude drew near, he was somehow raised up on a throne. I can't say he went into the air, I can't really describe it. All I knew now was that people were running all over the place, they had entered rooms in buildings and were exploring. All the while he was there on this throne that everyone could see and praise him as they explored. Well it was mad, people were just ecstatic, they kept going in and out of buildings and back outside where the land was so beautiful. The sheer clamour of joy as they embraced each other in delight was exhilarating. This was sheer delight, a multitude had come in and it was still so spacious.

Today is a day for celebrating the birthday of Claire Stoddart, but her most dramatic birthday was the day of her entry into this most amazing place. She is in Heaven now but has something yet more wonderful to look forward to: the wedding feast of Jesus when he calls in his bride, the church, to join him in the place he has prepared. The Bible talks of a new Heaven and earth which makes me wonder if Claire and Jen are in a place which Jesus is still preparing. These are things too marvellous for me to know. Any insights into the beyond are given to encourage us to live well for him today. Telling others with total confidence that his promises are true, bearing trials with joy because of what is set before us.

Tuesday 3 October *Visiting the grave*

I finally got round to visiting the place where the girls discarded skins were laid to rest. The place hasn't seen me since July and I was intrigued because Heather tells me it's quite a sight. I thought I'd be all choked up so I stiffened my lip and cycled there, ipod booming away to songs that spoke of the wonders of God. Flowers and cards covered the grave remembering Claire's birthday, along with little plants dug into the ground. Not a weed was in sight and a small wooden cross had been firmly dug in with a gold-coloured plaque stating the girl's names. Heather told me Bernard and Hannah (their aunt and uncle) had done this as there won't be a proper gravestone for a couple of months yet because the ground has to settle first.

This prompted me to start looking around at the gravestones nearby. Only a couple of them spoke of any real Christian faith. I was looking for give-away Bible verses or statements of faith but hardly anything. Well I will trumpet the destination of my girls in any way I can on their gravestone. I'm not interested in this "dearly departed stuff", I want everyone who looks on their graves to encounter the promise of God which is the resurrection of the dead and the joy of Heaven awaiting all those who fall asleep while trusting in Jesus and who are therefore to be judged righteous. As for me at the grave, well I tried to be sombre and focus on the girls and my loss, but I couldn't do it. In fact I felt defiant of death, like it was a defeated enemy that deserved nothing but contempt.

Sorry death, but all I could do was to look and consider where the girls are now. I contemplated the grave and simply saw the victory achieved on the cross. Once again my thoughts turned to Jesus and the tears filled my eyes. In my humanity I am weak and so often troubled by bad dreams and despairing thoughts, but in my spirit there is another story, one of life and victory and almost uncontainable admiration for their saviour and mine. Viewing the grave is a profound experience but not a desperate one. It is my relationship with Jesus that serves as the point of connection with the girls. When I focus upon him, they are there too, part of the promise of what is to come. Something of Heaven lives inside of me already; it is the deposit of the Holy Spirit which is placed in all believers. This is why I do not need to visit the grave much, for I am not dealing with dead people.

Thursday 12 October *Jenny's 16th Birthday*

It would have been her birthday today. She'd have woken up and we'd have all gathered on our bed still in our nightwear. All the presents received in advance would be in the middle of the bed, waiting to be opened and we'd all have ours ready to give to her. Claire would have been complaining that we were taking too long and that Dad should have been ready earlier

– a common Claire complaint. Her present would have been costly for she made a point of giving good presents, possibly a CD and some jewellery, although this year she would have been away at university. Amy would have made a card and got some smelly soap or jewellery maybe. Heather would have helped Tom do a card and the parental present would have been something agreed in advance – almost definitely an ipod this year.

Whatever the gifts, Jenny would have shown equal appreciation to everyone; she'd have read every card carefully, tidied up her presents to go to her room and (perhaps) even helped to clear the wrapping paper away. Heather would have noted who sent what and Jen would have later written thank-you notes to people. During the day, her friends would have plied her with cards and presents, either at school or they would have come round afterwards. She would have made plans in advance to celebrate – a whole horde of them perhaps having a party at home or going out somewhere. The difficulty as ever would have been how to fit so many people in when spaces were limited to car-seats or grumpy dad constraints on numbers allowed in the house.

Jenny was a much-loved girl. Her gentleness and energy were evident to so many people. She was liked in church by young and old alike and popular with school teachers because she wasn't rude and took responsibility for her work. She organised her friends, sorted out lifts, babysat for no pay and generally made time for people. Tom adored her, he still remembers her as the 'best' sister. Was she perfect? Of course not. When roused her punishments were vicious, I was always careful to tease her with a wary eye as to where her feet were and she was fully in charge of Amy and Tom. The warning would come "I WILL hurt you" and she did. She refused to be outdone. If you got the last hit in, she'd remember for days until revenge had been achieved. Nevertheless, Amy was always prepared to take the risk with both Jen and Claire. The problem was their clothes. Amy needed them and too often became a slippery thief creeping into their bedrooms to remove the latest outfit. She suffered mercilessly at their hands.

I yearn for Jenny and Claire; quite a few of us do. Parents, brother, sister, family and friends all miss them so much. None of us will ever see them as we remember again for they are changed. As they wait for the day of judgement, the wedding feast of Jesus and the full appearance of the new heavens and earth, I believe they are utterly happy, joyful in the presence of Jesus. They are yet to receive their new bodies but they are conscious and active. So much of life beyond mortal death is veiled to us.

Friday 13 October *The Newspaper report*

"A 22-year-old man appeared in court this morning facing multiple charges relating to an horrific car crash that killed five people. Ben Morphey, appeared at Lowestoft Magistrates' Court facing five counts of causing death by dangerous driving following the two car collision on the A12 at Blythburgh, near Southwold, on July 1. The crash claimed the lives of Lowestoft sisters, Claire and Jennifer Stoddart, 18 and 15, their friend Carla Took, 18, and Simon Bonner, 40, and Kim Abbott 41. The case was sent to Ipswich Crown Court, where Morphey will appear on October 24 at 10am." Source: Eastern Daily Press

Ben. I think about you often and what you must be going through. I wonder how troubled you are and how you feel. In 1984 I became a Christian at the age of twenty-three. I had lived quite recklessly until then and been in trouble with the law. I did things that were dangerous to other people and I have done so since. More than once I could have caused the deaths of other people and today I see and hear of people all around me breaking laws as they drive. The extent of your recklessness will be made known soon, but we are all guilty to some extent. Your crime will be greater than some, it will certainly be less than others.

On that night in 1984, I had an encounter with God and more specifically Jesus Christ. For hours I sat in this couple's house, asking about other religions and for proof that the God of the Bible was real. As the conversation continued I became less concerned about finding reasons to disbelieve and more compelled to meet this God who they kept saying was so wonderful. That night, I took a step towards him and he met me and has continued to meet with me ever since. I now cannot imagine life without him. I am utterly convinced and intellectually satisfied that Jesus is all he says he is and more.

Is this relevant to you? Well I became very aware that God was perfect and I was not. The Bible says all of us have done wrong and are not worthy of him. He showed me how dirty I was in his sight and that one day I would be judged and punished. But he also showed me that he loved me and that he didn't want to punish me. Instead he offered to put my punishment on Jesus who suffered for all of us that we might be forgiven. What I had to do was to come to him, turn away from my wrongdoing and follow him. So I did. I said sorry for all I had done wrong. I put my trust in his authority to forgive and today I walk tall as a free man. Even when I do things wrong now, I simply say "sorry", and try to address my wrong actions. The difference now is I want to live life for him, so I hate doing wrong almost as much as he hates wrongdoing – if that were possible.

To help us, he sends the Holy Spirit. The Bible talks of followers of Jesus receiving the 'Spirit of Truth' or the 'Counsellor' so that they are able to live for him. It's like something of him living inside you and it is amazing. Jesus is able to forgive anyone, even us who are the very reason he had to be crucified. Imagine being put through terrible pain, tortured by your own children and yet still having nothing but love for them? That is what Jesus is like. He offers forgiveness to any who will come to him with sincere hearts. Finally, consider this; he says anyone who receives his forgiveness will also forgive others as a consequence. A mark of the Holy Spirit living within a person is that they do not hold on to grudges and forgive freely as they have been forgiven themselves. I am a man who truly bears the mark of the Holy Spirit and bitterness finds no home within me.

Thursday 19 October *Thankful*

I wonder what it would be like to truly experience the heart of Jesus as he surveys people. All people whether Christian or not are his concern. Yesterday a crew from ITV Anglia were round our house and the graveyard filming us and some of Jen's friends. It was for a documentary called "Dying to Drive" that will go out in November and concerns young people, road safety and the need to change the laws concerning driving. We will feature with other families who have lost loved ones.

As the day progressed we learnt of other people affected like us. From the TV crew, and from a family who arrived at the graveyard with flowers for their lost one, and also from a conversation later in the evening, we heard of the aftermaths of events, some much further back than our day of July 1st 2006. Few parents had returned to work and we discovered we were highly unusual in this respect. An alarmingly significant number of parents had, or were, in the process of splitting up. Affected siblings were struggling to cope with school and behaving irrationally.

Jesus' heart is such that he closely watches these people. I know he does, I feel something of his heart for them. He looks upon anguish and despair and I actually think he cries. For so long he has held out his hands wanting to comfort them but in their pain and agony they receive nothing because they do not come to him. I am so thankful for the day I acknowledged those hands held out to me. To think that there was a time when I thought I didn't need Jesus; that I was so invincible that I could get through life with my own strength.

I talked to God way before I responded to the message of the cross of Jesus. I remember often yelling out to him in anger and crying for help when I was scared. I knew full well that by choosing to live life according to my rules I was doing wrong. Why I felt that way is now obvious to me, but the point is

I knew what I was doing and thought I could get away with it. I now know he tolerated my self-centered lifestyle because he loves me. I don't understand why it was in October 1984 that I humbled myself before him and not before or after. I only know that during that time I was a convicted man. I couldn't get him off my mind. How could I have known back then how significant this day was going to become?

All I thought of then was being set apart for Heaven. I experienced for the first time the incredible joy of forgiveness. I knew I had to change my lifestyle and live for him but this seemed worth it. The full implications of this were lost in a sort of spiritual honeymoon. Today, I am more aware of the benefits of knowing Jesus personally. Families are suffering in a way that mine is not. Churchgoers need also to be aware that just having a belief system isn't really good enough for dealing with bereavement. Knowing about the things of God only gets you so far. The Bible helps to focus your mind on what is true and to mentally reject the nagging fears of the night. Often I can overcome bad thoughts by simply focussing on where the girls are, our eventual re-union and the wonders of God as revealed in the Bible. But nourishing the mind alone is not enough, something more is needed.

Experiencing the presence of Jesus, the Holy Spirit and living amongst his church is the full package. There is something inside of me that cannot be defeated. It's the deposit of the Holy Spirit and it is so powerful that when he comes upon me it is often just too much to handle. Even now, it just happened: suddenly this welling up from inside, a sort of shaking and then a pouring of tears. Are they tears of grief? No, because there's no sadness in them, they are tears of joy. I know him and something of him dwells within me. Only those born of the Spirit can experience this. He renews my zest for life. In fact I'm going to stop writing now and go and do something lively. A big fat grin is here again!

Friday 27 October *Parallel worlds*

All my life I have lived within two parallel worlds that I have never been fully aware of until now. One is happy, energetic and carefree, the other is dark and woeful. Mostly I have walked in the nicer realms, experiencing the warmth of living particularly since becoming a Christian. I have been and continue to be surrounded by so many positive people who radiate the joy of Christ. Even those who don't know him seem to have something of him in them, whether it be a cheerful personality or kindness or loyalty or a seemingly unquenchable thirst for living. All good things come from the Author of Life and man is made in the image of God. Therefore it is very rare to find a person so distorted by sinful living that nothing good is evident.

So have I wandered through a carefree world. Occasionally darkness has crept in and I have slipped into darkness and known something of the other world. In no particular order but during my teenage years the family dog died young and my Grandad died from a stroke while being cared for in our house. My parents separated, I changed house and school in the final year, I bodged all my exams and left home at a young age. I was selfish and insecure and a burden to raise. Occasionally I felt I had no home at all and lost all sense of belonging. In my old diaries I have records of intense loneliness and it is not hard to see why I lost track of responsible living and felt no urge to pursue a normal career. There was a scar on my forearm which took years to disappear. Two words were carved in with a scalpel that described my attitude perfectly: "F*** Life". Yet still I retained a carefree approach and lived recklessly, able to smile and laugh and enjoy the good times.

When I became a Christian so much changed. I found purpose
and a person who had answers. For twenty years he has walked
with me and brought changes within, through the Holy Spirit.
A well of joy has been created and I have been gifted with
a wonderful family. Laughter and abundant life, much more
than alcohol or drugs or anything the world has to offer, has
been mine, is mine and will continue to be so. Yet today I walk
in two parallel worlds more than I have ever done. During
the emptiness and loneliness of years gone by I have never
known what it is to lose someone who I really loved. Time
does nothing. It does not heal, it does not replace and it is not
something to wait for. Time is merely the setting within which
we must face our battles and stand by our choices. We are
forced to walk truly dark paths now. Bereavement comes with a
honeymoon; the feelings are new and as on a honeymoon the
couple are the main focus. So we were surrounded by many
people, but the honeymoon is over and the marriage has truly
begun.

There are the pictures of Claire and Jenny. We used to see
them and talk of them freely during the honeymoon. Now the
merest thought brings a wrenching pain to my stomach. A few
days ago we were at the University of East Anglia; what a lovely
place, full of happy people – Claire would have been amongst
them, but at Nottingham. People want photos to remember
them by – I can barely look at one. I just went into the living
room and there was Tom crying while kissing a picture of
Jenny. Heather's eyes seem always so tearful while Amy will
speak in her own time - I don't feel right to talk about her here.
None of us will ever see the girls again this side of life. It hurts,
God it hurts and he knows and it still hurts. Every morning,
every time the mind is allowed to wonder, every connection
and it actually physically hurts. Deep in the pits of the stomach
it wells up and can only be countered by forcefully taking
control of one's thinking.

So doesn't your God work then? I guess that's your question. When it really comes to it, what's your God made of? You don't realise how strong we are because of him. The evidence speaks for itself. We need make no defence because we remain standing. We walk in dark places but we carry bright lights. These paths do have to be trod sooner or later, imagine walking them with no light as some do? We will walk and if we see you fallen along the way let our light become your guide too. The Stoddart family is a family to spend time with; we are not gloom and doom, on the contrary we are conquerors of death, yet it still hurts so much.

13 No letting up

Why?

Why oh why oh why
Why them, why me?
Why do I walk into their bedrooms
What am I expecting to see?

People are carrying on
Another tragedy has passed them by
Someone they know lost their friend
And some parents lost their daughters
Some little folk lost their sisters
But they're only young, they'll be ok
Life moves on, let come what may.

There's fresh news on the telly, more tragedy, more losers
I've had my time to grieve
So I need to stand aside for another loser.
In fact, let me offer my most sincere apologies
After all, it was only a death or two
I see that you've all moved on now
And I'm stretching your patience.

Oh Jesus, it always comes back to you
The world moves on uncaring, but not you
Death and despair invade my dreams
But disappear when you draw near
Your church is close beside you
And I know I will not be defeated.

Two departed faces greet me every morning
But you are always between them
When my stomach churns with longing
And my mind reels with knowledge of a lifetime's absence
My thoughts keep turning to you.

When I meet you for real I am going to fall at your feet
And wipe them with my tears
Because if it wasn't for you there would be no hope
No day of rejoicing, no re-unions with loved ones
Who fell asleep trusting that when their day came
They would spend forever with you.

I can survive today because my eyes are fixed on tomorrow
I have a place reserved in Heaven
I am invited to a party where joy and celebration await me.

Thursday 9 November *The pain within*

Coming home from visiting places is so hard. You spend some time away and take in new experiences and then you come back home and the photos stare at you. Each picture holds a memory and today I've been sorting a bit more of their stuff out and it is grieving to do so. To remember these happy, bustling lives when all was well and life bore no pain. They laughed and hoped, they had so much to look forward to and then one day they died.

Jesus is not harsh, I know that. Everything I've come to experience of him tells me he is not harsh. I know that nothing holds sway over him or happens outside of his control. He could have stopped the crash, he could have, but he didn't. Yet I know he is good. Just the merest revelation afforded to me by his Spirit and I melt. I know I am faced with an incredibly good saviour. I think of the pain, the moment of impact, how two young and vibrant lives could be just smashed to pieces. Yet he is good. If anything, I will love people more, I will move amongst unbelievers with more compassion than I have ever known because something tells me that whatever the circumstances of life, what matters most is that people are saved from the horror of Hell.

God can bring good from the darkest of situations. I am convinced that there will be some people in Heaven because of the forfeit of their lives and the way God's people responded. Our loss, the tears that fall, the pain that so many of us feel, somehow that is the price that must be paid to live on this desperate planet. Death comes to us all, even lives as precious as Claire and Jenny's were not exempt. But Jesus still is the one to trust; the man who suffered is also God who saves. He is not the bringer of doom; rather he is the answer to it.

I have never known pain like this. It eats at me, it grows in my stomach, there is nothing I can do but come to my saviour and friend. He is the only one who can make sense of all this. I trust him utterly. I cannot conceive of how I can get through this without giving up unless I stand on the rock who is Christ. Why oh why do people reject you Jesus? How blind can they be? Do they have too much pain, too much fear, or are they just so blind that they will not come to you and be saved?

Friday 10 November *Not God's fault*

I've wondered sometimes whether Jesus homed in on Claire and Jenny as lambs to be led to slaughter so that others could live. I think not and actually the thought goes deeper than just one or two lives. People are being killed every day and experiencing similar losses to us, sometimes better, sometimes worse. Everyone with a faith in God could say their loss was part of God's strategic purposes to bring more people to him. This would give us a very harsh God indeed.

No, the real question is why does a loving God allow suffering to happen at all? The answer is perhaps startling, it is because of love. God's starting point with humanity is free choice. He could have made us so that we did not have the capacity to do anything other than serve him. Instead he chose to give us the choice to belong to him or not. Basically he let go and look what happened: murder, lust, envy, greed, you name it. Once we were on our own way the wars and famines followed and the result? Suffering the world over and we are the ones who cause it. Mankind has turned its back on God and so we have to live with the consequences.

All through this, God has looked upon us with utter and complete sorrow. His answer? One man, innocent of the crimes of mankind, to be punished so that all could once again belong to him. Jesus' suffering on the cross enabled us to come to God and be forgiven and restored into a fantastic relationship. Something he has done enable others to come to God.

The suffering of a Christian is also able to produce something good. If through our pain we can testify to the goodness of God and his ability to help us in our sufferings then those who do not know God can plainly see we have something more than mere words. By our testimony, people are turning to Christ and so it is not because of the deaths of Claire and Jenny that people are being moved to seek him but rather because of the amazing way God has moved amongst us. He has comforted us and the hope of Heaven has shone ever so brighter amongst us. Is this just true for Heather and me? No the whole church, young and old, including their best friends have all encountered the amazing love of God through this time. He is faithful. I have experienced the death of my daughters yet I have a joy inside me that cannot be quenched. But go ahead and listen to the cynics who call it brain-washing.

Wednesday 15 November *Looking for Jenny*

For a few brief moments I searched intently for Jenny but she was nowhere to be seen. Another memory seeping out into today's realities. The last bell at school had gone and although the main surge had passed, there were still a few stragglers making their way home. Year Eleven girls, nice girls, alert and well-presented: Jenny's year and Jenny's type. There seemed to be an abundance of them, from my school and hers and automatically I looked and wondered if I would see her on my way home, but there is no Jenny, at least not like these girls. I can look all I like but I won't find her, not in this world. People seem so invincible sometimes. In the light and normality of the day it is hard to conceive the thought that life can end, that people can actually die. It seems so amazing; almost as incredible that people can live is the concept that they can actually die. How is it that a normal person full of energy and hope, and a simple trust that her time will be at the normal time in the far flung future, can be smashed up in the time it takes to blink?

My situation is most ironic. Jenny would have been in Year 11 in September for the first time in her life. Although I have taught this year-group for six years now, I have never been a form tutor for them before this year. Everyday I sit in front of people who dress like her and have their hair like hers. I experience with them the demands of their particular year, the never-ending coursework, mock exams and whether to stay on at the sixth form.

Sometimes I will finish the day not long after them. As I cycle home I begin to leave the students of my school behind and begin to ride past the students of Jenny's school. A few of them I know and acknowledge, but sometimes I see Jenny. "That's roughly how she would have been now", I think to myself, but when I get home there'll be no Jenny, no room will house her.

The last time I saw her is etched in my memory. I stood one side of the hospital bed and Heather stood the other side. I prayed to God, I asked him if I was to pray for her to be risen from the dead. I know God can raise the dead, I know my God can do anything. Yet, there were simply these few words from him to me in response to my prayer… "No, I have taken her. She is with me now". Somehow, these words were a comfort. I knew the God of Heaven was in control.

The way had been opened to trust God for the passing of her life some twenty years ago when I first trusted him: eternal life for all those who put their trust in Christ. Do I still believe it or not, simple as that. Do I believe that she is now in a far better place and having been there would not want to come back and live as we do? This is what the Bible says. Do I trust God to be my comforter and my refuge? Do I believe the promises of God? Yes, again and again. There is something inside me which is assured. It can only be the Holy Spirit who gives such conviction. I walk dark paths yet carry a light that no darkness can touch.

Friday 1 December *Christmas begins*

I'd like to say it's Christmas and it's just so, so exciting. The houses of the brainwashed are being draped in cheap lights and gimmicks far too early. The novelties this year are Santa scenes in plastic bubble balls, pegged down in front gardens with fake snow falling within. Everyone knows that we probably won't get any snow until February and by then who'll care anyhow?

Claire was fantastic at giving presents. I began to really notice it in the last few years. Her presents just got better and better. I remember her saying that cheap fake stuff just bugged her so much, so when it came to her presents she would give good ones. How many times I thought to myself, "how can you afford to buy these things?" but she did. All our family got good presents from Claire. We had traditions for Christmas. At the foot of every bed there would be a stocking filled with little goodies. Claire insisted that she was never too old to have a stocking. Heather had to lay a mince pie and a glass of sherry for Santa by the fire every Christmas Eve and no change was allowed.

Christmas morning was a ritual of taking it in turns to open our presents. Being Dad I had to open one present to every two of everyone else's. This annoyed Heather and Claire so they made sure I had more presents in the latter years. Every present was opened well. No tearing open the paper without considering the gift tag. Who's it from? what does the card say? Endless banter and hills of presents developed in different areas of the room. We have our last present opening session on video, but will there ever come a day when I will be able to bring myself to watch it?

So what about this year? What price Christmas? Go on world, go on celebrate, eat your fill. I can't wait until you're over, I would leave you now if I could, but how selfish to walk out on you. To just end it and leave people to sort their own lives out. Would I leave a son and a daughter to grow up without a father and would I leave a widow? Would I pack up all my bags, the countless experiences of Jesus, the love he has shown me and just tear it all up into little pieces, knowing that if I did he'd still accept me? That is an incredible thought. I could blow my brains out and saunter into Heaven and still he'd accept me. I could heap more sorrow and despair on my family and still I could walk in. His grace is unconditional and my saving is a result of what he has done; it is not dependent on my works - or lack of them, more to the point.

But there would be no joy. I would see him, the one who had suffered and had drunk every last drop of the cup of sorrow he was given and I would weep. I would have repaid the saviour, the shining one, the one who is perfect in every way with pure selfishness. Oh Jesus, you heaped treasure upon treasure into my lap but I threw it all away! How would I look him in the eye, knowing he had given me everything I need to see life through to an end of his choosing, yet ended it at my choosing! Is that how I want to enter Heaven?

I want to meet him and stand with Claire and Jen in ecstatic rejoicing. I want to celebrate and go wild knowing that I was faithful and that my life demonstrated to the world that he was worth it, that his grace was sufficient for my every need. It's got nothing to do with reward. I love him so much, even more now that I have seen him that I want to one day come to him knowing that I did something for him that mattered. What matters now is that I stand triumphant in the face of death because I listen to the song of Heaven and not the stupid tinsel trappings of the world or this body that just wants to give up and say goodnight.

I have a message to tell and I will not be quiet. He melts my heart and when I consider him I often find it too much for my body. How can I explain it? It's like a surge of emotion, a flash of insight into his very being and I shake with the knowledge. My eyes stream with tears but it's because something has to come out. The pressure on the plugs is too much and they just cave in. I really just don't understand how anyone can look on him at all. He really is just too awesome to behold. He's so perfect and you realise you are nothing before him; everything you are is because he allows it. I would just dissipate, fade away into dust if he so wanted, yet he doesn't want that. He wants me to exist and in some marvellous way he reveals himself in a way I can just about accept. The other day, in a sort of vision I was sat before the river again and he came near and appeared young and friendly. He can look how he wants to. He appeared like this because he wanted me to know that he was my friend, that I could talk to him about anything just as friends do. Friends understand what their friends are going through and he appeared to me as my friend. I can't explain what this means other than that it melts my heart to know he can do this. HE IS SO AWESOME, I really can't write any more.

Wednesday 6 December *A cruel twist*

Last night I was having one of those insipid uneventful dreams where the brain seems set to "random play" and all the songs are the 'maybe' songs, the ones which you have to get through before you get to a classic, but then the scene changed. I was lying in my bed and then through the door, Claire and Sarah appeared. I looked in astonishment at the two girls who were shadows of their former selves. They were like skeletons, they were so thin. They were both in pyjamas and Claire's top was open revealing a sunken chest where all the ribs could be counted, there just wasn't any flesh to spare. It was almost as if their skins were a few sizes too small for them.

Claire was fighting back tears and I noticed her right leg was so lame that she could hardly walk; there was just no bend in it. "Claire?" I muttered in amazement as she drew near. "How?" I was now hugging her, full of joy, taking care not to hold her too tight for her body was so frail. Thoughts raced through my mind such as the slight problem that we'd told the world she was dead and the issue of university: would she be able to take up a place in Nottingham for next September? She began to speak through her tears. "They kept me alive but wouldn't let me see you, and I feel so guilty about Jenny."

"What?" I replied. "Claire, it's alright, Jesus met with us at the hospital, he took responsibility for her, she's with him; there really is no problem". I couldn't believe it; she was wracked with guilt, worrying that people were blaming her for Jenny's death. "You were on your side of the road, you were driving well within the speed limit, you drank no alcohol, why would anyone blame you?"

I was ecstatic, she was back and then my logic kicked into gear. All around me was dark once more, I was awake, it was just a dream, but why did this happen, what made the dream come? My mind was fully awake now, bothered by another night of broken sleep and the prospect of more hours of unwanted wakefulness. The possibility dawned on me that when dreams seem so real it wouldn't be that far-fetched for their ghosts to appear. After all I now had to go to the loo and a nice dark corridor would be an apt place for a visit. Suppose they did appear and engage me in conversation?

In my disturbed state I began to focus on Jesus and peace began to soothe my worries. If they did appear, it wouldn't be them at all, just tormenting spirits taking on their appearance. I would tell them the light of Jesus was within me (as if they wouldn't sense it anyway!) and I just know that his presence would be enough to address the situation. I remembered all those weeks ago when on the day of the car crash I sat propped up against the garden fence, unable to stand in my grief. I remembered how he, or perhaps an angel, stood over me. I could sense it; it was like a powerful warrior was standing over me, protecting me from harm. Nothing would get past him then and that same protection remained with me now. Satan and his demons cannot harm me.

Minutes passed and I began to consider the implications of the dream. Why was Claire limping so badly? I remembered Heather saying if either the girls had survived, they would have had to live with terrible injuries. I think I saw Claire as she would have been, trapped within a mess of a body. And then there was the guilt. Although no guilt was due, she still would have struggled with coming to terms with being the driver. At times, fault would have been irrelevant to her. Her logic would proclaim her innocence yet her mind would play cruel tricks. What would her dreams be like? Even with the knowledge of Christ within us, we still have weak human emotions. The Christian does not escape bodily injury and does not escape emotional injury either. Jesus would have come alongside Claire as he does with us, but like her parents, she would have still had to learn to walk with him along a dark and uneven road, trusting in a bright light that is the very presence of Christ.

Wednesday 13 December *Being happy*

Well we got the Christmas stuff up at the weekend, a real tree, some lights and a bit of tinsel. I insisted on a more under-emphasised Christmas this year and Heather pretended to play ball, comfortable in the knowledge that Amy would intervene. Sure enough it ended up as a gunfight stand-off. Knowing that the washing needed bringing in from the garden, I smiled and said sweetly that I would open up the attic where the rest of the festive garbage lay if she collected the washing.

Of course, teenagers are allergic to such mundane activities, so it seemed my strategy was secure. However Amy retorted she would get the washing in – but only if I opened up the attic. So the two gun-slingers faced each other resolutely and unprepared to budge an inch.

There was only ever one winner. Using her buddy Lauren to help block my every move, she trod on my toes and crowded my personal space until I succumbed and now there's even more tinsel up and the wheels of Christmas roll on. This is the time to have an air rifle. The inflatable targets of Santa and Homer are in abundance in many a garden this year and I really am compelled to shoot them.

I had a good day at school today, seeing everyone good-natured and excited about Christmas, the grand old deceiver. Why is it that we all get so caught up with it? Big grins on our faces and then comes January and folk do about-turns and get all grumpy. At this point the travel industry kicks in and says "DON'T WORRY! It's almost summer time. Beat those winter blues with sun, sea and warmth. HOT PRICES, hot deals", blah blah blah.

So I was cycling home early again and passed the kids from Claire and Jenny's school on their way home. The kids are all separated out into houses with different colour shirts. I like the way they manage to adapt the imposition of colour shirts to their own fashion. Whether they wear bright yellow or football-pitch green or pretending purple (the colour no one really likes but makes the effort with because it's different) the girls still all look impeccable. They would all make fantastic shop window dummies such is the current trend to look perfect. Straightened hair, mascara and eye liner, how much time do they spend to look like this? And even the lads are spraying themselves and moussing and gelling their hair. This is the most vain generation for decades. What a bunch of posers, sold out to Calvin Klein and Givenchy.

Lost in my thoughts as normal I cycled home. You'd be right in wondering how safe I am on the roads. I rarely concentrate on my bike, such is the wandering of my mind. I was struck with feeling happy, I had little voices in my head saying you really should not be feeling happy. Why not? Oh yes Claire and Jen are gone and I'm never going to see them until I'm with Jesus myself. Cast yourself down you fool, you're alone and no one can comfort you. Why? Why can't I be happy? I begin to reflect on them again. My thoughts major on Jenny this time, possibly because I associate her more with school-kids now than Claire: it is her year group I see on my way home. Life is fun and she's missing it. She'd be having a whale of a time if she was around now. She'd have gone out for a meal with the church youth group last night, buzzing with excitement. Claire would be about to return from university as well, delighted to meet up with folk and compare situations. What fun they're missing.

The thought then dawns on me, "but they're with Jesus. Is there anything I can conceive of that would beat being with him?" And then the tears come again. I perceive the Glorious One, those dazzling white robes, the sheer joy that radiates from his being. I have been brought to tears more by the perception of his being than I have by the loss of Claire and Jen. This is no lie. I can be happy and I am at liberty to be happy because despite the fact that I have to live without them, I can rejoice in the saviour. He means everything and reduces me to tears at just the slightest revelation of his presence. What he has done in saving my daughters is too wondrous to contemplate. I cannot but weep with thankfulness and trust to my balance that I won't fall off my bike.

I am incredibly hurt but I am equally happy. It is possible to bear a wound and still be full of the joy of life. Some days are better than others and I cannot guarantee always being able to be full of his joy. Yet I have tasted it and I know where to come when I am thirsty and desperate. I am incredulous that he has revealed himself to me. Whenever I see him, when the Spirit draws aside the veil and allows me to glimpse him, it is just too much. Yet without that revelation, life would be so much harder. What mercy, what grace, what a saviour, what a friend. Oh Jesus.

Saturday 16 December *Facing up*

Somedays you just can't face the crowds. You can't even face the people you live with. Somedays you can't even face yourself. You look at the people around you and think "it doesn't really matter to you, does it?" You lost someone you knew, one of the crowd, that's all, just one of many, so you can't feel it like I do. I want to hear them come through the door, want to see them walk down the road. I want to reach out and touch them. I want to engage, I want to hold them. How can people die? How is it that life can end, how can a mind stop thinking; how can existence stop?

It can't. I know that. I know they live on. Yet however happy they are, however transformed they are into beings so unimaginable, they're still no longer my girls. The girls I knew don't exist any more and knowing they are more than they were doesn't always help. I want to talk to the girls I knew, not mega beings, not immortals, just them, as they were, not as they are… and I can't.

I want their humanity. I want their grumbles. I want Claire's dodgy opinions and judgements. I want Jenny's bursts of pure anger. I want their challenges, their struggles. I want their humanity, not their perfection, but I don't really, I'm only being selfish. If God would grant these desires, would I really deny them their current reality? Would I have them brought back to life as I know it? Do I really think they would come anyhow? Can anyone taste Heaven and settle for something less?

The thing I dread most is returning to life as I remember, the days before July 1st when I sat comfortably in my heavenly status. No

real cost to count, no need to depend on Jesus. After all,
I had a comfortable middle-class existence, a fun family, excellent
friends, a vibrant church, a relatively easy job. I knew Jesus as
Lord but I only really needed him for my ticket to Heaven.
I didn't need him to live. Now I depend on him utterly. I cannot
handle my loss unless it is placed firmly within the context of
him. I cannot contemplate death without what lies beyond,
I can only accept loss in the face of the good shepherd who
came to seek and save the lost. If not for him, I wouldn't bother
you know. If left to my own devices, don't think for a moment
I'd have returned to work so soon, don't think I would have even
bothered to live normally. You cannot lose your children and
live life to the full unless you have Christ. It's just not possible.
Whether bitterness, revenge, despair or depression, something
will get you. I don't get anything but ups and downs. When I'm
down, I know I have the up. I always know that no matter how
low my feelings can go, I can see him and he doesn't change.
How can you fall when he is holding you up?

Thursday 21 December *Bits and pieces*

Christmas. The first one without the girls. We kicked it off with
a sort of party by inviting Claire's friends around from both
church and school and a few nights earlier had Jenny's friends
around for pizza and stuff. Why? There's something so refreshing
and attractive about youth. I love the idealism, the energy, the
drive. I like being with them, although not one of them. As
an older person you can do that, you have no agenda (other
than keeping your furniture intact). You can delight in their
biased opinions and social stumbles; no need to take sides as
they come out with wondrous statements about each other.
Everything is up for grabs, the issues which are already settled in
my mind have to be re-visited because they are still exploring.

Claire and Jen would have flourished in such situations.
Sometimes I wonder if we are feeding off the energy of their
social groups as a way of coping. I don't think so, I've always got

bored quickly with middle-aged scepticism. That's the attraction of youth, they keep your thinking young. To be "childlike" is not a bad thing at all, it's far too easy to be so hardened by life that living becomes a drudge. I hope I never fall so far as to become a perpetual grump. Does anyone think of me as such? I blame teaching and losing my hair if it really is the case.

Another thing about today was that the man who caused the accident was due back in court to face charges. We had been prepared for it to be done and over with but now there has been another delay. It's not going to be until June now and there was a plea from the defendant of 'not guilty' which means a full-blown trial. I have no interest in it at all. It's not where my focus is and I don't want to make it that way. My task is to deal with the loss and tell as many people as I can that Jesus is enough to see us through. We cope because of him. That's all. Justice and punishment is not my concern, it all lies in the hands of God.

Still, I wish the girls were here. We've had cards saying, "thinking of you" and it really is hard of late to not get lost in emotional pain, thinking about them, choosing whether to dwell on memories or not. It is like that, you get a memory come into your head and you have to decide whether to pursue it on the basis of whether you feel strong enough to handle it. Well, whether strong or not, the Stoddarts are still very much alive and kicking. You see we have a rather large and unbreakable backbone. I wish I could claim some sort of credit for it, but I cannot. I know I'm a wimp, I know I have no strength of my own; yet he stands over me. I cannot vouch for tomorrow, I cannot look to any strength of character within me that will see me through. Yet I know that he is faithful. I know that when it mattered, when I could not even stand on my feet that he was there. If he was there for me then, he will be there for me tomorrow.

Tombstone, St Michaels Church, Lowestoft

14 Tell the good news

You people

You people who have heard about Jesus
Who are happy to walk with his people.
From time to time, they will tell you about him
"Follow him and he will lead you to safety".

Let us be quite plain for a while and consider that you have
indeed heard how to meet him
How his blood was shed instead of yours
So that you may escape the judgement of God.

What are you doing? You're playing with fire
Have you decided the day of your death?
You must have because you say
I might follow him when I'm a bit older.

What do you mean when you say
I'm happy that you've found something
But its not for me
How can the Author of Life and Death not be for you?

Are Christians mad or just deluded?
Please tell me your thoughts
What evidence of madness is apparent?
Maybe they've been hit on the head;
Perhaps they're emotionally weak and manipulated?

Or are you scared, do you think you may become trapped
Locked in with no way of escaping
After all what will your friends and family think
The teachers, the medics, the apes, the cynics?

Just maybe, you don't want to know
Maybe there is a God out there but why should you
Why lose your lovely life and miss out on all the goodies
No sleeping around, no bitching, no living?

Well I'm sorry I'm such a loser
I'm gutted when my daughters died that I only had loser
Jesus to call upon
I'm sorry that I found an answer to death.

When I'm in Heaven with Jesus
I wonder if I'll remember you
What blinded you? what made you so reckless?
To think you knew more than your creator?

Sunday 21 January 2007 *Graveyard*

I cycled to the graveyard today and hadn't been there for a while. I did my usual circuit: first Carla's ashes plot, next Claire and Jen's grave, then the grave of the girl who was murdered a bit further down. Finally I sit down on the bench near to my girl's grave and think and pray. What people have to put up with! For every grave there is a network of people who have to learn to live with the emptiness within. Nothing can satisfy their loss, not people, not things, not time and not even knowing God, at least not fully, not yet. Whoa! What are you saying? You're a Christian. Yes I'm a Christian, I'm filled with the Holy Spirit, I'm part of an excellent church and still I say it.

God never intended any of this death stuff for any of us. He didn't intend Claire and Jen to die like they did. He didn't intend that poor girl to be murdered. Was he helpless? Why didn't he stop it? And when it happened to us: Christians, part of his church - why didn't he stop it? And after allowing it, why when I stood over Jenny still being kept breathing by some machine, why didn't he do something? I prayed, "God, will you raise her from the dead?" He answered, "no, she is with me now." I knew his voice and I knew there was no debate. I also knew he stood with me. I think the hospital people thought I was a weirdo, but better to be a weirdo with hope, than 'normal' with nothing. God never stopped Jesus dying on the cross either.

In fact that was the express purpose why Jesus came among us. God never stopped some of his most obedient people suffering grievous deaths either. Why?

Well the blueprint of life has been perverted. Sin dominates this world and we all suffer under it. Jesus provides the way back to God and putting our trust in him means that one day we will be part of a new heavens and earth, living forever with him: the Bible is clear about it, the Holy Spirit affirms it. I am filled with hope and am convinced of this. I have taken my stand and it is based on trust and conviction. As for knowledge, I am satisfied with the logicality of my belief as much as I can be. Yet while I am here, I am buffeted by the winds of sin. The sun shines and the rain pours on the righteous and the unrighteous alike. Whether Christian or not, sin strikes at all people: we age, we suffer the loss of loved ones, we die – and sometimes way before we get old. Pain and grief will never disappear, not even for Christians, not until that day when they are with Jesus forever. Until then I must learn to live with the pain of what has happened and there is surely even more to come.

I have lost my loved ones and I sit on the bench, thinking about what people who don't know God have to put up with. How can they do it? How can they bear the loss, the biting pains within, to live without hope, with no saviour to trust in? I am crying for I experience something of the pain, Oh God. And then he speaks to me. "Everything you have put your trust in is true. I am the same, today, yesterday and forevermore. You have been laughing at the mean and miserable compensation the world is offering you for your loss. I tell you that when you come into your inheritance, you will receive more than you can ask or imagine. There is nothing that you will lack when you meet me and see your daughters once again. Your gain will outstrip your loss beyond your imagining. This is my word, now work with me, tell these poor and desperate people about my love. I love them so much. I am so desperate for them to come to me." His words are written on my heart and I cannot but tell of his goodness. Another victorious visit to the graveyard: perhaps the most painful yet, but still victorious.

Monday 22 Jan *Speaking out*

Our church held an Alpha supper in a pub last night. It started with a meal and I was the speaker. Since mid-December a leaflet had been circulated advertising Alpha and me speaking about the "End of Death". I accepted the invitation to speak quite readily. I know I have to speak about the goodness of God to me and my family since the events of July 2006. It's like he's written it on my heart and I don't particularly have to prepare much, I can recite it word for word at any time it seems.

But Christmas had gone and the day was but a few days away and I began to think I ought to think about what I was going to say. The Alpha supper is a pre-cursor to a course where Christians invite non-Christians to investigate the validity of the Christian faith. The supper is meant to be like a taster, and involves a meal and a talk, which is the layout for the course. Alpha in principle is great. You get a free meal and afterwards there is a short presentation on some aspect of the Christian faith. After this, you discuss it on your meal table and give opinions. When done properly it is a great context to explore ideas. At the end, people might or might not want to become Christians. There's no pressure to do so and if folk choose not to, then that is their choice, take it or leave it.

So at this Alpha supper there were around fifty people if not more and I was the speaker. More than half knew little of God I reckon. But how can you enjoy a meal when you have to speak afterwards – especially to strangers? Well I did a pretty good job actually; I've been in similar situations before and know how to block out nerves so that I can enjoy food. And I did, I sat and managed a half-pint of beer and all of the meal. Someone bought me a second beer but I knew better than that and left it until afterwards. Finally the moment came. The first half was about how little we know about the universe we live in and about how I became a Christian. All of this was carefully thought through. The second half was dealing with the loss of Claire and Jen. No notes were required here. I couldn't re-visit the memories in my preparation and just trusted to God's assurance that these things were written on my heart – no preparation needed. Far too painful you see, I only go there when I really have to, for him and his kingdom.

So I talked and suddenly half an hour had passed. There was adrenaline, elation, a late night and then exhaustion the next day, but no emotional pain. It is strange but true that whenever I talk about the events as a witness for God it seems I am spared the cost. I believe this is part of his equipping, whenever I talk for him I become like a soldier who has a captain in control. I am a standard-bearer in such times, not through any doing of mine. It is his strength. I have come to believe that those who stand for him in adversity receive strength beyond what they have. I cannot pinpoint it but I can testify to it.

What it means is this; if you have put your trust in Jesus and you have taken your stand you need not worry about the day when your time of adversity comes. He is faithful and you will be strong on your day. Therefore do not fear the evil day for your saviour will not let you down. You will stand, not because of your own strength but because he is faithful. Believe this. It is as fundamental to your faith as what you have believed for your salvation. If Jesus will not stand with you and strengthen you on your day of need then he will not stand with you at all. Do you believe he has paid the price for you and that you are destined for Heaven? Then believe what I am saying as well.

Tuesday 30 January *Most of our Universe is missing!?*

A few months back I watched a programme on TV called "Most of our Universe is missing". They claimed that everything was made of atoms: me, you, houses and cars, the mountains and oceans, the planets and stars. In between the atoms was nothing, just space. According to Isaac Newton, famous for his observations on an apple falling on his head, atoms moved according to the various gravitational pulls upon them.

Furthermore, gravity is universal, the same rules apply everywhere. "In the same way that the sun controls the orbiting planets by exerting gravity on them, galaxies must be controlled by the gravity-giving black hole at their centre. So when we think of our sun, it exerts a gravitational force such that the planets closer to it travel in an orbit that is faster than those further away. In short, Mercury travels much faster than Pluto."

This was all great as theory but then there came the discovery that although the gravity law appears true for our solar system it does not appear so elsewhere. In spiral galaxies the stars are racing around the centre at approximately the same speed. So they concluded there must be something extra that is providing the gravity force to provide the extra speed. The problem was that according to their instruments there was nothing – at least nothing made of atoms, so they came up with the idea of dark matter and dark energy to account for what was missing – a staggering 96% of our universe (according to best estimates).

Something is driving our universe which they cannot account for. So they coined the phrase "dark matter", its definition being something that must exist to explain our understanding but as yet we cannot detect – and what's more, it's all around us. Some of them propositioned that thousands of tonnes of dark matter pass through the earth everyday. So at the bottom of Europe's deepest mine in Cleveland, UK, away from all influences, they placed a detector but sadly for them nothing doing so far.

As the programme went on they put forward that dark matter actually only accounts for 21% of what is needed to drive the universe. Why? Because rather than diminishing – as they previously thought – stars are actually moving further away from each other. This means the universe is expanding at a certain rate and the other 75% is needed to explain and drive that expansion.

As they debated and argued, one scientist concluded "We don't really know anything at all."
Source: www.bbc.co.uk/horizon

Could there be a God? 96% of our universe is missing or not made of anything that we can detect or understand. We can neither prove nor disprove God by means of science. Most of our universe is undetectable.

Yet here am I, a small speck of humanity who is convinced that he has met the living God. What's more, I claim this meeting is not by scientific detection nor by any of the senses we rely upon so much to explain the environment we live in. Rather I claim that I met him simply because he revealed himself to me. Not in his entirety, not in his grand majesty, but rather in a way my being could cope with and make sense of.

I believe he is the God none other than the one described to us in the Bible. This is the God who knows us by name personally, and what's more, who loves us. As our creator he has an undisputable claim on our lives. We have no right to reject him although we are free to do so. If we do reject him, he will reject us and he will have every right to do so. No one will be able to stand before him and say they have the right to escape his judgement. He will rightfully decide our eternal destiny which awaits beyond the grave or cremation furnace. Is it valid to make a stand on something other than science? The scientists themselves say we really have no answers. I suggest that they do not know because God has chosen to deny them a way of finding him by their own means and cleverness… which is his right to do so.

Friday 9 February *The Comforter*

So often Jesus is alone. He was alone in the garden of Gethsemane though his disciples were close. They could not help him in his anguish; there are some things other people cannot touch. No one could know his dread and he suffered both torture and crucifixion alone. None of us can even begin to comprehend his descent into death and separation from his father. When I pray and see impressions of him, so often he is alone – even now. I believe he appears this way to us as a way of meeting with us deeply. I am alone and my soul cries out for one who can meet me in my loneliness. No angels or other magnificent beings stand beside him when he comes to me. He is personal, his agenda is simple: him and me. Experiencing him with me in this way is my continuing comfort and right as a son of God, given to me as a gift from him.

When I come to him, I know now not to speak first of my failings, nor look to my feelings or fears. I have gazed upon him who melts my heart. I know I am loved incredibly; he and I stand together united, we face my fears together, my feelings and my failings. I am not alone, I share my burdens with the one who has freely offered to carry them, but first I will gaze upon my friend and saviour. May I never again come trembling into the presence of God in the foolish belief that any situation or failure would ever obstruct his primary desire to love me, to cleanse me and to stand me on my feet. If need be, together we will look at my sin and he will show me my error, the pain it has caused and what to do about it. No shouting, no punishment, we are together him and me.

He will stand beside me and we will look beyond. Together we will see people and I will ask of him. Sometimes there are clear answers; many times I am aware of his deep passion and concern for them. To have a sense of how he loves other people is an awesome and deeply humbling experience. My humanity can barely care for my family, yet he burns with desire for every living being. Other times he will show me how to deal with situations. He is so much more than a comforter. Towns and cities, nations and continents lay bare before him. A son of God is also a soldier, I am comforted because he loves me and I am comforted to bring his comfort to others. This is the joy of knowing God; perfectly loved and perfectly equipped to hold his banner high. Joy is not complete unless I obey his promptings and share in his work.

One day, many people will be gathered around a huge banqueting table at the wedding feast of Jesus and how much happier will be the workers than those who were not. Our place at the table is guaranteed by the cross, but our joy at the meal will be influenced somewhat by what we did with what he gave us. Did I do what he asked of me while on earth? If so, then I was there in the battle for souls. The feast itself is a celebration of Jesus victory but I'll celebrate more if my life displayed in whatever way it could just how great his victory was.

Wednesday 14 February *Claire's Mr Valentine*

Every year Claire received a mystery card through the post. It was all very secretive. More than once I suspected Heather, as did Claire, but we never really knew and I still don't. The 'Claire' world of romance was always a guarded secret, kept to the confines of friends and in the latter stages the walls of Jenny's bedroom. Even Heather knew things which I did not, although the occasional whispering reached me unintended. I know names and even now the knowledge causes a wide grin across my face. Perhaps the very reason I knew so little had much to do with the reason for my grin! Claire knew that knowledge in my hands was a dangerous weapon, although I like to think I keep close the things that matter. Perhaps the problem was that we had widely differing opinions over what mattered and what did not.

On occasions I reflected upon how much boyfriends mattered to Claire. Some girls her age were in long-term relationships and I know it must have been an issue to her. Yet I wasn't seeing a troubled life and if anything there was a social mega-star in the house. Looking back now, I thoroughly recommend her lifestyle to anyone her age. She was well-balanced; she worked hard at school because she had considered what she wanted to do in life. Her level of organisation was scary. When I had to sort out all the practical problems of her leaving the earth, I found her documents all sorted and easy to deal with. From mobile phone contract to university finance, from work contract to receipts and guarantees, it was easy. She had done it how I have all our stuff – but she lived at twice my pace.

Claire's balance extended to enjoying life. She spent lots of time with a wide range of friends because she wanted a life that danced. She had energy to burn and so much to do. I remember her complaining once that she didn't have enough time to revise. When pressed she revealed a rather large social diary which wasn't up for amending. There was also work to fit in. How did she manage to accommodate all this? Sometimes with flying colours, other times the cunning schemer drew upon ways of which one is not permitted to tell.

Finally and most importantly there was her relationship with Jesus. It turned out he was her Mr Valentine all along. From an early age he wooed her in private and the evidence is that she loved him back. So Claire wasn't in love? Her diary says otherwise; many passages talk of a love affair transcending the superficial garbage of relationships based on physical pleasure. Her Bible is underlined in many places. It did not stop her having an excellent life, rather her lover protected her from damage. Only a man who knew Jesus in the same way would have been acceptable to Claire. I do not know why Jesus did not prevent her life here being taken away from us but I do know I trust him. Her life was not wasted, nor has it ended, nor what I loved about her will ever be lost. I am convinced that although my memories will fade, all will be restored to me. This is part of her inheritance and part of mine. If you counted her amongst your friends it is yours too if you belong to Jesus.

Wednesday 21 February *No chance to say goodbye*

I just so wish we could have got to say goodbye to you both. I wish it could have been like the day before you were off on a long trip somewhere, that we knew you were going to be away ages and that we could send you on your way. Even more I wish we could have known of the place you were going to; perhaps to have already been there ourselves and met the people you were going to be with. We could have helped you prepare, sort out the things that were being left behind and make sure you had what was needed for your journey. Then we could have seen you go with peace of mind, happy in our minds that all was well.

We'd feel sad as you both went. We'd know our lives would be changing and that there would be something missing that could not be replaced, but no matter, we'd know where you were and that was what you wanted. Of course, you'd be in touch soon and there's always instant messaging on the internet. Contact would no longer be close but we'd still have you at a distance and know how things were going.

But we were denied such a parting and I didn't even see either of you on the day of your journey. I don't think I hardly spoke to either of you the night before. Everything was wrong; you both went on a journey you had no intention of going on and none of us had made any preparation, or had we not?

Oh yes we had. In fact all of us had been prepared; we just didn't realise it. Each of us had made personal journeys some time before and those previous journeys turned out to be all the preparation we needed – you two were able to reach a destination far beyond your wildest dreams and us? Well we already knew something of the place you'd gone to and we knew plenty of who you had gone to be with. It may be a while now before I get to hand over a daughter in marriage. It may not happen at all but if it does I hope I will hand her over to someone I can trust. Someone who I know will never abuse her and will love her beyond the realms of self-gratification. Is there someone who will love her more than he loves himself? Perhaps not, but a father can have no greater hope for his daughter than this.

I got to hand Claire and Jenny over to you Jesus and no one can ever know what that means. They may think they can but oh no. A flood of tears erupt from me at this knowledge. I got to hand them over to you! Can there be any comfort greater than this? Of course, they never belonged to us anyhow. They were always yours and we were nothing but stewards charged with looking after them. But something in our lives worked; for all our failings and weakness, our daughters were helped on their way by how we lived. Yet it still remains that we can have no contact. We talk to you Jesus and you always assure us of their utter joy and well-being. I sense and know by spirit and mind that they are a source of merriment to you. I know that their distinctive personalities are not lost. I also know that my stomach hurts and that I still can't wander freely in the memories of times gone by. It is not right that a family should be separated like this, yet your heart for the lost burns within us. Though we are hard-pressed we must continue, as must all who bear your name.

Why? The lonely suffering of unbelievers and their eternal destination are at stake. Ours are not. For a while we are what the apostle Paul describes as "drink-offerings" – living sacrifices poured out for the sake of others. We must accept the provision he has given and prove his love. The grace and power of God at work in us is a signpost to people who have not knelt at the cross. A quote from the Bible: "When the day is over, the night will come when no one can work." We must work while there is time to work and rest when he calls us home. I want to walk into Heaven with pride, not with a tail between my legs.

Tuesday 27 February *Jenny's fruit*

The really sad thing Jen is that you're not here to see it. Although if you were here, would it have happened at all in this way? Because of you and Claire getting all smashed up and having to abandon your bodies early there's all these things happening and such was your nature that you'd have been so thrilled by it all. I haven't a clue as to how aware you are of things down here but you've been a focal point for quite a few people and they've looked for God and some of your friends have become Christians. What's more, some of the friends you had who were already believers have become sort of radical for God. They have this determination inside them, something made of steel. No longer are they timid teenagers and I suspect if the devil punched them in the face they'd get up like pronto. I think they've taken their place on the battlefield; they've become fighters and people are noticing and the church is growing.

I came home after school tonight Jen and your mum was sat with a Bible with a bunch of your friends and they were learning about Jesus. If this was your diary then you'd write down every one of their names with little "wows" after certain ones. You loved your friends Jen. After the Bible they had pizza and garlic bread and doughnuts in the most bizarre order. They survived a few Tom attacks and they left with 'New Day' leaflets. Then all through the evening the phone kept going. It's now half ten and mum's still on the phone. Do you know Jen there's seventy people signed up already, loads tonight. Mum says we'll need two coaches this year and we'll have to take more cooks! There's folk from my school signed up tonight. It's hilarious, even they're interested in God!!!! There's so many who will be going either as new Christians or as still just looking into it. I wish these stupid atheistic television and newspaper people could just see what's happening but even if they could they'd call it brainwashing, anything to deny Jesus. But we love him Jen and you see him face to face; how amazing is that?

I can't say that all that's happening is down to you and Claire
my darling because God's so much bigger than you and us
but you've played your part. The little you were able to give in
your short life seems to have been taken by him and made into
something big. I don't know if you can place a value on human
life but I honestly believe that some people have come to God
because of your life and your faithfulness to God. Those little
times Jen when you stood up for him, when it was difficult to say
you were a Christian. When you didn't do something because
you knew it would offend God or when you did something
purely because you knew it was right. I see it Jen, I see that it
mattered, every little bit mattered. Some people have found the
way to eternal life because of you. I stood over your dying body
and I still stand Jen. I'm sort of like you in a way. Death came to
you and you passed it by and death knocked on my door and
tried to destroy my life but it couldn't. It tried to destroy your
mum and you sister and your brother Jen, it tried to do your
friends in Jen but it couldn't. Only Jesus Jen.

15 Uneasy bedfellows

Mind storm

If I could stand in a hurricane
Walk on a bed of flames
Climb over a precipice
Walk into my memories
I'd gladly be ready to do it.

If I could burst into Heaven
Talk with the angels
Hold onto my daughters
Gaze on my Saviour
I'd truly be happy to do it.

But I'm held in a living cage
Propped up on a theatre stage
Where the audience interest is gone.
They've moved onto another film
And I'm left with a silence so bare.

What shall I do with what's left of me
How long must it last
Shall I end it all rapidly
Face it all cowardly
Run away to the greener grass?

But there is no liberty to end it
I have been bought with a price
Death is not mine to choose
For my life belongs to Christ
And I have to do what's right.

I'm as strong as I want to be
It all depends on my faith
Do I love it or leave it
Reject or believe it
And deny the Lord of Life?

He's guided and cared for me
Looked after me lovingly
Stood over me when I wept in my grief.
He put his arms round my daughters
He chased off death with his laughter
How can I deny the Lord of Life?

I will live well, I will smile and laugh
I am stripped yet unharmed
I will tell of his glory, though my emotions overwhelm me
I will walk tall in his victory with salvation written over me
A son of eternity destined for happiness
Wonderful worship and joyful abandonment await me.

Jesus you amaze me, to see you it breaks me
I cannot contain you, how long can I gaze on you
You are truly beyond me, so awesome to see
I perceive you and know that I am nothing

Yet you love me perfectly.
I only want to love you
For there is nothing greater than this
I want to die knowing
I loved you more than my life.

Monday 5 March *Day and night*

It's strange that day and night should come night and day whatever. Perhaps a better way to order this planetary routine would be to let one reign until its power was spent and then let the other take over until all was done and we were left with neither. God could do that; a few mechanical changes here and there, hardly a problem.

It's strange that I should have something like two natures inside me since I became a Christian. On one hand I live for God and count his blessings. I proclaim the realities of Heaven and the magnificent victory of the cross. There are times when I can be so full of his Spirit that I cannot contain the life within me. All is fine, I've met him enough times to know all that he has promised can be trusted. I tell people about him with sure conviction because I know of the joy and peace he brings. I know it works. There are even occasions I can talk about Claire and Jen as though they've just popped down the road. I'll see them later, no problems. I can glance at photos and smile as though they're still around. I can talk about them freely… and then I realise I can't.

Night follows day and just as surely as I have been walking in the light of day, something of the light disappears and night time approaches. It is different to the falling of the sun; that which no man can stop. It is something I feel I ought to be able to do something about, yet I can't. I cannot sustain such strength and I know I am not meant to. I cannot ask of my body that which it cannot do. I cannot deny my emotions; after all I am only human. If God were to ease me of such things I would cease to be human. He gives me enough to live, that is all I can say. It is sufficient; it is by no means a feast. Yet the more I teach myself to trust the voice of God the more I grow into my new nature.

Sometimes, no many times, the voice is small and can barely be heard. Yet it is never lost and I learn to walk and to understand that little bit more, the plights of people far worse off than me.

Jesus walked in weakness voluntarily; compassion can come from no other source than from those who have walked the same paths. That's why he emptied himself and came to earth. That's why he became a man of sorrows. No one can accuse him of not being able to identify with their sorrow. No one therefore can claim a situation beyond his reach. His church must also walk such paths and, like Jesus, prove that there is no situation too difficult for God. The good news is for everyone.

So, sometimes it is day and sometimes night. Darkness: when I don't seem to be able to draw upon God – or I simply don't want to. I'm never going to see my girls again and it hurts and makes me angry. Why should they be denied the right to life? How can people just die? How can lives which had so many hopes and passions just be taken away? How can I let them go, yet what have I got to hold onto? I can do nothing to get near to them and sudden rushes of anger abound. I can make no sense of death. We all carry on with our lives, yet they die. Why is there this waste? Why should I want to live when they are not? Why didn't I die instead, why didn't you?

That's how it is, that's how grim I can be. I can withdraw for hours and harbour these thoughts and not talk to anyone. I wonder who else can also be like this? Yet I cope and come round, for the small, small voice of God is never silenced. Would any fool be stupid enough to ask God to hold back the Holy Spirit until the day you die? Maybe that would be better than this roller-coaster way of living. Maybe it would be better if night didn't follow day like it does, but only a fool would think so.

Saturday 17 March *Claire, my darling*

I remember the day when it was just you and me. We went down in the blue car, the one which you were going to die in, to Reading for your interview at the university. You took charge of the music because you assumed superiority. It was funny how we both assumed the better taste in music and how it wasn't even up for debate in either of our minds. You were happy to let me drive because you didn't like driving on the motorway. I remember you set your ipod to play songs which you thought I'd like. It still bugs me that after those few years of early teenage awkwardness and keeping me firmly away from your social world that you'd finally become happy to let me in. I was enjoying you. You were no longer fighting me and you were making me smile lots and in ways I'd come to regard you as a friend. Not just a daughter, a friend; someone who I liked to be with, who could make me smile.

It's funny how a father and daughter can be. We were so alike. You're mum used to laugh at the striking resemblance in our personalities. Neither of us held back our opinions, we were both so forceful, yet I loved how you had come into your own. You'd arrived to say the least. Also, you knew how you and I were and you'd obviously recognised that we clashed in some things but you'd made a decision to love me, despite the ways in which I would annoy you. I'd opted to love you as well. No fatherly duty, I loved you more than that. God does matter when it comes to accepting people. In hindsight I was able to recognise where you were at and still love you. Love doesn't depend on people's actions it's far deeper. Love accepts people despite their actions. God taught me that and I think you had grasped that as well.

In fact, the last year spent with you was at times as good as the old days when you were young. I remember at New Wine, that conference we used to go to, when you and I would disappear for ages to read Enid Blyton. I would get you a king size mars bar and read you a chapter in the Grandstand on our own. We had a special relationship and we'd spend ages together when you were young. There was a long time when Mum was working and I was at college and looking after you full-time. She said often that you were a dad's girl and you were, and that's why it hurts so much. I can't say it hurts more than Jen, because me and Jen had mega-times concocting weird stories.

We had our own world too and I don't really want to compare. Sometimes it's Jen that causes me to cry, sometimes it's you.

I loved the way you had such energy and drive. You were so clued up, more than I ever was. I just dossed through my teenage years but you did them in style. Now you were virtually an adult. You'd got yourself baptised and I was just an onlooker at the service. Mike and Jamie and Erin baptised you and prayed over you, but I was so proud. You were just a body to some folk but to me you were exceptional. I knew your heart and there you were, taking your saviour full on. No half measures with you, no half measures with me. I wonder if I would have cried then like I'm crying now, if I'd have known just how important your relationship with Jesus would turn out to be?

I so want to make contact with you. Anything would do. I keep knocking at the door and all I get is Jesus. But you know that's how it is. It's like the boy who fancies the girl and he keeps coming to her house and knocking and the dad keeps answering the door and you can't get past him. In ways I feel like I'm an outsider. If I could get through the door I'd see you but the dad won't let me. I'd like to end with a Bible verse to say it's ok but why pretend? All I know is that you're safe and well. Thank God for that, thank God that we met him, thank God that one day my darling I will read to you in paradise and look to our saviour with an overwhelming gratitude that I will struggle to contain. I cannot understand how anyone can look at him, perceive what he has done and not weep. His presence commands my being, my emotions cannot be contained and yet I only see him in part. HOW can anyone see him in full and contain it? Unimaginable.

Wednesday 21 March *Never lose sight*

There is certainly nothing boring about life at the moment. I am part of a community of people, believers and non-believers, people who don't care, people who don't know. There are 'don't-knowers' and 'do-knowers' - hesitant, perhaps scared of stepping into God's family. There's a lot of variety and energy and lots of things happening and God is so visibly moving. It's exciting and tiring, challenging yet satisfying, it creates in me a yearning for more. Yet it is so easy to get caught up with this bustle of activity and start to miss out on the sustainer of it all.

I have tasted what it is like to be in the very presence of Jesus. It is no wild claim nor dramatic exaggeration. No one should be surprised that a son is visited by his heavenly father or that he should see something of the visible expression of the Godhead: Jesus himself. It would be very easy to get caught up in all that is currently going on and let the activity dominate, let the people I enjoy being with become my nourishment. Like people who have no personal relationship with God at all, like I used to be, I could live an acceptable life even though my daughters are gone. I could recover from the grief simply by feeding off the relationships and activities I have now. And what a fool I would be to do so or even believe I could.

I spent time with Jesus this morning, reflecting on this. It's his presence which is my food. This is what it means in the Bible when he calls himself the bread of life. There's something about seeing him and being with him that gives strength beyond my ability to describe. Here is the one before me who loved me so much that he allowed himself to be crucified, to be beaten up and nailed to a cross. At any time he could have stopped it happening, but he saw it through - for me. Only by experiencing him personally can a person have any sort of idea what this really means. Head knowledge is good but we are not just intellectual beings, we are so much more than that.

My daughters are enjoying Heaven because of him. Only a spiritual experience of this – something beyond my ability to explain – is real food. Head knowledge again is good but not enough for a hurting heart. I trust him because I experience him and I trust his word accordingly. He is not one who should lie, he is God. My daughters are indescribably happy because of the faith they came to in him. They were not born that way; they submitted themselves at the cross, just like I did. The result? I'm like someone who's learning to drive a sports car yet has to go round in an old heap. I'm impatient for the real wheels. Living well is all about nourishing the spirit within which knows no boundaries. There is something about me and you, so much more than our bodies. That's why we read in the Bible so many warnings and pleadings to live accordingly.

It is so bad when we live just for bodies, treating ourselves and others with such ignorance of who we really are. Lads, never EVER let the physical beauty of a woman be the basis for which you treat her. That is such an ignorant thing to do. Ladies do not abuse your good looks or live down-trodden because of your own or others perceived lack of them. They are ignorant. Our bodies are just tents. Yes we treat them with dignity and respect because they are God's provision for us. No we do not serve or idolise them, neither our own, nor that of any other person. Tough call I know.

Monday 26 March *Another death*

Another little girl died today, just up the road from where we live. She was riding her bike at a school crossing when she collided with a lorry. I think she was aged six and I wonder how many entries this time to the ranks of the bereaved? Somewhere a mother and father are beside themselves with grief, perhaps a sister and brother too. There'll be grandparents, aunts, uncles and cousins and some close friends of the family too. From the wider community there'll be the police and hospital staff, the school to where she was riding to. There will be the witnesses and the driver of the lorry and his family. These people will all be affected to differing degrees and some will be viewing their new surroundings with dismay. They are in a different world now, where everything is tainted by death and loss. Life has lost its colour and they cannot perceive how they will ever smile freely again.

Can anyone help you if you have joined these bitter ranks? To some extent, yes of course. I only hope you have people who can offer comfort, who will spend time just keeping you from being alone. You're scared of the loneliness now aren't you? Don't want to be left with just your thoughts, pummelling you mercilessly, bruise after bruise. Going to bed is the worst, the prospect of hours churning over the harsh reality of your new surroundings. There is no escape from your mind, no hiding place where you can be free. You are naked. You fall at the slightest touch, you have lost the will to live. Your legs have become unstable and your stomach is a huge knot of despair. Is there not anyone who can help you?

On my date with death, my friends didn't let me stay alone. They became like bright little fires that provided comfort on a dark and cold winter's night. In terrible darkness you are desperate for any light, no matter how small. You make for it, you stay by it because the darkness is so fearsome. Yet they were only little lights and I had a far greater light than them, a light that could not be extinguished. Darkness could not overcome it.

HE stood over me as I lay so terribly wounded, awesome and majestic; an impression of a mighty warrior was forged upon my mind. I lay collapsed upon the grass of my back garden, stricken with grief and I was suddenly filled with the knowledge of his presence. A mighty figure in gleaming white, one who was much mightier than death was here. My daughters, their destiny and my grief seemed like they had all been weighed up. It was as if their full measure had been considered and counted way within his capability. Nothing was happening outside of his authority. He stood there sombre and in full defiance of the situation. I had a sense he regarded it as a personal attack on him. Considering it now, I realise it was. The freedom we all have to choose right or wrong, to accept or refuse him, results in much death and sorrow. Every offence against his creation is an attack on him. I had no doubt that mixed in with his love for me was a burning anger. He was here to fight, to stamp his authority on a desperate situation. No wonder he has been described as like a lion.

The only real remedy for grief is knowing Jesus. Time is no healer and friends are just as helpless as you. Alcohol just creates greater despair; there are no physical pleasures that can deal with the pain of loss. Thirst for revenge is pointless and only creates bitterness inside. You have lost someone and you will never see them again. The loss can become unbearable. It is both emotional and physical; your stomach, your legs, your sleep. Your hands shake, you are truly crippled.

I know Jesus and it counted. The blow of grief was softened because I knew my daughters had gone to be with him. I didn't just hope this, I knew this, because I have met him. I know where they have gone and I know to whom they have gone. I know that one day we will be together again and I am fully satisfied within. They knelt at the cross and so have I: the promises of Heaven are granted to us because of this. Their lives now are incredibly more amazing than my life now. Therefore the saying, "what a waste of such young lives" is not appropriate in the case of Claire and Jenny Stoddart. Sorry, but look elsewhere for tragedy and woe. Don't look to them for it, they never knew it. Try victory instead, try death defeated and life without end. Try Jesus.

16 A hard road

For a friend of Jenny

How come you're leaving so soon?
I thought you were here for good
I know when you first arrived
You'd come intending to stay.

No need to tell me the path is so hard
I keep falling over myself
Blood on my knees and big black bruises
We can compare the knocks if you want.

I don't enjoy life too much either.
Do you think of death too much
Puzzle over how to end it
And what it would mean if you did?

When you lost your friend
It was like a bullet through your heart
It came out of nowhere but brought you to Jesus
Where else was there to go?

So you joined us in the house
And together with him we stood
He became our food and drink
And led us beyond our understanding.

Wasn't it amazing back then?
So warm in the hands of God
His presence was infectious
Tears of sorrow kept turning to joy.

So how come you're leaving so soon?
Perhaps you no longer need him
You've learnt to cope with the loss
Got what you needed, now moving on.

Or doesn't he love you like he used to?
You're lonely and hurt but he's distant
Perhaps the rocks have just got too big
So you're bailing out, not turning up anymore.

Please don't walk away
You're listening to a liar.
As if the man of the cross could ever stop loving you.

Yes the path hurts but at least it's a path
The mountain still has to be climbed
It all ends at the top and those other paths you see
Just look easier but get worse up high.

His presence is still here
It's just different now, keep walking
You're not to be carried into Heaven
Sometimes he stands back a bit so you can learn.

If you walk there yourself
You'll be so pleased when you enter
Heaven's crowds will applaud all the more
Over the faithful ones

Be faithful, you'll be so glad you did
When you see him
You will want to give him everything
But all that you'll have to give is your faith that proved
"With my God, all things are possible"

Sunday 15 April *Death is a fighter*

Death, even deprived of victory and sting is still death. It still represents a door firmly closed and I am not permitted to open it. I cannot walk through and pass back; there are no windows, it remains a mighty force that often makes me angry. While we were away last week, two milestones happened, the first was April 1st, the nine month departure anniversary. October 1st was Claire's birthday, swiftly followed by Jen's. January 1st is our wedding anniversary. April 1st was in the Easter holiday and holiday times seem to be particularly difficult. More family life is happening, giving more time to reflect. Soon it will be July 1st, one year on but before that comes the June court case.

The second milestone was the tombstone finally went up in the graveyard. It reads:

In loving memory of

Claire Stoddart. 1st October 1987 to 1st July 2006
And
Jenny Stoddart. 12th October 1990 to 1st July 2006

They lived together as friends, sisters and believers in Jesus their Saviour.
They died together in a car crash and are now enjoying eternity with Him.

"For God so loved the world that he gave his one and only son, that whoever believes in him shall not perish but have eternal life."
John 3:16

"Where, O death is your victory?"
1 Corinthians 15:55

I remember compiling this inscription months ago. The words came out so fast that it was like they had been pre-assembled and just needed bolting together. They should point the reader to the total and utter defeat of death at the hands of Jesus. Where O death is your victory? The power to totally destroy a believer is broken and so life does not end. In Sleeping Beauty the princess is cursed to die but those flowery-dressed little fairies turn the curse to mere sleep. Similarly death is permitted to rule in this age but its power is lessened. Believers suffer the deaths of their bodies alone, their spirits are unharmed and of course, the resurrection bodies await. But even in defeat, death still delivers the most vicious of blows.

Today the sun shines and people walk about in shorts and all is so seemingly carefree. But Claire and Jenny are not here. I have to die to see them. Sometimes it feels like a prison where no rattling of the bars and no tantrums or fits of rage will move the guards to release me. I am truly stuck!

This makes me think about what the mindset of a life-time prisoner is like. Do they rattle bars in anger, becoming more furious as time ticks on? Do they wail and gnash their teeth in the same way as the inhabitants of Hell will? Is part of the torture of Hell the continuing knowledge that you cannot get out? And, of course, you are surrounded by desperate people, angry and violent, lashing out at whoever and whatever they can.
I wonder if such people will even have the hope that one day their suffering will end and they will know oblivion. In Revelation 20v14, John sees "death and hades" thrown into a lake of fire which is called "the second death". But worryingly verse ten comments on the "devil and the beast" thrown into the lake of fire and surviving to be tormented day and night forever.

Does there ever come a point when a caged person becomes weary of anger and rage? Do those serving life-sentences ultimately just give up and neglect to live? I have felt something of that and what it is like to be reckless. There are times when I just don't care about anything and rehearse crashing a car at high speed to make the journey beyond. I imagine the pain of impact, what would it be like – surely swift, just focus, concentrate and do it.

Yet there is so much to live for. In truth I have so much. The feelings of recklessness have to be firmly placed into context. They are blows from death, stings that hurt, a dying enemy who is lashing out in anger. I am blessed in life and I have my God. I re-iterate I want to make the journey beyond with my head held high. I don't want to risk living through eternity knowing I was so self-absorbed that I even took my own life. If laying down your life for your enemies is the most selfless act that can be done (Jesus on the cross) then surely taking your life (suicide) and forcing bereavement on friends and family is the most selfish act of all.

But to anyone who is feeling suicidal, I am aware that I am not someone in an unbearable situation as you may be. I simply want to see my daughters. I am not suffering from any physical pain, I am not a prisoner, I am not emotionally destroyed. You may be experiencing pain beyond anything I have known. Please come to Jesus first before you visit death. For someone like me who has feasted upon his presence, who has known such blessing and healing, to take my life would be utterly selfish. It would be throwing hatred into the face of love. It would be an evil choice. I am not one who would seek to judge you in any way but we must all one day account for our lives and the choices we made.

Tuesday 17 April *Changeover time*

Somedays I wake up feeling like nothing is right. The whole world is irritating and nothing is good. Such a day was today, first day back at school after the Easter break and all I could think about was the continued absence of Claire and Jenny. I feel as though approaching the end of a changeover. Mere months ago I was in one place but now I am in another. Why is this?

What seems like months of God's presence is now so hard to know. Back then, it seemed so easy to dwell upon the wonders of Heaven and in particular the carefree laughter and joy that so characterises it. So many times, a river surrounded by beautiful countryside would come into my mind as I prayed. It would be graced by his appearance and he would sit with me and I would be filled with a peace so still yet so powerful. There's something about his being which is hard to describe. To be in his presence is not just a visual thing, it is more about perceiving. To see him is to be filled with a sense of wonder as if somehow you can comprehend him. But it also becomes like looking into the sun and your eyes cannot long contain the sight or the perception of who he is. Many times I shook and cried at the one who stood with me. Even now, just talking about it does something to me I cannot explain. And I saw something of Claire and Jen and the blissful existence they are now living.

Now is different. A hard road filled with struggle and requiring grim determination to travel. Sometimes the churning in my stomach and panic-filled feelings of despair seem so powerful. God's word feels inappropriate and weak, utterly unable to provide the slightest jot of comfort. On occasions I will even refuse to contemplate him and instead, turn my thoughts elsewhere and let anger dominate and fuel my thoughts, so that my tongue can become a weapon of malice. At this point I have to decide my path, because that is my responsibility and mine alone. There was a time I recorded how he stood over me like a mighty captain protecting his wounded soldier. He knew I could not stand alone and I think he stood over me for months.

Now is different. He wants his soldier to stand. Jesus said this in the Bible: "You shall know the truth and the truth shall set you free". There is no lasting benefit in being kept alive on visions and physical outpourings of God's presence. We mature by faith; learning to trust him is what makes us more like Jesus. He told his disciple Thomas, "Because you have seen me you have believed; blessed are those who have not seen and yet have believed". What happened to me back then was amazing but it was also yesterday's food, provided by a loving father for a desperate son in his hour of utmost need. Now is more of a time for saying, "come whatever, however I feel I will trust the words, the promises of God more than I will trust anything else".

Claire and Jenny are not to be associated with death and separation, true that these things are. Rather they are to be associated with Jesus and Heaven. One day, I will stand in glory and I will behold him and them. He will present them to me and me to them. I must stand on this promise and allow the truth to set me free. Free of what? Free of grief. I can live looking backwards so my life becomes a memorial to their lives or I can live looking around me to those that remain – all as loved and cherished by Jesus as Claire and Jen were and are. I can also live looking forward to that great day when he returns with all those who have died trusting him.

It is not an insult to Claire and Jenny to move on. Their memories fade even now and they will continue to fade. Already I struggle sometimes to remember some things and a year has not yet gone by. They would not want any of us to live stricken with a grief that does not stop. There is a time to grieve and a time to stop. I will remember their lives in a wholesome way, free to look back and laugh, free to sometimes cry but I will not live defeated by death. I firmly believe that everything I need to fully enjoy our re-union is being safely kept in the hands of Jesus. In the darkest of nights the Christian is still called to live "life in all its fullness".

Monday 23 April *Reflections*

I took so much about the girls lives for granted. During the hustle and bustle of daily living I rarely stopped to consider the evidence of Jesus at work within them. Both of them set standards for friendships that were unusually high and similar to each other. How often they were organising social events, taking responsibility for planning things and spending time with a variety of people. Both had equally strong friendship groups and both enjoyed their church friends and non-church friends alike. Neither of the girls was prepared to be confined to one group alone and I regard that as an excellent pattern for any follower of Jesus.

Of course, their friends were virtually all good-natured folk and had a basic respect for others and a desire to get on in life. I come across a lot of young people at school and it is always so refreshing to communicate with the ones that don't have to swear in every sentence or pick on someone during the course of the day. The ones that realise teachers and adults are of the same species as them, the ones who don't get their enjoyment out of other people's miseries.

The Bible tells us to have nothing to do with an evil person and Claire and Jenny certainly didn't. They got irritated by thuggish behaviour and I remember their outrage at the idiots who had annoyed them and everyone else at school. I don't tolerate such people and neither did they. The girls didn't get their laughs from putting people down but they still had a joy and laughter about them that was infectious. In the weeks leading up to the car crash they became so loud. Sometimes Claire would have so much to say that she couldn't quite get the words out of her mouth quick enough. They often took to spending the end of the night in each others bedrooms and the noise they generated as they talked about people and who they fancied was like there was a party going on.

I suspect strongly that God had put a massive dose of life into them in these weeks. As if instead of one sugar in the tea they had received three or four. They were on such a high. I also remember them discussing boisterously in our car how they wanted their funeral services to be – the songs they wanted in particular. God foresaw this car crash. I accept that he foresees all things and there are many things he could have stopped but didn't. I understand that death is the price we pay for the fallen world we live in. But is it possible that in those weeks we witnessed an outpouring of the joy of the Holy Spirit upon them?

Wednesday 23 May *The gloom*

Sometimes I just don't know what to do with myself. There is tiredness filling both mind and body and everything I take an interest in has lost its appeal. Even thinking itself becomes tedious and I become like a computer closed down to standby mode, having enough power to be alive but not enough to do anything more than breathe.

I have lost any enjoyment in my work. I rise every morning and steel myself for the day ahead. There is no satisfaction there, nothing to inspire, the work is drudgery. I attempt to teach that which I have no interest in. The subject-matter has become mind-dulling and year after year I will have to repeat it and achieve results. If students fail it is not their fault. Even if they make no effort from the start and disrupt entire classes it is still my fault. The fact that they cannot behave or lack motivation is overlooked. Blame the teacher for this (of course).

Being a Christian is so hard. Everyday I am asked to lay down my life and put Jesus and others first. I have a little problem called me and it is tiring me out. I am supposed to be motivated and telling people good news so that they can be saved from Hell and I am too tired to do it. I also understand that death offers no escape from responsibility. We all think of it as the last resort, that when it comes down to it, if life is getting too unbearable we have the power to end it and take our own lives.

But there is no real escape. Hours, days, weeks and months of suffering on earth will only be replaced with an eternity of it by those who don't belong to Jesus. And there will be no last resort, no getting out of Hell once you're in. Even for Christians, I don't believe that taking one's own life would bring the great escape we think it would. Eternally forgiven as I am, I have a safety-net of mercy and so even though it would be wrong to take my life, I sill would make it to Heaven. But I'm a fool if I think God would overlook what I had done and that I would emerge unscathed.

No, it is at times like these that I feel I am cursed with life. I didn't ask for it and feel as though I do not want it and am powerless to end it. Death is merely a crossing from one level of existence to another. I am immortal unless God decides otherwise and I have no say in the matter.

So I look for friends but where are you? I wonder why it seems that other people have places to go in the evening, have things to say, but I am confined almost every night to four walls with nothing to say and no one to say it to. And what about you God? You are after all the comforter of my soul and I need your presence right now more than I need just knowledge of you. I don't know how bad I would feel if I knew nothing of Heaven. But right now I need to experience you. My entire being is worn out and you're the only one who can bring me a drink.

Monday 28 May *Bad week, worse weekend*

I didn't really expect such a dark and gloomy week. I guess I had the thought nursing in the back of my mind that this week was to be the last week in school for the Year Elevens. Jenny would have been leaving Year Eleven, looking forward to a prom party and nights out to celebrate. As a teacher I get invited every year to my school prom and Thursday night was my third in a row. This year was different as my form had moved up to Year Eleven and so I was seeing them go. They entered the school at the same time as me and some had been in my classes throughout their high school lives. They had become more than students and moreover some of them had known Jenny and had cried with me during the farewell service held for the girls at their school. Others had sent me letters of support and when I returned to school, only two months after the crash, they did much to make my life as bearable as possible while teaching.

All through last week my thoughts seemed locked into Claire and Jenny. It's been almost as if I've had a second wave of grieving. Gripped by memories of them being around, there were times I just cried out for them and then had to face the oppressive reality that never, never in this life will I encounter them again. At times it made me angry, but most times just weighed down, barely able to speak. Locked into loneliness, it was unbearable and for some reason I couldn't bring myself to pray.

I knew that only a meeting with the Lord of Life, the one who is their current reality, could get me out of this pit. But I didn't even have the energy to do it. I despaired of living and it wasn't until Friday night laying awake in bed at some stupid hour, that it dawned on me I had once again to let go. They wouldn't want to see me like this, defeated and drained of hope and they are NOT dead. They are gone but they are not dead. They do not live in my memories either; they live in a way beyond my imagining and which is also my destiny.

So close they have seemed this week but the photos haven't helped. I put large photos up on the wall in the living room and the computer room a while back and all they have served to do is cause me to live in a memory. So I determined to re-allocate the locations. Their portraits along with Tom and Amy's are now in the corner of the living room. All other large photos save one, are now in a room upstairs. This one photo is of them in a crowd of Christian friends at the New Day event and that photo makes me smile and they are not overly prominent. It also reminds me of the great re-union that we will have in Heaven, that the girls were part of a community, one big family, all Heaven-bound. It's just that they got there sooner.

So why the move? I want to choose when to remember. If I want to see their faces I now have to either physically look to the corner of the living room or go upstairs. They no longer dominate our house. Heather quickly agreed to this change, it seemed they had been affecting her as well. Letting go of the girls is not a one-off event.

The court trial starts on Monday 4th June and their death-day anniversary follows on from that. Whether it's the foreboding of those events or the Year Elevens last week of school, the large photos or just the recent good weather and times similar to how the girls left the world, I don't know, but all in all, a week I'm glad to be rid of.

Torment

A downward spiral
Down and down and down
Each step just plummets
And my stomach gets more unbearable.
I have searched my mind
For somewhere to go
A place where I can rest
And be happy, just that, quite simple really.

But there isn't anywhere
I can't even see Jesus
No hope of Heaven is strong enough
It is just another of those things I can't touch.
Living is a curse
I don't want it, yet here it is
Forcing my feet everyday
Every waking moment an intolerable prison.

I don't want this life
Yet there is no liberty to end it
I don't own it, it isn't mine
No rights to claim.
No escape beyond the grave
It is too much to bear
Yet no choice exists
Live and die with no control.

I want my children back.
Life is unacceptable without them
There is no hiding place
Loss is a barren land, an endless desert.
Somehow, I have to meet with Jesus
Knowledge of him or Heaven is not enough
I have to meet him
Nothing less is good enough.

I am desperate for you God
If you will not meet with me
Then life is over, it is not worth living.

Grief

Not a torrent of water
That suddenly appears and overwhelms
But then is gone.
More like the waves of the ocean
That well up slowly and creep in gently.

Grief builds up to a crescendo
And crashes down at the shore
Then swiftly retreats
Only to return as before.

I checked my diary
Just to make sure
That a few days of grief
Had not been pencilled in.

So just how did it happen?
Perhaps a few glances at the photos
Of two departed daughters
Gave birth to the wave.

And maybe my defences were down.
Not enough time spent in the presence of God
Chewing slowly the words of truth
And swimming into heavenly waves.
The hope of Heaven, the victory of the cross
The promised re-union with loved ones.

So for days I have only considered the loss
Their faces have become projections onto others
I saw Claire eating at the dining table today
And Jenny passed me by on the stairway.
I cannot cope with a lifetime without them
And my eyes cannot hold the waters much more
My stomach is knotted and my hands are shaking
There is nowhere to cast my mind and suddenly the wave.

Grief

Not a torrent of water
That has come but is now gone.
It will come again and again
And I am lost in a storm.
Flee the waves, don't let them crash over you
Run for your life
Hide yourself. Where?
The Word of God
I am desperate for you Jesus
Only you, only you.

17 Judgement

Tuesday 5 June 2007 *Fathers' tell of grief after A12 tragedy*

Below are extracts from an article which appeared in the Eastern Daily Press 5th June 2007.

The fathers of three teenagers killed in a road crash have spoken of their relief after the man accused of causing their deaths changed his plea to guilty just days before he was due to stand trial. Army corporal Ben Morphey, 22, is facing jail after admitting five charges of causing death by careless driving while unfit due to drink. Lowestoft teenagers Claire Stoddart, 18, her sister Jenny, 15, and their friend Carla Took, 18, died after the two-car crash on the A12 at Blythburgh, near Southwold, on July 1 last year.

Ipswich Crown Court heard that Morphey had drunk a "considerable amount" of alcohol during the night of the crash and ploughed head-on into the car being driven back to Lowestoft by Claire Stoddart. "Judge John Holt said sentencing would take place during the week beginning June 25 and warned Morphey that a prison sentence was inevitable.

Phil Stoddart, the father of Claire and Jenny, said he was relieved at the change of plea by Morphey, particularly as it meant two other teenagers who survived the crash were spared the trauma of giving evidence. "The last few months have been really horrible for us," he said. "Right from the start we knew Claire had been driving on the correct side of the road and that she wasn't speeding. There were two other people in the car and they would have had to go through the whole trauma of being witnesses. For them to avoid this is really good news."

Mr Stoddart, 44, added: "In terms of a custodial sentence, we've got mixed feelings. On the one hand we don't see the benefits of him going to jail, because he didn't set out to kill our daughters. But on the other hand, if you don't pass a hard sentence for drinking and driving, you encourage other people to do it. Justice has got to be shown to be done."

The teenagers' friends Sarah Mitchell and Adam Cox were injured in the crash. Two passengers in Morphey's Renault Laguna, Simon Bonner, 40, and Kim Abbott, 41, both from Yoxford, died and Morphey was treated for leg injuries. Prosecutor Simon Spence said Morphey had been drinking at a club on the night in question. Witnesses said he had stopped drinking quite early, but tests carried out after the accident revealed he must have consumed "a considerable amount".

The collision happened during the early hours of 1 July and experts estimated that Morphey was driving between 50 and 55mph when he drove onto the wrong side of the road, which has a 60mph limit. Initially, it had been suggested by Morphey that lights on the Vauxhall Astra being driven by Claire Stoddart had dazzled him, but expert examination of the wreckage revealed the lights were in a dipped position. He added that as Morphey had pleaded guilty to the five new charges it was not in the public interest to pursue the original five counts of causing death by dangerous driving.

Although the guilty plea was heard on Friday an order was made postponing any publication of the hearing until the victims' families had been notified. James Onalaja, representing Morphey, said it was not claimed that anyone else had played a contributory role in causing the accident and that the crash had been caused by a momentary lapse of concentration from his client. Morphey was granted continuation of his bail until the hearing at the end of the month. He was made the subject of an interim driving ban ahead of sentencing. A spokesman for the MoD said he could not comment on Morphey's future career in the Army until after sentence was passed.

Wednesday June 6 *Why forgiveness is so important*

I appeared on a regional BBC News programme yesterday and announced I harboured no feelings of enmity towards the driver of the car that caused the deaths of my daughters. The interview was edited to fit into the time-constraints of the programme and ended with an assertion from me of forgiveness. I attempted to indicate why during the interview, but the attempt did not make it past the editor. Now it appears the issue of forgiveness has caused a divided reaction amongst some people and so I want to make plain why forgiveness is important and indeed essential for anyone wishing to recover from a grieving process.

Firstly in the New Testament, God commands us to forgive those who do wrong to us. The Bible goes on to make clear that if we do not, it will obstruct our relationship with God and cause nothing but sorrow to those around us. As a Christian, this in itself is enough for me – if it's there in the Bible I will do well to heed the instructions therein. However, the past year has also taught me the wisdom of forgiveness. Bearing a grudge is a bitter path to choose. You become consumed by hostile thoughts towards the wrongdoer, and desperation grows for justice. Yet when the day of justice finally arrives, it only leaves you flat for it can never be enough. So whoever offended you is now starting their sentence; has it really done you any good and have you got back what you lost? Did not your quality of life deteriorate in the process and where is the satisfaction you thought would be yours on the day of reckoning?

No, there is nothing. It was the focus of your mind and you used it deflect the loss but now the loss must finally be faced. The truth is that negative reactions such as revenge have no power at all. Only the positive love of Jesus is strong enough to deal with the enormous hole in your life.

On the day of the car crash, I honestly believe Jesus met with me. One of the most emphatic things he impressed on me was not to question him. He was there for my comfort, to let me know that he was bigger than death, that death itself was subject to him, but he was not there to be questioned.

I believe that deep down the grudges we bear are actually against God himself. How could he allow this to happen? I remember another Christian in my family saying, "why take two of them, wasn't one enough?" When I saw Jesus, I sensed his love for me was deeply beyond my understanding. He was not one to be questioned; rather he was one to be trusted. If I had taken the hostile and bitter path I am fully convinced that I would not have been able to experience him as I did on that day and in the days to come. There is no darkness in him and grudges are dark, bitter roots that result in much evil in this world. Forgiveness is essential to living well. It is a daily choice, a deliberate act of the will. I will not fill my mind with hostility, rather I will focus on the good, the positive, the Lord of Life and being a benefit to those around me.

Thursday June 7 *Hero for a day*

I feel sort of bemused. One day you're alone and the next you're the man on the stage. It started at 7am on Tuesday when BBC Radio Suffolk wanted an interview. I was in a deep sleep and came round to Heather prodding me to take the phone. It was rather similar to the morning of the car crash but this time I said "no way" and fell back asleep. Later I gathered my senses enough to realise she had done an interview and that a number of people who knew her had listened and been touched by her words.

The Eastern Daily Press contacted me the previous evening and quite large articles now appeared in their paper and that of the East Anglian Daily Times. The Daily Telegraph also published some blogs I had posted on their website so Heather went out to get hold of the newspapers. Then the phone kept ringing. There were national newspapers and magazines and they wanted exclusive rights to an interview. Some were prepared to pay for exclusivity while others seemed to think the privilege of appearing in their rags was enough in itself.

I must confess to being a bit bewildered. So we were heroes for a day. David Bowie did a song about that, heroes just for one day. The BBC arrived – a camera man and a reporter. I liked them because they were a laugh. We cracked jokes about some of my more extreme facial features and I enjoyed them being here.

A magazine reporter was also pretty impressive, she took time to treat us as people. Then some national press started getting in touch. One reporter really annoyed me – I was just another story, less than human, privileged to receive their publicity.

An agent acting for News of the World turned up in the early evening. I liked him because he wasn't pushy, so he got a cup of tea. Then a national radio station phoned up for an interview – I didn't like them, wish I hadn't spoke to them at all: abrupt rude man who treated me like a piece of meat. Heather did a two and a half hour magazine interview and promptly collapsed in a heap on the settee afterwards. I finished off with talking to a nice woman from a local paper and that was that.

A hero for one day; well thank you very much, but why?

Why didn't we just tell them all to go away? Well we have a message to tell and the message is valid and true. Jesus is no mere concept of the mind, no product of a wishful heart. He has made a difference and the evidence is there for all to see. The interesting thing is I am just a quizzical, just as sceptical as the most ardent of non-believers. I don't care too much about proving to others that the road I have travelled for the past twenty years or so is valid; at least not for my sake. What I really care about is that when it comes to the crunch, is the one in whom I have placed my trust present and reliable? It matters more to me that I can say, "YES, he is" more than any need to convince anyone else. Ultimately you have to be honest because what other people think only matters so much. When it comes down to it, is Jesus there when it matters, like he promises he will be, or is he not? Yes he is. I cannot look back at the last year and come to any other conclusion.

Friday June 8 *Right to say it as it is*

Quite a few comments have come back from the blogs I've done on the Daily Telegraph website. Here is what I wrote in response today.

"I really appreciate the comments people have left on my previous blogs to do with the A12 car crash and forgiveness. I apologise to folk who think they're a bit too Bible-based but I cannot divorce my experience from my faith. These blogs are simply an account of my life and that includes both God and the Bible. All I wish for is honesty and I note a lot of honesty in the comments from people who do not claim a similar faith. That's fine. Every individual has the right to be respected for their beliefs. I should be at liberty to talk about mine as should everyone else.

This liberty is gradually being eroded and it all happens when governments decide what people should believe or when individuals become intolerant of beliefs contrary to their own. At the heart of everything lies the integrity and value of the individual. I want the right to tell a person, if they are willing to listen, what I believe and in return I should do likewise. What scares us all so much about religion are the people who seek to manipulate it to gain power over others.

This is a can of worms but it really is not wrong to want to tell others about something you are convinced is true; but it is wrong to force your beliefs on people. You will always get this right if deep down inside yourself you realise the value of other people is equal to that of your own value. You would want no one to take advantage of you so don't take advantage of anyone else. In short "do unto others as you would have done to you" - but that's getting biblical again, oops.

None of the above is what I was going to write about. There's a person who posted a comment about losing his 16 year old daughter in a car crash this January. You bought tears to my eyes. I am so incredibly sorry that you are now right in the heart of grieving. The thing with losing teenagers is you've enjoyed so much life with them because they have so much life about them at that age. I was particularly enjoying the company of my daughters when they were killed. They had become like friends, we traded banter and then they were gone. I note you too trust in Jesus and I rejoice that you are not facing the ordeal alone."

Sunday June 10 *A final ten minutes*

We've been camping for the weekend with a few folk from church although some of us had the luxury of dry caravans where sleeping a few feet off the floor was a big bonus in the damp conditions. I finished the stay chatting to my friend and talking about how God can bring good from bad circumstances. We got round to talking about Claire and Jenny's deaths and how God had worked such good from such tragedy when he revealed he had been in touch with the person who had spent the last ten minutes with Claire before she died.

I was stunned and my stomach turned over and I wanted to cry. This person had been in the car behind and had held Claire's hand straight after it happened. It seems she survived for ten minutes but didn't speak during that time. I thought she had died instantly, one moment chatting, the next face to face with Jesus or at least an angel. I knew that someone had sat with Jenny in the ambulance for a while before she slipped away but not Claire. So she had been conscious for ten minutes or so and just as with Jenny, someone else had held her hand, not me.

Even while continuing to talk with my friend, my mind had become firmly fixed on Jesus and my stomach was churning. Was she in pain, in agony? I reasoned the body closes down on the point of death, even though conscious in some sort of way and I doubt either of them would have been too aware of their injuries. But more comforting, even before I had finished talking with my friend, that familiar sense of Jesus' presence came upon me and these words in essence: "Do you think that I, the Lord of Life, was not there for both my daughters throughout that time? Do you think it possible my love for them could ever have been less than perfect? I draw near to you every time you totter on the point of utter collapse, I assure you I was there with them throughout."

My eyes are streaming now. Lord how could I ever, ever doubt you? You astound me; just to be with you is to be filled with a deep assurance that you are indeed perfect. I will not walk in any fear of the agony they may have endured. It is enough for me to know that you were with them. You will be with all those who belong to you when their time comes. Perfect love drives out all fear.

Tuesday June 12 *A glorious final 10 minutes*

The knowledge of the extra minutes of life for Claire plagued me a lot on Monday. I was in work but I couldn't focus. I kept getting bad images in my mind and tears kept coming out. At the end of the day I excused myself from a meeting and went home my mind in a whirl. I knew Jesus was with them both throughout their passage from earth to Heaven but the possibility of suffering still gnawed at me. It was time for a break for I was in no state to work. It was time to meet with God and Christians who I could talk to and pray with. Having friends who share the same faith, who are like-minded and utterly convinced of the power and love of God is an amazing privilege.

It was like calling on the cavalry! In the evening I went round someone's house and was cheered up immensely just being able to talk freely. We just don't realise how helpful to each other we can be sometimes, unaware that within each of us who belong to Jesus there is something of him, something radiant and refreshing. Sure, not one of us is perfect and Christian friends annoy one another all the time, but this does not diminish the work of the Holy Spirit within.

The next morning I knew God had something special. I sensed this was a day away from school commanded by him. There were no phone calls from the media and another friend was available to meet and pray. He came with that something 'special' and it was almost as if I was waiting for it. Not knowing what I wanted to talk to him about and while showering that morning, he felt God say to him that just as he was fully focussed on the shower and the force and heat of the water, so Claire and Jenny were fully focussed on

Jesus in the time after the crash. Like we become unaware of our bodies under the hot gushing water so were they unaware of their bodies as they heaved and sighed and finally closed down. They weren't aware of it, for they were focussed on him.

The cynics among you can say I'm being soothed by the most convenient suggestion possible. Go ahead, doubt and undermine my God. My belief is that I perceived the nature of their departure before I heard anything from my friend. I just needed to hear it from someone else I guess. I trust Jesus; I trust him that Claire and Jenny are radiant with him NOW; I trust him that I will one day stand radiant, clothed in gleaming robes of righteousness before him. I trust him to speak to my spirit deep truths and I also trust him to speak through his people when he chooses to do so.

Thursday June 28 *The sun shone in July*

It only takes something small to become lost in a memory. A glance at some vibrantly coloured flowers on the window sill in the morning sunshine became that something. Back to that funeral day, the eerie calm and beauty of last July, back to the masses of flowers dressing our house and their aromas; back to death again.

It seems a bit odd that the days holding our farewells to Claire and Jen and the sickening grief that was so overwhelming, should have been such marvellous days of summer. Odd maybe, but not inappropriate; in fact, I couldn't think of a better backdrop to such an amazing event as the passing of the girls to a level of glory that our minds can barely contain or imagine. I know for some, that the summer beauty was a mockery of the situation. Their loved ones, their friends had passed into some unknown uncertainty and all they were left with were memories to pit against their loss. How dare the sun shine! It should have thundered and rained and the days should have been grey and dark.

For me, I look back and see it as a celebration of the wonders of Heaven. The colours of nature on a bright summer's day remind me of the new heavens and earth that are to come. I've seen something of where the girls walk, only small glimpses, tiny impressions but it really is the place to be. The very atmosphere is filled with the presence of God and perfect knowledge permeates through every being. The joy and energy I've sensed among people who are there is pretty amazing but nothing compares to the presence of Jesus.

In some marvellous way, his very being fills that place, yet at the same time he can appear in person because he also has a body and substance. Whenever I have become aware of his presence I have been awestruck and so overcome that I cry, sometimes uncontrollably. Even the little I see is too much to contain. Yet the people already there can contain him, they share the deep sense of joy and awe that I have but they are able to handle it in a way my body just has not got the capacity to do.

It could have been a summer of grey clouds, rain and darkness back then, but it wouldn't have made him shine any less to me. It was just nice to have the beauty of nature so evident. In fact, it strikes me now that my most compelling experiences of God have come in the darkest of times. And I am changed. Any amount of time spent in the presence of Jesus cannot fail to have an effect. The reason some of those apostles could write things, like they count all their personal achievements as rubbish when compared with the glory of knowing God, or while being stoned or beaten up could pray for their enemies forgiveness, was because they had been in his presence.

None of us are capable of doing these amazing things we are told to do. I walk in peace and forgiveness and assurance of where Claire and Jenny are because I have met Jesus and because the Holy Spirit is at work within me. It is not mental gymnastics or some discipline I have achieved; it is merely a submission to his presence, a simple acceptance that he really is pure light. No darkness within him, no need to doubt or question him. He really is beyond that. Don't ever think you could come into his presence and debate with him. You see him and just know that he is right and good.

18 Anniversary

The first face that they saw

Was yours the first face that they saw
Or was it the face of an angel?
I can only guess, I can never know for sure
Who met them at the door.

Did they spend any time with the lights out
Unable to make sense of their surroundings?
Were they alone without anyone to hold to
Before the light of day appeared?

How much did they know about the crash
Did someone tell them life was over?
All that they'd known had come to an end
And a new day had begun.

Were they able to think of us
Fallen to ground in our sorrow?
Legs so weak we couldn't stand up on our own
Or rise to face the day.

I wonder if they cried when they knew
They'd never see their friends or family
Until the day when we take the same journey
And stand bewildered at your door.

Now they're spending time with you
Walking freely in the garden
Constantly amazed by the marvellous sight
Of the lion and the lamb, who is both God and man.

Do such wonders fill their thoughts
That memories of earth are now distant?
Have the healing leaves of Heaven brought such joy to
their hearts
And driven out the pain?

Or is it that now they're so changed
They're able to deal with all that's happened
Able to praise and dance and joyfully laugh
Knowing that God will meet our needs?

I will never see them as they were
And when we meet I too will be changed
Healing leaves will wipe the tears from my eyes
And a white robe will be mine to wear.

That's how I'll be coming to the party
Clean and full of joy and praise.
I'll see the girls and go wild at their beauty
And worship the saviour all my days.

Death-crash sentence attacked

The following article was printed by the Eastern Daily Press on Saturday 30th June 2007.

A drink-driver who killed three Lowestoft school friends was jailed for eight-and-a-half years yesterday, provoking an angry response from parents who described their own ordeal as a "life sentence". Ben Morphey, of Yoxford, had been drinking with friends before the accident on the A12 near Blythburgh which claimed the lives of Carla Took, 18, and sisters Claire and Jennifer Stoddart, 18 and 15. The teenagers were returning from a concert in Ipswich when the car driven by Morphey veered onto the wrong side of the road and hit their car head-on in the early hours of July 1 last year.

Ipswich Crown Court heard the 22-year-old could have drunk almost twice the legal amount of alcohol before causing the crash, which also killed two passengers in his own car. Judge Neil McKittrick told him the accident was caused by a "clear, gross error of judgement", but he would be credited for his guilty plea. He also disqualified Morphey from driving until 2017 and said he would serve half of his sentence in custody.

Following the hearing, Carla's parents Angela and David Took, of Lowestoft, criticised the sentence as inadequate. "We were hoping this court case would send out a clear message to the public that there are serious consequences if you drink and drive, but I don't think it has," said Mrs Took. "He has been given eight-and-a-half years but we have been told he will only serve four. It will never be enough. He has killed our daughter, and given us a life sentence. It has been the worst year of our lives. We have had all the firsts - the first birthday without her, the first Christmas without her, and this Sunday we are at the end of that year."

Morphey, an Army aircraft technician, pleaded guilty to five counts of causing death by dangerous driving on July 1 - just three days before his trial was due to begin. Mr Took said: "This was a clear-cut case, and he should have been tried before Christmas. The evidence was stacked against him." Sgt Steve Knight of Lowestoft police said: "I think it is a fair sentence and the judge has clearly taken all the evidence into account. Whatever the sentence is it will never compensate any family for their loss."

Phil Stoddart, father of Carla's friends Claire and Jennifer, was not at yesterday's hearing, and chose not to comment on the sentence. Morphey's passengers Simon Bonner, 40, and Kim Abbott, 41, also died as a result of the accident. The court heard Morphey had been handed the car keys by Mr Bonner after a night out drinking, and was chosen to drive as he had had the least to drink.

John Madden, for Morphey, said: "He accepts that he had been drinking that night. He accepts full responsibility, and indeed his life has been devastated by this incident, although it cannot be compared to the loss of the families of those that died." Mr McKittrick said there was no suggestion Claire Stoddart, who had been driving the other car involved in the collision, had done anything wrong. Benjamin Britten High School will

open a memorial garden in memory of the three teenage
pupils this Sunday, on the first anniversary of the crash.

Saturday June 30 *A comment on the sentence*

Whenever I've written stuff, so far, I've been inspired to do so.
The words have been easy to come by. Today I find it hard
to know what to say at all. The trial finally happened and we
chose not to go. We didn't really see what was there for us
and felt flat and uninterested. The press kept getting in touch
wanting our opinion but I was weary of them. I think they
wanted Heather and me to indicate what would satisfy us: five
years, ten years, life, hung, be-headed, perhaps the defendant
sliced up into a thousand pieces?

I have recently felt so empty of anything but sorrow for us, for
the other families involved and for the Morphey family. One
stupid decision, one reckless act and there the lad was, alone
with his own feelings and a messed up life. He too is a victim
of his behaviour on that night. Like the rest of us he has to live
with what happened. But what about your daughters
Mr Stoddart; what about your family and all the suffering they
have been through? Yeah, what about us, does someone want
to suggest we should have been there, seeing that the girls got
justice, getting some sense of closure, some sort of satisfaction
out of the punishment of a man?

Our comfort lies elsewhere, we sit with Jesus and his church.
We are not looking for closure, rather we are looking forward
to our heavenly inheritance of which Claire and Jen are
now a part. This has nothing to do with a court trial or
punishment. The sentence can neither satisfy nor intensify
what we are going through. Our concern is daily receiving the
strength that comes from God that enables us to deal almost
contemptuously with death.

I love Claire and Jenny to bits. Often my eyes are filled with
tears that they are no longer here. I yearn for them and there

are times I can hardly bear it. But then there is Jesus and the cross and "I know whom I have trusted and I am convinced that he is able to do more, so much more, than I can think or imagine (quote from the Bible)." It's him and glimpses of Heaven that comfort and heal us. The world cannot do this.

Please be careful about getting involved in judgement, don't become part of a crowd that one day gathered in indignation at a woman who was found in the act of adultery. "How dare she spoil her husband's reputation!" someone yelled out. "Filthy whore", another added, "she's betrayed her children" came another cry. "Tell us Jesus, what shall we do with her? Our law says we stone her to death."

Jesus, for some reason, had been writing in the sand on the ground while the crowd vented their fury. When there was quiet, he straightened himself up and looked the crowd in the eye. "Stone her then", he said casually but then added, "only let he who is without sin be the first among you to throw the stones".

The crowd slowly started to break up, first the older men slipped away, then the younger men. Finally, Jesus stood alone with the woman. "Is there no one left to harm you?" She looked around and shook her head. He picked up one of the stones left by the crowd and caressed the jagged edges and looked to Heaven. Only he had the right to stone her for only he was spotlessly innocent. Instead he silently acknowledged yet another crime to be added to the punishment waiting for him at the cross. He dropped the stone and looked her full in the eyes. "I too do not stone you, now go leave your life of sin." (story adapted from the Bible)

Sunday July 1 2007 *Anniversary*

Well today was the anniversary and I'm so glad that it was on a Sunday. We started it in the best possible way, worshipping God amongst our friends at church. The speaker, Mike Betts, reminded us all of the promises of eternal life and afterwards we held a barbeque in our garden for anyone preferring not to be left alone with their memories. A number of Claire and Jenny's school friends had joined us at the service and they were there at the barbeque too. It was quite ironic to consider that exactly one year ago our garden had been packed with a similar crowd.

Unlike then, today was mostly a light-hearted atmosphere. I realised afresh that many present have known the closeness of Jesus and have learnt how to focus on his promises during this time of sadness. I also think some people without the same faith as us have taken comfort in our reaction over the past year. Whether intended or not, together with close family friends, we have set a standard, a banner of hope, to which some people have rallied.

During the barbeque we walked the short distance down the road to the girl's school to the opening of a small landscaped garden dedicated as a memorial to the three girls. Together with Carla's parents we placed special stones into a rock-pool and mixed with the large crowd who had gathered to mark the occasion. It struck me just how much these deaths have affected the local community. I think I know why this is, it's the worst fear that a parent can have and it's all a bit too close to home for them.

I almost feel that Heather and I have become marked people. I sometimes notice people looking at us perhaps a little bit longer than they normally would, where a casual glance becomes a lingering stare. I wonder if we now represent their worst nightmare; they see us and wonder what it must be like. Perhaps they consider the inevitability of death visiting their loved ones, that one day they will be us. Maybe they have already lost people and maybe they suddenly remember their grief and emptiness.

Wednesday July 18 *Active memories lost to photos*

It's turning out to be another difficult week. Images and thoughts of Claire and Jenny keep flashing into my mind and

making me feel sick. How can they be dead? How can I live?
How can I really enjoy living anymore with them gone? It's just
a constant battle. What do people mean by this term 'closure'?
Closure – when you finally put something to rest, when you
walk into a new chapter free of what has gone before. I really
do not see how 'closure' can apply to anyone in my family.
There is no such thing as closure. How at any point in my life
will I ever even want to forget them?

What bugs me a lot nowadays is that my mental images of them
are starting to become the photos around the house. Real active
memories are being lost to photos. I don't like this, it's another
connection being broke; perhaps this is a moving towards
closure? Well I reckon to achieve it you have to want it and
I can't say I do. This is the battle, the constant challenge to defeat
utter despair with the promises of Heaven. Every time I have to
combat the loss with what they have gained and with what I am
promised, an ever constant friend called Jesus walking with me
all the way to Heaven. There wait wonders unknown.

But saying it is one thing, doing it is another. You cannot defeat
bereavement and grief by a mental exercise. Both of these foes
hit your mind and body and they are powerful. I have to focus,
it's not enough to read the Bible, I have to know the presence
of God. The devil knows the Bible, scholars know it, anybody
who wants to can pick it up, but for me, the words within
proclaim the truth about Jesus. They help me to understand
him but meeting him is the real deal. Perhaps the words
of a book like this are able to soothe a wound like a dab of
antiseptic cream, but meeting him, experiencing his presence,
sort of blows the foes away. Sure, they come back, but then
again so does he!

This is why I hate sin. When I bow to it, it hinders the meeting
with him. I need these meetings, I need to come to him
without holding things back because the more I'm living for
him, the more he's active in me. Sin is holding onto things,

holding on to the rights to do something. You hold onto sin at your own expense; you keep it, you miss out on him. I can't afford to be reckless with sin. I know that when life's major blows arrive, an open walk with Jesus makes all the difference. Today you sin, tomorrow you lose a loved one and only the conqueror of death, the Lord Jesus, can truly help.

Wednesday 25 July *Seeing the girls again*

Someone who lost his father in quite tragic circumstances told me a pretty bad time for grieving is around an anniversary. 1 July came in a bit of whirl as it was caught up with the court sentencing on 29 June and the opening of the memorial garden. Rather than going to the trial I issued a statement to the press. We had two reasons for staying away, the first was we didn't want anything to do with the sentence, to either criticise or agree with whatever punishment was handed out. The second was because we just didn't want to go through it. For us, it seemed right with God to have nothing to do with the proceedings (as much as is possible) and where there was a choice, to keep away.

I don't know why he prompted us in this direction but I suspect it is to demonstrate forgiveness with dignity and quietness. The press knew the stance we had taken and I think they wanted to make a real point of contrasting it against the "norm" of what they were used to. In the closeness of the situation this would have been insensitive and perhaps might have made us look like we were boasting; floating on some moral high ground at the expense of others. Nothing could be further from the truth. Our stance is born out of necessity and it is a survival instinct straight from the Spirit of God who is part and parcel of our lives.

Yet overall, it seems the whole event has passed by quickly and without too much emotional hassle. But looking back over the last few weeks I realise how withdrawn I have become. I have absented myself from as much social activity as possible, including the end of school gathering with free food and drink. I am also struggling with a constant desire to be alone and yet when I am alone, I want to be with someone.

It all became quite overwhelming yesterday when once again the loss seemed so unbearable. Fortunately a friend had come round to pray with me and I told him how I felt. As we prayed we both saw a vision of Jesus standing with Claire and Jen looking at me. The thing was, when I've seen them with him before, they weren't aware of me. This time they were and it was because he had allowed it. The first thing that struck me was that this was not something he did often to say the least. It was a concessionary gesture made to me that involved them. I knew they had been summoned or perhaps brought by him to this scenario. They had briefly turned aside from their paradise, that garden which I have glimpsed so often, to see me.

What they saw made them cry and it made me cry even more: a distraught father. It seemed wrong that they should see me like this. I became aware that soon they would return to the fantastic lives they now have, perhaps where memories would once again become dim because of the amazing presence of Jesus. That is what it's like for them and the picture emphasized that when I finally go to where they are, there will be full recognition and memory and such a wonderful meeting. But the joy I know at that time will soon be eclipsed by Jesus and the place he has prepared for us.

So why was I seeing this? I might have dismissed the scenario were it not for my friend seeing the same as he prayed as well. I must confess I don't really know. What I do know is that somehow it strengthened me, added resolve to overcome the struggle. The best I can make of it is that even if I could somehow talk with the girls as they are now, it wouldn't be long before the light of Jesus would become so bright that our conversation would cease in the face of it. Beyond Claire and Jenny is Jesus and he meets with them in Heaven and he

meets with me here on earth. The desire to see them again is
not the end aim, it is only a stopping place on the road to him.
This is spiritual knowledge and the significance can only be
understood in the spirit. The satisfaction of my soul does not
lie simply with being with the girls again, fantastic though that
will be.

19 Back to New Day

A song of understanding

May I be to you as clay in the potter's hands
Easy to mould shaped to your command
Filled with your Spirit in abandoned overflow
Giving strength to my heart and joy to my soul.

Oh Jesus, I fix my eyes on you
I gaze upon such glory
There's nothing I can do
To contain what I receive
Or even think to speak
What can I say to one such as you?

Will you take me now for earth has lost it's hold
The house I built is ruined put up for sale and sold.
Take me to the new house the one that you've prepared
For my heart is for my home and it is there.

"A few hours more
Just a few hours more
The cup is made for drinking
Not for hanging on a wall
You are tired from the usage
But the night has not yet come
The drinking must go on
Until the work is done."

I have seen you
I have no questions
I know that you are good
And in you lies the answers to any doubts I hold
I know you break my heart
So that love will drive me on
I will not come to rest
Until my work is done.

Last year there were around fifty of us that attended the New Day youth event, this year there were double that number and it was nice to see some more of Jenny's school friends present. I must admit that even though it was great to see so many teenagers and twenties going for God, I was struggling with my personal walk. What was really bugging me was that life was continuing and Claire and Jen weren't a part of it. It was as if their deaths no longer mattered, just an irrelevant statistic consigned to the scrapbook of time. It was hard to deal with mentally because I knew the very joy of Christ that enabled people to move on was my lifeline too. It had to be this way for it was right and proper, a natural progression.

I felt Jesus was saying that the battle of the last year had drawn to a successful conclusion and now there were new challenges to meet for his kingdom was always advancing. But something inside me couldn't quite go with that. A voice within demanded that everything should stop, God should halt and the church refrain from all activity. In fact, the voice was really saying Jesus really ought to return to earth right now and God should commence the final judgement. My world had been booted into touch so why shouldn't everyone just call it a day? Ridiculous really, but that was the voice.

Maybe it was the lack of control I had, the fact that a large part of me still wanted to die and be with my girls, but I couldn't. It just wasn't that easy to let go of all the memories and to trust that everything lost would be restored. So I began the event in mental turmoil and perhaps it was not surprising that rather than go with everyone else to the meetings I went by myself and stood amongst strangers. But Jesus still sought me out and over the next few days I knew much blessing as can be seen from the entries below.

Friday August 3 2007 *New Day: The great congregation*

I am standing amongst thousands, freely in the presence of the Lord Jesus. There is song after song and I cannot help but raise my arms as high as they will go. Somehow I am trying to touch this magnificent presence which fills the atmosphere and which is him. If creation apart from humans can praise God then surely this is the nearest I've ever come to understanding how this can be. The very atmosphere is charged with him.

My eyes are firmly closed but they are seeing so much. There is a great multitude reaching out to God and this gathering within a big top tent has become part of it. There are banners being waved with strange symbols upon them, not the flags of nations or organisations, but bearing his many facets. Each in itself is glorious but when they come together you see something of the plethora, the many, many aspects which make up the character of God.

There is this underlying bass and drum sound that is deeper and richer than any sound of nature I can think of. Not the roaring of the sea, nor the cracking of thunder, not even what must be the catastrophic sound of an earthquake or volcano erupting could get anywhere near to matching this sound. I am also aware that not everyone assembled are human. I sense the presence of majestic creatures, perhaps white horses charging around somewhere behind me. I am standing at New Day, yet I am part of the great heavenly host, a congregation beyond my senses.

As I start to try and make sense of what I am seeing I reluctantly become aware of my body and the experience passes. Worse, either a demon or my own mind is trying to accuse me, remind me of how sinful and dirty I am. Surely I cannot belong to this congregation. It is too incredible, too marvellous, too good to be true. Perhaps the sighting is a taunt, a mighty show of all I will be missing out on because of my inability to conquer sin?

Remind yourself Christian. You are part of the family by grace; sin and death were defeated at the cross. The very fact of your unworthiness is part of what all the ecstatic worship is all about. This is a love story. The great lover has set his bride free and she can do naught but love him for it. How can I choose sin when he breaks my heart like this? The smallest wrong I do is a blow that he freely took on the cross. And I have seen him, glorious, exalted and worshipped by incalculable numbers yet he loves me personally, infinitely. He left glory in Heaven to set the likes of me free. All who are part of that great congregation are lost in wonder and awe because of what he did on the cross. No human deserves to be there and the heavenly beings themselves are cut to the core at the greatness of his love. I am back worshipping again, seeing more.

Saturday August 4 *New Day: Two crosses*

Caught up in worship, my mind still must wander towards Claire and Jenny. They are here, somewhere within this crowd. What comfort to know that here, in the presence of Jesus, there is no dividing wall between life and death. I am born again, my spirit is alive to God and that within me which is born of God, is part of the same congregation that worship him - whether in Heaven or here on earth.

In this place there is no separation, there is no death because he has destroyed it. In Heaven the cross is outstanding. I keep being drawn to it and see a gleaming white, shining symbol that dwarfs everything else. Just to gaze upon it is to know how much was accomplished by it. No one who sees it can pass it by. It is the cornerstone, the chief stone of a new creation built upon love and sacrifice. Yet as I gaze at this magnificent sight I also see an ugly, shrivelled wooden cross. It is a sobering and hateful sight, reminiscent of thorns and stinging nettles and wasps. It makes me think of bad-tempered outbursts and cruelty and selfishness. It is poisonous to view and I want to strike it and swear. I wish it would go away.

Jesus, you took it all upon yourself. Before the shining white cross that trumpets your glory could happen, you smothered yourself in all that is disgusting. Every last drop of filth was upon you and we all drew round and kicked you and swore at you. Even your father turned away when there was no more that you could take and then you died and all us dirty scumbags were made clean. But that ugly wooden thing is what makes the gleaming white cross so glorious. I don't think I will ever be able to look upon the cross and just see one or the other – it has to be both – your sacrifice and your great accomplishment.

Somewhere my darlings you are among this crowd and we are both full of love for our saviour. Together we gaze upon him and weep for joy. Who are we that he should love us this much? I cannot think of a better place to be than where you girls are. I so want to be with you and see him like you do but it's not my time. I accept this because he wants to do more in me and through me before I come. I need his heart, a heart that knew all too well of the wonders of Heaven and yet still chose to leave and labour on earth for the lost.

Sunday August 5 *New Day: Too much to contain*

Another worship time. Even singing the words becomes too difficult. The weight of his presence is upon me and it is all I can do to hold myself together. My arms keep reaching high towards him but they get weary. The heavenly songs are flowing and I don't want to miss out on one moment. I can barely move my mouth, my eyes are streaming, my nose is dripping and my head is pounding: this body is inadequate for worship like this.

I knew I had to come to him this morning. I have to be here because there is no one else to whom I could go. I cannot live in victory over death unless I come. Why do you allow me in so freely Lord? I am covered in filthy rags of sin and I've got nothing I can give you. I do not even dare make promises to you because I cannot trust myself to carry them out. Could it be that the verses in the Bible that tell me to not make promises to God, to just let my 'yes' be 'yes', are there to protect me? Rather than a stern warning, are they my Lord's yearning to spare me from the burden of guilt and shame when I fail to keep them?

There is a silence in my mind and then he speaks. "I am just so glad that you come in this way. You come like a child, you are humble before me and I love you dearly for coming to me so empty of pride and with nothing to give. I am not looking for anything from you. Only you, I only want you".

My eyes break into fresh streams at these words spoken from Spirit to spirit. Someone in the meeting on the stage starts talking in a 'tongue'. Although I do not understand the words, the presence of God within them is a fresh source of wonderment and when the interpretation comes, the words take the form of tides and waves of the oceans; the endless, relentless crashing of God's love upon his people and upon me.

What my spirit is receiving is beyond my mind and body. One day my spirit will be housed within a new immortal body that will not be so utterly inadequate for the worship of him. No one who has tasted heavenly worship could have problems with the idea of worshipping him forever and ever. The presence of Jesus is infinite; there are no ends to his wonders. Yet I know part of Heaven will also be about inter-acting with all those who are there with me. I can only suspect that somehow my new body will be capable of doing this and seeing him face to face. If I was to enter Heaven with this body I would be able to do nothing, for I would be consumed by his glory.

Tuesday August 7 *New Day: The feet of Jesus*

Glimpses of Heaven are a privilege of belonging to Jesus. The Bible encourages us to fix our minds on things above and this has certainly been a major feature of my life since the girls I love went there. These insights give a deep sense of joy, refreshment beyond the reaches of anything worldly, but they are also dangerous.

I know that the Awesome One, Jesus the King, reveals these things to me because I need to see and live with a heavenly perspective. I think I would have crumbled in despair had I not seen something of Heaven revealed. But the danger is to become so obsessed with a home where I have not yet truly arrived, that the journey there becomes unimportant and of no interest.

During a worship time, I was prompted away from the great celebration and sensed him saying to look at his feet and to know that his joy is also there. He says, "I am found when you gaze upon me in admiration and when you look for me in humility and weakness but I am also found in your service."

Words similar to those spoken in the Bible come to me, 'if you love me you will do as I do and you will learn the joy of deeds.' Simply put - doing good to others for no reward other than knowing that they touch the heart of Jesus. Within the heart of a person who gives in this way is a deep understanding, hidden to most, of Almighty God. The heartbeat of Jesus is to Heaven as the ticking of a clock is to us. All that we do is within the context of time. All that happens there beats to the heart of the One who gave everything 'for the joy set before him' as the Bible says.

I look downwards and see his feet of burnished, glowing bronze. How lightly they move amongst people stricken to the ground in their sickness and sorrow. I sense the joy and compassion within him as he does this and know he seeks no rewards. He only rests when needed and bids me to do likewise. I flinch at this, what about me? My life? Time for me? Seeing him makes the questions seem absurd. Of course, how utterly natural that where he walks, the losing of self-seeking is the finding of real life. The Bible is full of this, "deny yourself, take up your cross", and far too often I've associated this with personal misery. It is for my joy that he exhorts me to do this. It seems so clear as I watch him; there is no real contentment at all in self-seeking. I am designed to love my God not to love myself. How can you find joy in doing that which you were not created to do?

A song of wonder

Of the wonders above
A mind cannot conceive
The glory that fills the universe unseen.
Where the One who is almighty
Sits upon the throne
And all bow down and worship him alone.

Such is your majesty
Such is your holiness.

Of the lamb who sits beside him
A heart cannot contain
All of Heaven sings out in praise;
"By Your blood you purchased men for God
from every tribe and tongue
Worthy is the lamb that was slain."

Father God, so wonderful your ways
Jesus Lord, I'm so thankful.

Who can comprehend the love
That bled and died for me
Who can understand the heart of God?
Heavy chains and filthy rags
Were overcoming me
Now my steps are light and clothes are ever clean.

I have come to the city of the living God
Where thousands of angels sing with joy
To spirits of righteous men made perfect
To the church of the Firstborn
But above all this, I have come to Jesus my Lord.

20 **Last words**

Friday 17 August *Daily Mirror feature*

An interview I did over the phone with a freelance journalist appeared in the Daily Mirror today. The interview and photos took up one page while a third of another page contained the headline; "He drank 10 pints then got in his car and killed our girls."

My heart just sank when I saw this. The article was to be about how God has helped us through grieving, not about Ben Morphey. I didn't even know he drank 10 pints until I read that headline and the police certainly did not reveal such precise details to me. One paragraph says "I felt numb as a police officer described the drinking that led to the car crash". The truth is that my mind was focussed purely on death and Jesus during the days and weeks after the crash. I was not thinking about drink driving at all.

The article also states that neither Ben Morphey nor his family have contacted me or shown any remorse since the court case. This is a loaded and unfair statement in that firstly, it suggests they should have made contact. Why? Put yourself in their shoes; would you pick up the phone to talk to us? Would you even feel allowed to? Would you think it appropriate? That family has enough on their plate without being made to feel guilty about something like that.

Secondly, how can anyone know whether any remorse has been felt? Who knows what is going through the mind of that man? I do not know and neither is it something on my mind. The suggestions made are not mine: they did not originate with me.

Finally, the rest of the article is well put together and a reasonable job has been done. But they made the mistake of presuming that the person responsible for the crash was on my mind in the way they have suggested. I re-iterate that my thoughts towards the Morphey family are not vengeful and angry. I did everything I could to ensure that article was about me, my family and God and not about them. Sadly the editor responsible felt that he had to sensationalise the crime and make the Morphey family appear heartless.

So why did I do the interview? Surely I must have suspected something like this would happen. I want people to know that God is good and can be our strength in times of tragedy. I want people to know that there is one who is greater than death. That just at the point when darkness seems so overwhelming, there is a light which cannot be extinguished. I testify that God is faithful to those who put their trust in him. This alone is my message.

Wednesday September 26 *The God-shaped hole*

It is almost fifteen months since that dreadful day and nearly what would have been Claire's twentieth birthday. I have become desperate again, struggling to breathe beneath the onslaught of yet another wave of grief that threatens to overwhelm.

I dreamt of Jenny last night. It was nothing dramatic, just time spent together, enjoying her gentleness. Yet when I woke the memory grew to become like a heavy weight as my mind went through it's daily instruction routine of what day it is, who I am, what I do and what has happened.

Everyday I have to go through this. It is like standing on a plateau then walking to the edge and looking down into darkness so far below. Memories and grief pull at me and the impetus is there just to let go and fall and drown in sorrow.

But there is a stronger voice within that bids turn and walk away from the abyss. It is a command from Jesus and I force myself to obey and listen to truth. I seem so quick to tears nowadays, like blood in a blister, the slightest touch and I bleed. I do not need to contemplate what the girls have missed out on for they have gained so much more than I can imagine. The blood starts to trickle. I do not have to worry about how I am going to get through the rest of this life, because Jesus is with me to the end of time. More blood, much more blood.

There is a familiar saying amongst Christians, that there is a hole in our hearts that is God-shaped and therefore can only be filled by him. I sort of understood it when I heard it, but now it has become one of the most profound statements of all.

It does not go unnoticed to me that meetings with Jesus always end up fully focussed on him. Nothing else can compete with him. Even the knowledge of Claire and Jenny fades before the glory that surrounds him. I fully accept, in fact I can no longer believe otherwise, that people who die and go to be with him are fully and utterly absorbed with him. The reason that loss and knowledge of loved ones are not present in Heaven is that there is simply no room for them. It's not that Claire and Jen won't be ecstatic when they meet up with us again, it's more that they are fully occupied with the wonder of being with Jesus. But, such is the heart of Jesus, when our meeting time occurs, he will give us in an instant all that we need to appreciate it to the fullest. Blood is running freely.

What is true in Heaven also has impact on earth. If I were to wake up tomorrow morning with Claire and Jen asleep in their bedrooms, I would still have a hole in my heart. The truth is that the people we come to love are not the right shape for the hole. I cannot be fully satisfied by human relationships and companionship no matter how dear they may be. They can do so much to make life pleasing to live but they cannot satisfy my deepest need.

I will never be truly satisfied until I am face to face with my creator and my God. That is how I have been designed and my whole being knows it. With him is where I belong. As a

Christian I have been given a taste of true life and the smallest
morsels indicate the meal to come. This is what is meant by the
"bread of life" which Jesus talks about in the Bible. Once again
I am forced to conclude that the only way to live while Claire
and Jen are gone is in the same way as when they were here.
Nothing has changed in this respect. There really is nothing for
it but to live for Jesus.

Monday 1 October *Claire's 20th birthday?*

If this really were me speaking now, what would you have
me say on what would have been my twentieth birthday?
Perhaps you'd want to know whether I'm aware that I passed
my A-Levels with flying colours but missed out on a place at
university because I died. And am I sad because I never fell in
love, never got married or had children of my own? Do
I miss you who were my friends, do I think of you who were
my family, do I sometimes wish I could talk to you all and enjoy
your company once again?

Let me assure you I am completely satisfied. I remember
everything that I once was and know that some of you will be
joining me here while others will not. I do not know who for
not all things have yet been disclosed. Like everyone else here
I look forward to the day when the Lord will be revealed to all
and the books are opened. It is the glorious wedding feast of
the Lamb who was slain and of the mighty Lion whose roar fills
the heavens. The Lion and the Lamb are one.

You may think I am concerned about those who will not be
counted worthy on that day. Indeed it is sad to contemplate
but you need to understand it is all but impossible to think of
the terrors of Hell when you are immersed in the wonders of
Heaven.

Try to imagine a bright summer's day of mountains and
meadows and waterfalls that pour into pools of warm water.
Carefree people splash and laugh and marvel with ever-

increasing wonder at their surroundings. It is not just the environment they are in, it is also the amazing people they are with and who they are themselves. And more, so much more, there is the Lord Jesus himself.

At times he is amongst us, young and fresh as the morning, like us and with us. At other times his presence seems to fill the heavens and we all just stop in amazement and worship him. Everyone is filled with the knowledge of what he has done on the cross. Everyone loves him and for us who were once on earth, we cry at the wonder of how he came down from all this into our world for our sakes.

Can you at least begin to understand now how different I am to how I was? If you wanted me to return it would be for your sake alone for I am truly satisfied here. I have no regrets. You say I was never loved by a man, that I never felt the warm embrace of human love. I am fully loved here. Does a person regret missing out on a morsel once he has been to a feast?

I worked so hard to pass my A Levels but did not live to see the results. What really mattered was that I gave my best. Beyond trusting in the saving power of the cross I tried to live a life worthy of Jesus. It wasn't brilliant and I'm sure you can remember things I did or said which weren't very good. I wish I had given more to living for Jesus and I know that on the judgement day to come there will be some things that I can be proud of and other things for which I will be ashamed.

One thing I do know is that however I behaved, Jesus will vouch for me on that day. My place here in Heaven proves it and it's all because I asked him into my life while I was still on earth.

Let me urge you to do the same and more, once you have done it, press on and serve him well. Because if you do, when you meet him your deeds will shine brightly and an incredible joy will surge throughout your being as you realise the Lord is so proud of all that you did for him. Wish you were here. Bye.

Friday October 12 *Seventeen (Jenny's birthday)*

I really wish there was a point
To hanging around at anniversaries
As if anything different will happen
Or there will be any changes.

So you would have been seventeen
And what if?
The college or the sixth form
English, Media, Art or Science?

Perhaps a boy you've met
And what of your new friends?
Who remains of the old gang
And who have you visited at uni?

But it's all gone.
I've searched the whole damn room
And there's nothing there
Nothing to be gained from might-have-beens.

I thought I was alone in this
But there's a few of us that feel like traitors.
So guilty for leaving you behind
And letting our memories fade

But there are no answers in memories
No solutions in the darkness of loss
We have to deal with reality
Where you are and what you have received.

I pity the poor folk who have no knowledge
Of what happened to you when you died
That as your body heaved and failed
You entered the gates of Heaven.

They don't believe it
They just hope it's true
They use it to disguise their terror
That death is the end.

> Jenny darling, I will fix my thoughts on truth
> I will let the joy of Heaven wash over me
> I will fall down before the One who saved you
> And let my tears be for joy not grief.

Thursday 22 November *Deluded?*

The question doesn't seem to go away. I thought it would and it's not often asked but when it is, it's usually after a few days immersed in work and tiredness; when you seem distant and a little unreal to me. I was just wondering how long I have to stay here? You see I'm a little bit desperate and have been thinking how nice it would be to go.

But then it strikes me Lord that I might be on my own. There's this little man within that doubts you and all I have believed. He whispers that I'm deluded, a wishful thinker who is trying to escape the grim reality that is upon him. After all, I am but part of a small minority and most people ridicule your existence. Yet the children of God shall be like the sands of the earth when they are assembled in your presence at the end of the world.

Sometimes – like now   it's hard to believe that I have a place reserved amongst them. Even worse, perhaps my daughters aren't with you either. As far as the world is concerned they no longer exist and there is no hope. So it is no surprise to them that the parents need to escape with a bucketful of religion rather than face their woe. Only recently I read in the news that a woman killed herself because her daughter was dead. "How can I live when my daughter is gone?" She found no answer and I wonder why that was.

It bugs me that I'm sometimes not sure what it takes to get into Heaven. Were my daughters lives good enough for you, and will mine be sufficient? We made a simple confession of faith and an attempt to walk in your ways. But for me, it seems that too often I've fallen over and taken far too long to get up. Are you really going to let me in?

For some reason (I hope I'm not misguided) that despite these nagging doubts I talk more to you than anyone. It seems you're written on my mind and I can't do anything bad without upsetting my conscience. How have you done this and why me? Is an open heart all it comes down to? I suppose the very fact that you're invited to walk wherever you want in my life speaks volumes. I never challenge your authority or think that I'm the one who's right. I just don't seem to be able to be perfect. Yet for all the failings I never deny you and somehow I know this is enough. And when I fall it's always you I run to – I guess that's what makes me know I'm a child of God.

It's the knowing of who I am that gives the strength for the battle of the mind. All those wonderful promises in the Bible, that anyone who sincerely comes to you will be saved; that Heaven and meeting you and glorious reunion with loved ones are all waiting. But I do not, indeed I cannot, fight just by knowing your word. It is the knowing deep within that I belong to you that really counts. This has nothing to do with how I perform. There is something stamped upon me that melts my heart and makes me cry. Something deep within that calls out "father", no matter what the circumstance. It means so much to know that I am loved by you.

Wednesday December 05 *Hidden Treasure*

Something I realised as I prayed today caused tears to run freely down my face. I was thanking Jesus for his goodness to me and also for the people of God who have been such a blessing during these last few years. My mind began to travel back to the events of July 1st 2006 and how it was that it had been such a special day with Jesus.

I could have been filled with anger towards a God who hadn't stopped the car crash. Yet all I could do was come to him as an injured child who falls into the lap of one of his parents and settles there. It strikes me now as interesting that I had no struggle with God over what had happened. In the hour of need there were no thoughts of blaming him, nothing inside me that even considered it. A scene in the New Testament comes to mind when a large number of followers were deserting Jesus. He asked the remaining few if they were going to leave him too, but Peter replied, "Lord to whom can we go? You have the words of eternal life!"

The reality is that when confronted with death there is no one but Jesus to go to. I knew that subconsciously from the start and I realise now that it is part of the deposit of the Holy Spirit living within me as a guarantee of things of come. All these years that I have spent struggling through my Christian life have not been without reward. Somehow, when it mattered, something I barely knew was there, shone out so bright that darkness could not overcome it.

If someone had said to me before these events that when the day of testing came I would stand, I think I might have smiled politely, but inside there would have been a cloud of doubt. Am I really strong enough, do I really believe all this, am I actually a Christian at all and when it matters will I just fall away?

What dawned in my praying today was just how little I knew of the strength of the light within. For years Jesus has been tending this light and I knew it not. I'm not sure I've ever thanked him until today for what he has done within me. I've counted it as something little, something that pales in comparison to what he is doing in other people. This is clearly not the case. I have to understand that there is something of God living inside me that cannot be defeated.

Yes I will fall down and the temptation of sin will remain camped on my doorstep for the rest of my life. But it will never defeat me because it hasn't any power over the light within. I quote from John the Apostle "In him was life and that life was the light of men. The light shines in the darkness, and the darkness has not overcome it." It is high time that I recognise the power of God within, and the uses of the hidden treasure that are mine to enjoy.

I am truly indestructible. My body can be killed but no one can steal what I have inside because no one is stronger than Jesus. I am stamped, sealed and delivered because of that terrible cross. The man who hung upon it loves me so utterly that he will never give up that which cost him so much to obtain. Jesus give up on his reward? How utterly ridiculous the thought. No, I am truly free to walk as befits a son of God. No condemnation, no accusation will stand. I am more than a conqueror through him who loved me. Hidden treasure indeed.

Monday January 21 *Death Defeated*

How can I stand
Against such mighty evil?
Death walks beside me every day
Never resting or forgetting to remind me
Of the loved ones whose breath he took away.

Not content with doing this
Death leaves his friend Despair
Who whispers words of ice to my heart
"Better to die than seek to live
Knowing you must live your years apart."

But this I know
My Lord can do more
Than I can ever imagine
There is nothing that I can ask
Beyond his power to perform.

Enemies much too strong for me
Halt at his command
And fall away defeated
Wherever his feet will stand.

Loved ones safe with Jesus
Are never quite away
For Heaven is where they are
And Heaven pervades my heart.

Sometimes I feel the songs of joy
That the dead in Christ are singing
Are bursting through the veil
That keeps Heaven and earth apart.

The sound of Heaven is truly overwhelming
Every creature is a living song of joy.
Filled as they are with perfect understanding
They marvel at the truths they hear
And proclaim wonders with their singing
That can never lose their allure.

Rejoicing now defines the loved ones
Who have left this fallen earth
And death seems strangely silent
As if it wasn't really there.

The cross of Christ now stands enormous
Shining in radiant white
The purity of Jesus
Has put my foe to flight.

Debbie Wicks and Heather

Hannah and Bernard Warnes

Mike and Sue Betts

21 Family and friends remember

Hannah Warnes. First contact

Bernard (Heather's brother) and I were woken in the middle of the night by Heather phoning us that Claire had been involved in a car crash and could Bernard come round to be with Amy and Tom while they went to see Claire. We prayed together for them, and then Bernard went quickly to their house. We waited for news and then Heather called to tell me that Claire had died and they were on their way to see Jenny in hospital. Up to this point we had no idea that the crash had been so serious, or that Jenny had been involved. The news of Claire's death was just terrible, but when Bernard came home to tell me that Jenny had died as well, we were devastated that the two had been taken. Bernard was so shocked that he could hardly speak and I cried inconsolably. We then had the awful task of telling Amy and Tom that their sisters had died and then had to tell Heathers parents.

In the days and weeks to come we found ourselves in shock and woke regularly in the night at the time Heather had called, sleep walking into our children's rooms to look for them, fearing that they were ill or hurt. Also, soon afterwards there was the birth of our third son, which although it brought us enormous joy, was in the middle of a deep time of grief and sorrow for the agony that Heather and Phil were facing. It was hard to understand why we had been given a life when two of our loved ones had been taken.

I had a very vivid dream soon after Claire and Jenny died, where I was tending their grave. I heard pure laughter behind me and, when I turned, Claire and Jenny were standing, still looking like them but totally beautiful and full of joy. They were asking me why I was digging soil and assuring me that I didn't need to worry; that it was all right for they were with God. So while I have many happy memories of them here on earth and miss and think about them everyday, I know that they are in Heaven and I'll see them again one day.

Debbie Wicks. All I could do

When my husband took the phone call with the news that Jenny and Claire had been killed I experienced the worst pain in my heart that I had ever felt. My immediate reaction was one for myself and then for Heather, I guess as a mum I felt for her. Our kids had grown up together; we had shared holidays, picnics, mothers and toddlers club and headlice! Within the hour I arrived at their house to be there as Heather and Phil got back from seeing Jenny. What I did for the next few days just seemed to come naturally. I made tea, cooked, cleaned, provided boxes of tissues, and supported Amy and Tom. For me it was all I could do.

Amy Stoddart (sister). Something that can never be replaced

It was roughly a month before my thirteenth birthday when I awoke to what seemed a normal Saturday. It was hot and sticky with a very distinctive smell of pollen in the air. As I lay in bed I could hear the little tapping of feet and realised my Uncle Bernard and Auntie Hannah must be round with their son Nathan.

I soon dragged myself out of bed to make some breakfast (cheese on toast as always) but once downstairs I sensed the mood was solemn and with little cheer. As I went into the living room, I saw my auntie's eyes were red and blotchy. She insisted I sat down for she had some dreadful news to tell me. Straight away I thought she had miscarried for she was pregnant at the time. I felt scared and worried and was not sure what to expect.

My auntie tried to put the news in the best words possible, but there weren't many ways to say something like this. She said "there's been an accident and last night when your sisters were coming home from the concert there was a collision with another car. Your dad and mum have already gone to the hospital but we know for certain that Claire and Jenny have both passed away. I'm so sorry".

I was in a state of shock and couldn't move or think straight. All I kept thinking was 'this can't have happened, not to me, it's impossible', but it had. I finally managed to say "really?" and then burst into tears that just wouldn't stop. I managed to ask for my best friends Lauren Martin and Lauren Shade to come round as quickly as possible. They came straight away, with messy hair and no make-up on. They both had obviously just put on any clothes they could find. They came in and automatically hugged me. My mum and dad still weren't back and my auntie didn't want me going out for a much needed walk until then.

So we waited and it felt like years, I just wanted to get out the house, get away from everything. After a long while my parents finally returned with bloodshot eyes and sorrowful expressions. I had never seen my dad cry before this moment, but now he was crying just as much as the rest of us. After that I just had to get out with my friends and for the first time I didn't care what I looked like. One of us had been clever enough to think of bringing a loo roll to carry as we walked around for most of the day, calling on friends.

I got back to the house for dinner-time but didn't want food for my mouth was too dry to endure the pain of eating. A lot of people were there and flowers had already been sent to us. Debbie, a very close family friend, had already organised a rota between all our friends so that for this week none of us needed to worry. She didn't want us to cook, clean or anything like that. When I went to bed that night I just lay there, until finally I drifted off to sleep which I wished to stay in for a long while.

The week to follow was a blur; I didn't go into school and I couldn't eat, I just didn't see the point in anything. But I did decide that I had to be strong so that other people wouldn't break down around me. One day I saw Jenny's two best friends, Bex and Amy Willis, going upstairs to her room. I followed them and got a shock, for I had forgotten what the room looked like. I had avoided it the whole week and it seemed strange without Jenny in it. I went inside and they were sitting on the bed with tears streaming down their faces as they looked at her art book. I came and sat down with them and also looked at the book. I had never seen it before and I never realised how well she could draw. Amy turned the page to one picture and I looked closer and it was me. She had got a photo of me and drawn me out so well. At that point I just broke down, it was too much.

We received so much support that week and my friends were with me at all times. Even when I told them I was fine they knew I wasn't and they stayed off school with me. We had flowers and cards sent for us from people who we had never even met before! We didn't know what to do with them, there were so many. July 1st will never be forgotten, it will forever be a day when I lost something that can never be replaced.

Matt Thomas. A milestone in my faith

You never think that you will lose the people that have always been there, those you grew up with. My mum told me what happened that Saturday morning and all I could do was stare until it sank in. It hurt, I was angry, confused, upset and for a time I hated God. It was a struggle but I had to put my trust in him and he was active in so many ways, and he comforted me. Now I try to actually live life, and enjoy the time I have with people. I still miss them and will always remember them for who they were. That time is now a milestone in my faith. No matter what pushes and pulls me, I can look back and remind myself to trust in God, from the power of Heather and Phil's witness and in how Jenny and Claire lived their beautiful captivating lives.

Jamie Wicks. More than just friends

I've known Jenny and Claire and their family for all of my life. They had become more than just friends, much more like the sisters I never had. Our families went on holidays together and some of my fondest memories involve both of them. The morning I heard of the accident was the most surreal and horrific time I have ever experienced. In the weeks after I began to realise the urgency in which the word of God needed to be told to as many people as possible, due to life changing events that can happen in seconds and completely change things.

Chris Clarke. Felt like my heart had been ripped out

The night before the crash I was surfing the internet, looking for a present for Jenny. I knew her birthday wasn't until October but I took great pleasure in finding unusual gift ideas and I knew she liked Amber. The next morning I was woken at six 'o' clock by my mother crying loudly in the other room. I dared not say anything because I'd never heard her cry like that. My door opened and she told me about the accident but I thought there had to be a mistake. Both dead! That can't be right, but it was. I felt like my heart had been ripped out. For over two hours I lay silently on my bed and just stared at the corner of the room, trying to take it in.

Strange as it might sound I knew that God had allowed this and that through it something bigger would emerge, giving him more glory. I just wished it wasn't Claire and Jenny. I tried to be angry with God but every time I questioned him, he butted in and reminded me of his love and how he was in full control of the whole situation. Then it hit me. They were in Heaven with him, by his side and the notion of that just blew me away. I said to God "I need your help so much right now - I don't know what to do". He replied with "I know". Without realising it I had been in full conversation with the Lord God, creator of the universe! Yet he had time for me when I needed him.

Since that day, the loss of Claire and Jenny has affected me everyday in some way. Losing them so suddenly has made me realise that life is so fragile and that anyone can die unexpectedly, even the good guys. Looking back I'm so grateful for friends and families support, but it was and is God who gives me strength and never fails me and I know that one day I will see them again.

Rebecca Pretty. Will Jenny recognise me in Heaven?

I'm known as Bex and was one of Jenny's best mates. I had known her for roughly six years and she started dragging me along to church when I was around twelve. Obviously the crash affected me loads and it was the worst time ever. We were so close but now we couldn't be further away and it really does suck.

I was at the Chili Peppers concert with Jenny and on the day it felt like we had never been closer. We were trying to edge our way forwards by chucking bottles in front of us, then picking them up and shuffling forwards. We found some guys from our school and talked to them for a bit and some really 'hot' random guys, but Jenny really wanted to find her sister.

In the train on the way there, we were counting the days we would get off school due to gigs and a festival. We were so excited and it's weird now to think she's gotten out of the education system forever!

The one memory I'll never forget is when the song 'under the bridge' came on and we were singing really loudly and everyone was turning their heads. There was a really creepy guy behind us though so we were trying to rush out when the gig ended. As we walked through the crowds, we were holding hands so we didn't lose each other and she said DON'T LET GOOO! She really wanted to buy a t shirt but our lift was here, then she found her sister and her mates. She wanted to go with Claire because their car listened to better music and it was more convenient so I went with the lift we were going to take. Her last words to me were I'll call you tomorrow!

I just can't help but think, I could have invited her to sleep at mine that night then she would have got in the car with me. When I was going to bed really happy, she was dying; how wrong is that!?

I'm really thankful to God for giving me that last brilliant day with Jenny, but when it happened I was crushed. For a while I grew closer to God but then I started to get into other things, mainly parties - not that I think they are bad, because they are wicked! But I always went over the top and hated myself for it. I think deep down I just couldn't understand why he would take her away, so I think I got depressed but just didn't show it and this is still happening up to this day.

I know I'm going to see her again and my relationship now with God has got stronger, but will she remember me or recognise me? Since she's in Heaven her eyes are only on God, the way it should be. But me being human and until I'm with God myself, I can't help but to ask questions about our meeting to come.

Amy Willis. We had so much to look forward to

It was the most devastating thing that has ever happened to me. I was woken on the Saturday morning with the news that my best friend and her older sister had died in a car crash on the way back from the concert we had all been at the night before. I felt guilty, as she should have been in my car, and angry, as we had so much to look forward to in life: our baptism, our proms, and all the plans we had for the future. But not that alone, I also couldn't understand why God would let this happen. Why Jenny?

But over time and through the amazing grace and comforting peace of God, that initial anger has disappeared. I am now more determined than ever to make the most of my life on this earth and since the accident my relationship with God has strengthened to an extent I never thought possible.

Having my relationship with God doesn't stop me missing
Jenny as nothing ever could. However, I can honestly say it
scares me to think how I would be now without it.

Abi Pike. I wanted the world to stop

It was around 7.30am and I remember resenting being awake
so early when my bedroom door slowly opened. It was my
mum and dad, telling me the devastating news that Claire and
Jenny had been killed in a car accident. I bolted upright and
screamed and cried out painful sounds that I'd never let out
before. There was absolutely nothing beyond the pain. I could
see no point in doing any thing else but crying and I thought
my tears would never stop.

Getting away from the pain felt impossible. Claire was my best
friend. I remember crying out repeatedly 'but I need her!' and
'I don't know what to do, I don't know how to do this!' I kept
shouting 'This isn't happening'. I felt sick and breathless and
couldn't move. Then somehow I managed to stop crying. My
parents left the room and I rested my head against the back wall
and just felt numb. My eyes burned and my head was thumping.

Soon I had to get up. Downstairs my mum was crying and dad
was on the phone. I went and sat on a cold step at the back
door and heard my neighbours in the garden. It made me
angry that everyone else was going on as normal. I wanted the
world to stop because it had stopped for me. It didn't seem
real. I started crying again and then some song lyrics came into
my head. They were from a church song:

'Hold me close, let your love surround me.
Bring me near - draw me to your side.
And as I wait, I'll rise up like the eagle and I will soar with you.
Your spirit leads me on in the power of your love.'

I remember being angry, desperately trying to get the words out
of my head, resenting the fact that they were there and even

resenting their amazing relevance. I knew God was there even if I didn't want him to be. I couldn't understand why he had let them die, such amazing and beautiful girls who loved him. It was like a picture of God holding me close and holding me tight while in my anger I kicked and thumped and thrashed about. All day I couldn't get the words of that song out of my head.

Later I decided to get out of the house and go for a walk. I took some music and a bottle of water and put my sunglasses on so that no one would be able to see me crying. I walked down the road in a complete daze, until a car screeched past. I freaked out, my senses alerted; every car was a killing machine and the noises were so loud and terrifying. I finally got into the park and walked along the river until I found a spot on the bank where I could sit away from everyone.

There were some teenagers messing about on the other side of the river. I thought 'that's what Claire should be doing with her school friends, celebrating the end of exams and dossing about on hot days'. I thought about all the things Claire would never do. I wasn't aware of how long I had been sitting there but soon I headed back and met my brother Jonny at home. There was nowhere I could go to get away from my thoughts.

That evening I didn't want to go to bed, so I searched frantically for any photos and letters from Claire since they were all I now had. I sat in bed but couldn't sleep. I texted Alice, Lauren, Sam, anyone who I knew would be struggling to sleep too. I couldn't turn the light off, I was too scared, it was like being a frightened child again. I didn't know what I might see if I turned the light off.

The next morning, details kept coming through about the actual crash. I spoke to various people that day and that helped because I felt pretty isolated in Cardiff. I would keep crying down the phone and would hear the other person crying too as we both tried to talk. I heard how the Stoddart garden had filled up with school friends and people from church since it was the only place people felt they should go. Erin said that even though it was horrific and there was so much grief and pain, that it was also amazing and that God was there in an awesome way.

I found it hard to understand what was going on in Lowestoft. This sort of awful yet amazing thing seemed to be happening. People said how powerful the first church service had been and that God was moving and really strengthening people. I didn't get it but was relieved at the same time that God had not abandoned us and was in control of the situation.

I told Erin that I was finding it hard letting God in and standing firm in my faith and she said something that changed my perspective. She told me that 'God is all we truly have - he's the only thing we can be certain of and worshipping him is the only thing we can do'. From then on I knew I had to lift my eyes to him and turn to him for strength. I was suddenly reassured that if I leant on him and fell back into his arms, I would be safe and he would make me strong. He was and is and will always be the only hope I have.

"The righteous cry out, and the Lord hears them; he delivers them from all their troubles. The Lord is close to the broken hearted and saves those who are crushed in spirit." (Psalm 34v17-18)

Erin Peace. Completely helpless without God

One of my favourite memories of Claire is from the very first 'Newday' festival we went to. On the last night there had been a really powerful talk by Dave Stroud and he asked people to go to the front if they wanted to speak in tongues. As I went to the front to pray with people I ended up next to Claire, and there was such anticipation of what God would do. I asked her if she wanted me to pray with her and she did. We stood there for about 10-15 minutes just praying and waiting expectantly. After a while I opened my eyes and Claire was praying in tongues; and after about 20 seconds she opened her eyes, looked straight at me and exclaimed in a slightly contemptuous but awestruck tone "I sound just like my dad!", to which we both burst out laughing with tears of joy.

The accident has made me evaluate my life entirely. In the weeks that followed my faith and relationship with God grew so much. There was so much sadness and disbelief but at the same time I have never known such reliance on him. I realised that when everything else is stripped away, only God is left, and I am completely helpless without him.

On 1 July 2006 after the news had spread, a crowd of us gathered at my flat and sat together in silence, with tears flowing and the occasional prayer of gratefulness for these amazing lives. It was a supernatural time which was marked by the presence of the Holy Spirit, who allowed us to grieve and at the same time reassured of his complete sovereignty over us. It was such a comfort to be with one another, finding comfort through friendships through the most horrific situation imaginable. My faith has grown so much stronger through this tragic time and my life will never be the same for having known such amazing people and for having the privilege of being friends with them.

Ellen Meadows. I became a Christian

I met Jenny in Year 9 of High School, and throughout the time I spent with her she never forced her religion on me or any of our other friends. I respected her for this as I had no interest in Christianity, God or whatever it was Jen believed. I went to a few events at church with Jenny but still had no interest in it.

On 1 July 2006 I was at home and when I got told the news I didn't believe it, "why Jenny & Claire???" is all I kept saying. This made me think "if there was a God he wouldn't let two of his devoted followers die like this!" But after a few months and spending time with the Stoddarts, I decided to do the youth Alpha course to find out more about Christianity and after six weeks I gave my life to Christ!! Eighteen months later I do not regret it one bit! Although it's such a shame a terrible thing like this had to happen for me to begin my relationship with the creator of the universe!

Jimmi Clarke. Hungry for Christ

When I heard the news I felt calm but didn't understand why, except that God felt close. I thought of the verse in the Bible where it talks of Jesus bringing a peace that goes beyond all understanding. Even though it was hard I knew God was in control and that he was now closer than I'd ever known. As time went on I soon realised that the life I was living wasn't all that it should be. I became so hungry for Christ and read my bible a lot. This was not because I needed answers but because Jesus was with me, and I loved it and wanted more of him. I read Ephesians 5 where it talks of being children of the light, I was thinking of the girls and the great example they were, they were children of the light.

Sam Betts. My soul woke up

The death of Claire and Jenny was a pivotal moment in my life. I had the privilege of being their friend for many years and

Chris, Sam, Amy, Erin, Abi and Dan. August 06

I can only describe the impact of their death as life-changing. My Christian life had been ordinary up to this point and my belief had perhaps not been a complete reality. Heaven and Hell were no longer imaginary or figurative expressions, nor were they psychological states; they suddenly became very real destinations. God was not a vague power but an accessible comforter at this time, biblical truths and the character of Jesus began to capture my mind and convict my heart. Put simply, my soul woke up to the truth. I realised that when life crumbles around you, the blank position of disbelief counts for nothing and cannot produce any sense of all life's realities. My attitude to almost everything in life changed and now I live unashamedly for Jesus in a largely God-less generation that does not pursue holiness. Being a Christian is not easy, it never has been and it never will be. Even so, God is the only firm foundation in this very fragile world, no temporary earthly possession or achievement will satisfy my whole being, for these things cannot be taken beyond the grave. With an eternal perspective I now appreciate that time is short and an urgency to tell the gospel is upon me.

Sarah Mitchell. Car crash survivor

I left the Red Hot Chili Peppers gig with Claire, Carla, Jenny and Adam. After the accident I have vague memories of waking up in hospital and having to be repetitively told what happened as I kept forgetting, due to the painkillers. I sustained multiple injuries, like breaking bones in my arm, elbow, leg, back and fingers. I cracked the bottom of my skull and hips and tore the ligament in my ankle.

I still have medical problems and may have further surgery to re-position my leg. This makes me scared of the future, but in a way, the more I feel healthy and well, the further away the girls feel from me - although I miss and need Claire and Carla just as much as I did then.

I have so many lovely memories of the three girls that I'm scared to forget. Claire always had the better memory, regularly reminding me of my timetable in school. Often when I was at Claire's, Jenny would come in to catch up with Claire and gossip about the family and Jenny's friends. Claire would always find earrings or something missing and say 'Ah Jenny!'

Claire often said how happy she was at the way Jenny had grown up to be similar to her. There are so many little memories I treasure equally; super noodles at lunch, revision and biology and our traditional chats about the events that happened at sixth form parties over a bag of crisps before bedtime. But I remember crying while writing a letter to Claire about how much her friendship meant to me, after one of the rare times we fell out. This was because I knew what I had before I lost it. Claire then shouted at me for nearly making her cry at work where she had read it.

Adam Cox. Car crash survivor

I became good friends with Claire at High School but had known her since Reception at Primary School, so to not have her in my life since the accident has been a hard adjustment. I too was involved in the car crash and to hear Claire, Carla and Jenny had died was heartbreaking. Surrounding myself with the group of friends and family who all shared a close relationship with Claire and support Sarah in getting better was my way of coping with their deaths.

Whilst I still miss Claire deeply, I remember the things she said, the way she would make me laugh, as well as her morals and outlook on life, from which I take inspiration from and will continue to do so for the rest of my life. Seeing the Red Hot Chili Peppers with Claire has been one of my best experiences and I will continue to treasure and use it to remind me of how awesome Claire was.

Mike Betts. Friend and Senior Pastor, Lowestoft Community Church

I shall never forget the phone call early that sunny morning, letting me know Claire and Jenny had been killed in a car accident. I shall never forget having to tell my wife and son the terrible news. I shall never forget the doorbell ringing and Phil and Heather standing there on their way back from the hospital. I shall never forget the church responding with such love and care in ways that only those belonging to Jesus Christ can. I shall never forget the thanksgiving service and the grace God gave to us all that day. I shall never forget Claire and Jenny who radiated the very life of God every day in every way.

How do people manage who do not know Jesus? I cannot imagine. The events of that weekend changed us all. We cast ourselves on God for his help. Some people look for mighty miracles and signs seeking to prove God exists and can affect our lives in dramatic ways. Look no further, Phil and Heather are living in the ongoing miracle of God's grace, which since the accident has daily sustained and strengthened them for life. They live in the frailty of human emotions and capacities, yet they live also in the strength of the one who has no limits to his power and grace.

Heather Stoddart (mother). With Jesus now

Jenny and Claire were beautiful, intelligent, loving and full of life. My last memory was the pair of them going round our garden and then the hedges around Benjamin Britten High School, cutting down branches to make themselves look like 'Ents' from Lord of the Rings. Half the branches ended up scattered over the garden and through the house!

July 1st changed my life forever and these last two years have been so hard to bear. Dealing with the loss is an ongoing heartache, although I know that both girls would be saying "Mum get over it – we're with Jesus now and it's amazing."

Knowing that both of them had a personal faith in Jesus and that they are with him now is the main thing that has got me through. I also have the very real presence of Jesus and I love him walking with me every step of the way. Even in the darkest and most difficult days he is with me. I quote from Psalm 23; "Even though I walk through the valley of the shadow of death, I will fear no evil, for you are with me. Your rod and your staff they comfort me."

Tom Stoddart (brother). Two people I loved

I liked it when Jenny bought me a big chocolate galaxy. She was nice and kind, she was always lovely. Claire let me watch 'Alice in Wonderland' in her room. They always tried to make me happy when I was sad. Jenny, Claire, Amy and me once stuck out silly faces for a photo at nanny's house. They always made me laugh when I was little. In 2005, we went strawberry picking and Jenny asked me if she could have one of mine and I let her. Claire bought me sweets from the sweet shop. I loved Jenny's long straight hair, it was really pretty. These were the two people I loved (written aged seven).

Tom, aged six. July 2006

Epilogue

An atheist dies

A heavy weight is pulling me down. A growing shadow that is dark and oppressive. I watched it approach and suddenly it was all around. A bitter coldness had invaded my land, numbing the senses as if a dressing gown of ice was being wrapped around me. There was no panic. I almost welcomed the approach as if ready and willing. It was easy to settle within this black ocean and accept the embrace.

Maybe the shadow had sensed despair; perhaps it had been waiting and brooding like a spider until the merest vibration upon its web would call it forth. It quickly came searching, eagerly anticipating the discovery of another wretched soul. Like a mother it came swiftly to comfort its child, speaking soothing words of dissolution as it spun icy threads around me.

"Let me cloud your vision then close your eyes completely. Let me spin a darkness so thick that you will lose all grasp of meaning. Thinking is pointless. I grant you oblivion, an eternal state of being where there is no need to worry or to care, for nothing matters. This is what you want; this is what you've always desired. Deep within yourself you only ever wanted rest. You only ever wanted an escape from consciousness."

"Mmmm. Thank you my mother. I am truly comfortable here, numb and lost in this thick black void where nothing is significant. Even the nourishment of my mind is unnecessary for I am of no consequence. Who am I, what is being? Don't answer, I desire no answers."

Time. I am trying to shut out time. How long have I been here? Where is my promised oblivion? Where is my utter rest? Where are you my mother? I still have being and I am dismayed.

Light. Somewhere over there I sense it; a disturbance, a pin-prick of light threatening the tranquillity. It offends yet it compels and commands attention, like the moon shining on the sea at night. As if from a dark cloud it emerges and the sea shimmers as a path of light is set before me. The darkness is evaporating before the advance of dawn and its outstretched arms of warmth and hope.

Music and singing. A sweet breeze carrying the scent of nature. Is that a waterfall I can hear and is there the sound of laughter mingled in? The light surrounds me now and I am focussed on its source. There's something there that I need to see, although all around there is a plethora of life stretching my senses. Sounds so rich, scents so diverse and breezes so fresh, yet warm. Closer, closer into the light where wonders untold await. I am going to see him, I understand now. He has drawn me in and my senses are reeling. Any moment now the end of sight, the Author of Life, the music is deafening, colours are colliding and I am now before him.

Silence and waiting. It felt like a journey through eternity but now I am here. Somehow, I don't understand how, I have the strength to pull my body up and kneel and raise my eyes towards him. Startled, I realise I know him. He is Jesus and he is perfect.

There are few words. We both look at each other longingly and a dreadful sorrow is creeping over me. I perceive him and all that which is his and know I have no part in this. I understand my life and know I alone am guilty. He died for me and I didn't accept it. I turn around and walk away, the full knowledge upon me. The singing grows quieter, the colours are fading, the warmth is cooling. One final time I look back and then jump into a lake of fire, wailing and shouting, sometimes despair, sometimes anger.

Man against God

Man's complaint:

Wish I never had come to this earth
Never been raised up from dirt
Never had a life for me prepared
So that I could love and hurt.

Tell me why did you do this to me
Why did you let me be?
Opened my eyes to your creation
Now let them close so I can leave.

They say that death is the thing to be scared
But I've never been more prepared.
Smash me in and stitch me up
Wash the blood out of my hair.

Lay the corpse on the hospital bed
Dress it up for those who are left
Maybe I shouldn't be so hard on them
Put them through all this mess.

But will you even allow me to die
Walk into the blackest of nights?
I'd welcome the touch of self-oblivion
No walk into an after-life.

God's response:

I am creator, I made you this way
I am a potter, I formed you from clay
I gave you life so you could know me
And enjoy the world I made.

I always knew that you would turn
Walk away from what you've learnt
Lose all trust in your creator
Trample my words in dirt.

So tell me what would you have me do
Stop creating more people like you
Put a full stop on my creation
Draw a line under anything new?

If you stopped looking in on yourself
And the tragedies giving you hell
You'd see beyond the flames that burn you
And trust me to see you through.

I never intended you pain
By allowing you to turn away.
Life was one gift, choice was another
The decision was yours to make.

Won't you freely give your life back to me
I will open up your eyes to see
The pleasure of walking in my wisdom
Friendship for eternity.

The world is growing darker each day
Men are walking in their own ways
They curse the gift of life I gave them
And plead for an end to their days.

Will you show them my hands and my feet
Where nails were drove into me
I hung on a cross to destroy the hatred
Put an end to this hostility.